ABOUT THIS PUBLICATION

FOR SERVICE ASSISTANCE

Customer Service
704.898.0770

North Carolina General Statues is published by The Muliti-Media Group of Greater Charlotte in Charlotte, North Carolina. Copyright 2015 by the Multi-Media Group of Greater Charlotte. This book or parts thereof may not be reproduced in any form, stored in a retrieval system, or transmitted in any form by any means—electronic, mechanical, photocopy, recording or otherwise—without prior written permission of the publisher, except as provided by United States of America copyright law.

The records required by U.S. Code 2257(a) through (c) and the pertinent regulations 28 C.F.R. Cli. 1, Part 75 with respect to this publication and all materials associated with such records are maintained by The Multi-Media Group of Greater Charlotte, Publisher and available for review by Attorney General.

www.visionbooks.org

Copyright © 2015 by MMGGC
All rights reserved!

TID: 5061447
ISBN (10) digit: 1502913178
ISBN (13) digit: 978-1502913173

123-4-56789-01239-Paperback
123-4-56789-01239-Hardback

First Edition

090520140547

Printed in the United States of America

2015 EDITION

North Carolina Criminal Law And Procedure-Pamphlet # 33

Printed In conjunction with the Administration of the Courts

North Carolina Criminal Law and Procedure
Pamphlet Reference Guide

Chapters	Pamphlet
Chapter 1 Civil Procedure	1
Chapter 1 Civil Procedure (Continue)	2
Chapter 1A Rules of Civil Procedure	2
Chapter 1B Contribution.	2
Chapter 1C Enforcement of Judgments.	2
Chapter 1D Punitive Damages.	2
Chapter 1E Eastern Band of Cherokee Indians.	2
Chapter 1F North Carolina Uniform Interstate Depositions and Discovery Act.	2
Chapter 2 - Clerk of Superior Court [Repealed and Transferred.]	3
Chapter 3 - Commissioners of Affidavits and Deeds [Repealed.]	3
Chapter 4 - Common Law	3
Chapter 5 - Contempt [Repealed.]	3
Chapter 5A - Contempt	3
Chapter 6 - Liability for Court Costs	3
Chapter 7 - Courts [Repealed and Transferred.]	3
Chapter 7A – Judicial Department	3
Chapter 7A – Continuation (Judicial Department)	4
Chapter 7A – Continuation (Judicial Department)	5
Chapter 7B - Juvenile Code	5
Chapter 8 - Evidence	6
Chapter 8A - Interpreters for Deaf Persons [Recodified.]	6
Chapter 8B - Interpreters for Deaf Persons	6
Chapter 8C - Evidence Code	6
Chapter 9 - Jurors	6
Chapter 10 - Notaries [Repealed.]	6
Chapter 10A - Notaries [Recodified.]	6
Chapter 10B - Notaries	6
Chapter 11 - Oaths	6
Chapter 12 - Statutory Construction	6
Chapter 13 - Citizenship Restored	6
Chapter 14 - Criminal Law	7
Chapter 14 –Criminal Law (Continuation)	8
Chapter 15 - Criminal Procedure	9
Chapter 15A - Criminal Procedure Act (Continuation)	10
Chapter 15A - Criminal Procedure Act (Continuation)	11
Chapter 15B - Victims Compensation	11
Chapter 15C - Address Confidentiality Program	11
Chapter 16 - Gaming Contracts and Futures	11
Chapter 17 - Habeas Corpus	11

Chapter 17A - Law-Enforcement Officers [Recodified.]	11
Chapter 17B - North Carolina Criminal Justice Education and Training System [Recodified.] Chapter 17C - North Carolina Criminal Justice Education and Training Standards Commission	11
	11
Chapter 17D - North Carolina Justice Academy	11
Chapter 17E - North Carolina Sheriffs' Education and Training Standards Commission	11
Chapter 18 - Regulation of Intoxicating Liquors [Repealed.]	12
Chapter 18A - Regulation of Intoxicating Liquors [Repealed.]	12
Chapter 18B - Regulation of Alcoholic Beverages	12
Chapter 18C - North Carolina State Lottery	12
Chapter 19 - Offenses against Public Morals	12
Chapter 19A - Protection of Animals	12
Chapter 20 - Motor Vehicles	13
Chapter 20 - Motor Vehicles (Continuation)	14
Chapter 20 - Motor Vehicles (Continuation)	15
Chapter 20 - Motor Vehicles (Continuation)	16
Chapter 21 - Bills of Lading	17
Chapter 22 - Contracts Requiring Writing	17
Chapter 22A - Signatures	17
Chapter 22B - Contracts Against Public Policy	17
Chapter 22C - Payments to Subcontractors	17
Chapter 23 - Debtor and Creditor. r 24 - Interest	17
Chapter 24 – Interest	17
Chapter 25 – Uniform Commercial Code	18
Chapter 25 – Uniform Commercial Code (Continuation)	19
Chapter 25A – Retail Installment Sales Act	20
Chapter 25B - Credit	20
Chapter 25C - Sales of Artwork	20
Chapter 26 - Suretyship	20
Chapter 27 - Warehouse Receipts [Repealed.]	20
Chapter 28 - Administration [Repealed.]	20
Chapter 28A - Administration of Decedents' Estates	20
Chapter 28B - Estates of Absentees in Military Service	20
Chapter 28C - Estates of Missing Persons	20
Chapter 29 - Intestate Succession	21
Chapter 30 - Surviving Spouses	21
Chapter 31 - Wills	21
Chapter 31A - Acts Barring Property Rights	21
Chapter 31B - Renunciation of Property and Renunciation of Fiduciary Powers Act	21
Chapter 31C - Uniform Disposition of Community Property Rights at Death Act	21
Chapter 32 - Fiduciaries	21
Chapter 32A - Powers of Attorney	21
Chapter 33 - Guardian and Ward [Repealed and Recodified.]	21

Chapter 33A - North Carolina Uniform Transfers to Minors Act	21
Chapter 33B - North Carolina Uniform Custodial Trust Act	21
Chapter 34 - Veterans' Guardianship Act	22
Chapter 35 - Sterilization Procedures	22
Chapter 35A - Incompetency and Guardianship	22
Chapter 36 - Trusts and Trustees [Repealed.]	22
Chapter 36A - Trusts and Trustees	22
Chapter 36B - Uniform Management of Institutional Funds Act [Repealed.]	22
Chapter 36C - North Carolina Uniform Trust Code	22
Chapter 36D - North Carolina Community Third Party Trusts, Pooled Trusts	23
Chapter 36E - Uniform Prudent Management of Institutional Funds Act	23
Chapter 37 - Allocation of Principal and Income [Repealed.]	23
Chapter 37A - Uniform Principal and Income Act	23
Chapter 38 - Boundaries	23
Chapter 38A - Landowner Liability	23
Chapter 39 - Conveyances	23
Chapter 39A - Transfer Fee Covenants Prohibited	23
Chapter 40 - Eminent Domain [Repealed.]	23
Chapter 40A - Eminent Domain	23
Chapter 41 - Estates	23
Chapter 41A - State Fair Housing Act	23
Chapter 42 - Landlord and Tenant	23
Chapter 42A - Vacation Rental Act	23
Chapter 43 - Land Registration	23
Chapter 44 - Liens	24
Chapter 44A - Statutory Liens and Charges	24
Chapter 45 - Mortgages and Deeds of Trust	24
Chapter 45A - Good Funds Settlement Act	24
Chapter 46 - Partition	24
Chapter 47 - Probate and Registration	25
Chapter 47A - Unit Ownership	25
Chapter 47B - Real Property Marketable Title Act	25
Chapter 47C - North Carolina Condominium Act	25
Chapter 47D - Notice of Settlement Act [Expired.]	25
Chapter 47E - Residential Property Disclosure Act	25
Chapter 47F - North Carolina Planned Community Act	25
Chapter 47G - Option to Purchase Contracts	25
Chapter 47H - Contracts for Deed	25
Chapter 48 - Adoptions +	26
Chapter 48A - Minors	26
Chapter 49 - Bastardy	26
Chapter 49A - Rights of Children	26
Chapter 50 - Divorce and Alimony	26
Chapter 50A - Uniform Child-Custody Jurisdiction and	

Enforcement Act	26
Chapter 50B - Domestic Violence	26
Chapter 50C - Civil No-Contact Orders	26
Chapter 51 - Marriage	26
Chapter 52 - Powers and Liabilities of Married Persons	27
Chapter 52A - Uniform Reciprocal Enforcement of Support Act [Repealed.]	27
Chapter 52B - Uniform Premarital Agreement Act	27
Chapter 52C - Uniform Interstate Family Support Act	27
Chapter 53 - Banks	27
Chapter 53A - Business Development Corporations and North Carolina Capital Resource Corporations	28
Chapter 53B - Financial Privacy Act	28
Chapter 54 - Cooperative Organizations	28
Chapter 54A - Capital Stock Savings and Loan Associations [Repealed.]	28
Chapter 54B - Savings and Loan Associations	29
Chapter 54C - Savings Banks	29
Chapter 55 - North Carolina Business Corporation Act	30
Chapter 55A - North Carolina Nonprofit Corporation Act	31
Chapter 55B - Professional Corporation Act	31
Chapter 55C - Foreign Trade Zones	31
Chapter 55D - Filings, Names, and Registered Agents for Corporations, Nonprofit Corporations, and Partnerships	31
Chapter 56 - Electric, Telegraph and Power Companies [Repealed.]	31
Chapter 57 - Hospital, Medical and Dental Service Corporations [Recodified.]	31
Chapter 57A - Health Maintenance Organization Act [Recodified.]	31
Chapter 57B - Health Maintenance Organization Act [Recodified.]	31
Chapter 57C - North Carolina Limited Liability Company Act.	31
Chapter 58 - Insurance.	32
Chapter 58 - Insurance (Continuation)	33
Chapter 58 - Insurance (Continuation)	34
Chapter 58 - Insurance (Continuation)	35
Chapter 58 - Insurance (Continuation)	36
Chapter 58 - Insurance (Continuation)	37
Chapter 58 - Insurance (Continuation)	38
Chapter 58A - North Carolina Health Insurance Trust Commission [Recodified.]	38
Chapter 59 - Partnership.	39
Chapter 59B - Uniform Unincorporated Nonprofit Association Act.	39
Chapter 60 - Railroads and Other Carriers [Repealed and Transferred.]	39
Chapter 61 - Religious Societies	39
Chapter 62 - Public Utilities	39

Chapter 62 - Public Utilities (Continuation)	40
Chapter 62A - Public Safety Telephone Service And Wireless Telephone Service	40
Chapter 63 - Aeronautics	40
Chapter 63A - North Carolina Global TransPark Authority	40
Chapter 64 - Aliens	40
Chapter 65 – Cemeteries	40
Chapter 66 - Commerce and Business	41
Chapter 67 - Dogs	41
Chapter 68 - Fences and Stock Law	41
Chapter 69 - Fire Protection	41
Chapter 70 - Indian Antiquities, Archaeological Resources and Unmarked Human Skeletal Remains Protection	42
Chapter 71 - Indians [Repealed.]	42
Chapter 71A - Indians	42
Chapter 72 - Inns, Hotels and Restaurants	42
Chapter 73 - Mills	42
Chapter 74 - Mines and Quarries	42
Chapter 74A - Company Police [Repealed.]	42
Chapter 74B - Private Protective Services Act [Repealed.]	42
Chapter 74C - Private Protective Services	42
Chapter 74D - Alarm Systems	42
Chapter 74E - Company Police Act	42
Chapter 74F - Locksmith Licensing Act	42
Chapter 74G - Campus Police Act	42
Chapter 75 - Monopolies, Trusts and Consumer Protection	42
Chapter 75A - Boating and Water Safety	43
Chapter 75B - Discrimination in Business	43
Chapter 75C - Motion Picture Fair Competition Act	43
Chapter 75D - Racketeer Influenced and Corrupt Organizations	43
Chapter 75E - Unlawful Activities in Connection With Certain Corporate Transactions	43
Chapter 76 - Navigation	43
Chapter 76A - Navigation and Pilotage Commissions	43
Chapter 77 - Rivers, Creeks, and Coastal Waters	43
Chapter 78 - Securities Law [Repealed.]	43
Chapter 78A - North Carolina Securities Act	43
Chapter 78B - Tender Offer Disclosure Act [Repealed.]	43
Chapter 78C - Investment Advisers	43
Chapter 78D - Commodities Act	43
Chapter 79 - Strays [Repealed.]	43
Chapter 80 - Trademarks, Brands, etc.	44
Chapter 81 - Weights and Measures [Recodified.]	44
Chapter 81A - Weights and Measures Act of 1975.	44
Chapter 82 - Wrecks [Repealed.]	44
Chapter 83 - Architects [Recodified.]	44

Chapter 83A - Architects	44
Chapter 84 - Attorneys-at-Law	44
Chapter 84A - Foreign Legal Consultants	44
Chapter 85 - Auctions and Auctioneers [Repealed.]	44
Chapter 85A - Bail Bondsmen and Runners [Recodified.]	44
Chapter 85B - Auctions and Auctioneers	44
Chapter 85C - Bail Bondsmen and Runners [Recodified.]	44
Chapter 86 - Barbers [Recodified.]	44
Chapter 86A - Barbers	44
Chapter 87 - Contractors	44
Chapter 88 - Cosmetic Art [Repealed.]	44
Chapter 88A - Electrolysis Practice Act	44
Chapter 88B - Cosmetic Art	45
Chapter 89 - Engineering and Land Surveying [Recodified.]	45
Chapter 89A - Landscape Architects	45
Chapter 89B - Foresters	45
Chapter 89C - Engineering and Land Surveying	45
Chapter 89D - Landscape Contractors	45
Chapter 89E - Geologists Licensing Act	45
Chapter 89F - North Carolina Soil Scientist Licensing Act	45
Chapter 89G - Irrigation Contractors	45
Chapter 90 - Medicine and Allied Occupations	45
Chapter 90 - Medicine and Allied Occupations (Continuation)	46
Chapter 90 - Medicine and Allied Occupations (Continuation)	47
Chapter 90 - Medicine and Allied Occupations (Continuation)	48
Chapter 90A - Sanitarians and Water and Wastewater Treatment Facility Operators	48
Chapter 90B - Social Worker Certification and Licensure Act	48
Chapter 90C - North Carolina Recreational Therapy Licensure Act	48
Chapter 90D - Interpreters and Transliterators	48
Chapter 91 - Pawnbrokers [Repealed.]	48
Chapter 91A - Pawnbrokers Modernization Act of 1989	48
Chapter 92 - Photographers [Deleted.]	48
Chapter 93 - Certified Public Accountants	48
Chapter 93A - Real Estate License Law	49
Chapter 93B - Occupational Licensing Boards	49
Chapter 93C - Watchmakers [Repealed.]	49
Chapter 93D - North Carolina State Hearing Aid Dealers and Fitters Board.	49
Chapter 93E - North Carolina Appraisers Act	49
Chapter 94 - Apprenticeship	49
Chapter 95 - Department of Labor and Labor Regulations	49
Chapter 95 - Department of Labor and Labor Regulations (Continuation)	50
Chapter 96 - Employment Security	50
Chapter 97 - Workers' Compensation Act	50
Chapter 97 - Workers' Compensation Act (Continuation)	51

Chapter 98 - Burnt and Lost Records	51
Chapter 99 - Libel and Slander	51
Chapter 99A - Civil Remedies for Criminal Actions	51
Chapter 99B - Products Liability	51
Chapter 99C - Actions Relating to Winter Sports Safety and Accidents	51
Chapter 99D - Civil Rights	51
Chapter 99E - Special Liability Provisions	51
Chapter 100 - Monuments, Memorials and Parks	51
Chapter 101 - Names of Persons	51
Chapter 102 - Official Survey Base	51
Chapter 103 - Sundays, Holidays and Special Days	51
Chapter 104 - United States Lands	51
Chapter 104A - Degrees of Kinship	51
Chapter 104B - Hurricanes or Other Acts of Nature	51
Chapter 104C - Atomic Energy, Radioactivity and Ionizing Radiation [Repealed and Recodified.]	51
Chapter 104D - Southern States Energy Compact	51
Chapter 104E - North Carolina Radiation Protection Act	51
Chapter 104F - Southeast Interstate Low-Level Radioactive Waste Management Compact [Repealed]	51
Chapter 104G - North Carolina Low-Level Radioactive Waste Management Authority Act of 1987 [Repealed]	51
Chapter 105 - Taxation	51
Chapter 105 - Taxation (Continuation)	52
Chapter 105 - Taxation (Continuation)	53
Chapter 105 - Taxation (Continuation)	54
Chapter 105A - Setoff Debt Collection Act	55
Chapter 105B - Defaulted Student Loan Recovery Act	55
Chapter 106 - Agriculture	55
Chapter 106 - Agriculture (Continue)	56
Chapter 106 - Agriculture (Continue)	57
Chapter 107 - Agricultural Development Districts [Repealed.]	57
Chapter 108 - Social Services [Repealed and Recodified.]	57
Chapter 108A - Social Services	57
Chapter 108B - Community Action Programs	58
Chapter 108C Medicaid and Health Choice Provider Requirements.	58
Chapter 108D Medicaid Managed Care for Behavioral Health Services.	58
Chapter 109 - Bonds [Recodified.]	58
Chapter 110 - Child Welfare	58
Chapter 111 - Aid to the Blind	58
Chapter 112 - Confederate Homes and Pensions [Repealed.]	58
Chapter 113 - Conservation and Development	58
Chapter 113 - Conservation and Development (Continuation)	59

Chapter 113A - Pollution Control and Environment	59
Chapter 113A - Pollution Control and Environment (Continuation)	60
Chapter 113B - North Carolina Energy Policy Act of 1975	60
Chapter 114 - Department of Justice	60
Chapter 115 - Elementary and Secondary Education [Repealed.]	60
Chapter 115A - Community Colleges, Technical Institutes, and Industrial Education Centers [Repealed.]	60
Chapter 115B - Tuition and Fee Waivers	60
Chapter 115C - Elementary and Secondary Education	60
Chapter 115C - Elementary and Secondary Education (Continuation)	61
Chapter 115C - Elementary and Secondary Education (Continuation)	62
Chapter 115C - Elementary and Secondary Education (Continuation)	63
Chapter 115D - Community Colleges	63
Chapter 115E - Private Educational Facilities Finance Act [Recodified]	63
Chapter 116 - Higher Education	63
Chapter 116 - Higher Education (Continuation)	63
Chapter 116A - Escheats and Abandoned Property [Repealed.]	64
Chapter 116B - Escheats and Abandoned Property	64
Chapter 116C - Continuum of Education Programs	64
Chapter 116D - Higher Education Bonds	64
Chapter 117 - Electrification	64
Chapter 118 - Firemen's and Rescue Squad Workers' Relief and Pension Funds [Recodified.]	64
Chapter 118A - Firemen's Death Benefit Act [Repealed.]	64
Chapter 118B - Members of a Rescue Squad Death Benefit Act [Repealed.]	64
Chapter 119 - Gasoline and Oil Inspection and Regulation	64
Chapter 120 - General Assembly	65
Chapter 120 - General Assembly (Continuation)	66
Chapter 120 - General Assembly (Continuation)	67
Chapter 120C - Lobbying	67
Chapter 121 - Archives and History	67
Chapter 122 - Hospitals for the Mentally Disordered [Repealed.]	67
Chapter 122A - North Carolina Housing Finance Agency	67
Chapter 122B - North Carolina Agricultural Facilities Finance Act [Repealed.]	67
Chapter 122C - Mental Health, Developmental Disabilities, and Substance Abuse Act of 1985	67
Chapter 122C - Mental Health, Developmental Disabilities, and Substance Abuse Act of 1985 (Continuation)	68
Chapter 122D - North Carolina Agricultural Finance Act	68

Chapter 122E - North Carolina Housing Trust and Oil Overcharge Act	68
Chapter 123 - Impeachment	69
Chapter 123A - Industrial Development [Repealed.]	69
Chapter 124 - Internal Improvements	69
Chapter 125 - Libraries	69
Chapter 126 - State Personnel System	69
Chapter 127 - Militia [Repealed.]	69
Chapter 127A - Militia	69
Chapter 127B - Military Affairs	69
Chapter 127C - Advisory Commission on Military Affairs	69
Chapter 128 - Offices and Public Officers	69
Chapter 128 - Offices and Public Officers (Continuation)	70
Chapter 129 - Public Buildings and Grounds	70
Chapter 130 - Public Health [Repealed.]	70
Chapter 130A - Public Health	70
Chapter 130A - Public Health (Continuation)	71
Chapter 130A - Public Health (Continuation)	72
Chapter 130B - Hazardous Waste Management Commission [Repealed.]	72
Chapter 131 - Public Hospitals [Repealed.]	72
Chapter 131A - Health Care Facilities Finance Act	72
Chapter 131B - Licensing of Ambulatory Surgical Facilities [Repealed.]	72
Chapter 131C - Charitable Solicitation Licensure Act [Repealed.]	72
Chapter 131D - Inspection and Licensing of Facilities	72
Chapter 131E - Health Care Facilities and Services	72
Chapter 131E - Health Care Facilities and Services (Continuation)	73
Chapter 131F - Solicitation of Contributions	73
Chapter 132 - Public Records	73
Chapter 133 - Public Works	74
Chapter 134 - Youth Development [Recodified.]	74
Chapter 134A - Youth Services [Repealed.]	74
Chapter 135 - Retirement System for Teachers and State Employees; Social Security; Health Insurance Program for Children	74
Chapter 135 - Retirement System for Teachers and State Employees; Social Security; Health Insurance Program for Children	75
Chapter 136 - Transportation	75
Chapter 136 - Transportation (Continuation)	76
Chapter 137 - Rural Rehabilitation [Repealed.]	76
Chapter 138 - Salaries, Fees and Allowances	76
Chapter 138A - State Government Ethics Act	76
Chapter 139 - Soil and Water Conservation Districts	76

Chapter 140 - State Art Museum; Symphony and Art Societies	76
Chapter 140A - State Awards System	76
Chapter 141 - State Boundaries	76
Chapter 142 - State Debt	76
Chapter 143 - State Departments, Institutions, and Commissions	77
Chapter 143 - State Departments, Institutions, and Commissions (Continuation)	78
Chapter 143 - State Departments, Institutions, and Commissions (Continuation)	79
Chapter 143 - State Departments, Institutions, and Commissions (Continuation)	80
Chapter 143A - State Government Reorganization	80
Chapter 143B - Executive Organization Act of 1973	80
Chapter 143B - Executive Organization Act of 1973 (Continuation)	81
Chapter 143B - Executive Organization Act of 1973 (Continuation)	82
Chapter 143C - State Budget Act	83
Chapter 143D - The State Governmental Accountability and Internal Control Act	83
Chapter 144 - State Flag, Official Governmental Flags, Motto, and Colors	83
Chapter 145 - State Symbols and Other Official Adoptions.	83
Chapter 146 - State Lands	83
Chapter 147 - State Officers	83
Chapter 148 - State Prison System	84
Chapter 149 - State Song and Toast	84
Chapter 150 - Uniform Revocation of Licenses [Repealed.]	84
Chapter 150A - Administrative Procedure Act [Recodified.]	84
Chapter 150B - Administrative Procedure Act	84
Chapter 151 - Constables [Repealed.]	84
Chapter 152 - Coroners	84
Chapter 152A - County Medical Examiner [Repealed.]	84
Chapter 152A - County Medical Examiner [Repealed.] (Continuation)	85
Chapter 153 - Counties and County Commissioners [Repealed.]	85
Chapter 153A - Counties	85
Chapter 153B - Mountain Resources Planning Act	85
Chapter 153C - Uwharrie Regional Resources Act	85
Chapter 154 - County Surveyor [Repealed.]	85
Chapter 155 - County Treasurer [Repealed.]	85
Chapter 156 - Drainage	85
Chapter 156 – Drainage (Continuation)	86

Chapter 157 - Housing Authorities and Projects	86
Chapter 157A - Historic Properties Commissions [Transferred.]	86
Chapter 158 - Local Development	86
Chapter 159 - Local Government Finance	86
Chapter 159 - Local Government Finance (Continuation)	87
Chapter 159A - Pollution Abatement and Industrial Facilities Financing Act [Unconstitutional.]	87
Chapter 159B - Joint Municipal Electric Power and Energy Act	87
Chapter 159C - Industrial and Pollution Control Facilities Financing Act	87
Chapter 159D - The North Carolina Capital Facilities Financing Act	87
Chapter 159E - Registered Public Obligations Act	87
Chapter 159F - North Carolina Energy Development Authority [Repealed.]	87
Chapter 159G - Water Infrastructure	87
Chapter 159H - [Reserved.]	87
Chapter 159I - Solid Waste Management Loan Program and Local Government Special Obligation Bonds	87
Chapter 160 - Municipal Corporations [Repealed And Transferred.]	87
Chapter 160A - Cities and Towns	88
Chapter 160A - Cities and Towns (Continuation)	89
Chapter 160B - Consolidated City-County Act	89
Chapter 160C - Baseball Park Districts [Repealed.]	90
Chapter 161 - Register of Deeds	90
Chapter 162 - Sheriff	90
Chapter 162A - Water and Sewer Systems	90
Chapter 162B Continuity of Local Government in Emergency.	90
Chapter 163 Elections and Election Laws.	90
Chapter 163 Elections and Election Laws. (Continuation)	91
Chapter 164 Concerning the General Statutes of North Carolina.	92
Chapter 165 Veterans.	92
Chapter 166 Civil Preparedness Agencies [Repealed.]	92
Chapter 166A North Carolina Emergency Management Act.	92
Chapter 167 State Civil Air Patrol [Repealed.]	92
Chapter 168 Persons with Disabilities.	92
Chapter 168A Persons With Disabilities Protection Act.	92

§ 58-10-30. Notice requirements.

(a) The transferring insurer shall provide or cause to be provided to each policyholder a notice of transfer by first-class mail, addressed to the policyholder's last known address or to the address to which premium notices or other policy documents are sent; or with respect to home service business, by personal delivery with acknowledged receipt. A notice of transfer shall also be sent to the transferring insurer's agents or brokers of record on the affected policies.

(b) The notice of transfer shall be in a form identical or substantially similar to Appendix A of the NAIC Assumption Reinsurance Model Act, as amended by the NAIC and shall state or provide:

(1) The date on which the transfer and novation of the policyholder's policy is proposed to take place.

(2) The names, addresses, and telephone numbers of the assuming and transferring insurers.

(3) That the policyholder has the right to either consent to or reject the transfer and novation.

(4) The procedures and time limit for consenting to or rejecting the transfer and novation.

(5) A summary of any effect that consenting to or rejecting the transfer and novation will have on the policyholder's rights.

(6) A statement that the assuming insurer is licensed to write the type of business being assumed in the state where the policyholder resides, or is otherwise authorized, as provided in this Part, to assume that business.

(7) The name and address of the person at the transferring insurer to whom the policyholder should send the policyholder's written statement of acceptance or rejection of the transfer and novation.

(8) The address and telephone number of the insurance department where the policyholder resides so that the policyholder may write or call that insurance department for further information about the financial condition of the assuming insurer.

(9) The following financial data for both insurers:

a. Ratings for the last five years, if available, or for any shorter period that is available, from two nationally recognized insurance rating services acceptable to the Commissioner, including the rating services' explanations of the meanings of their ratings. If ratings are unavailable for any year of the five-year period, this shall also be disclosed.

b. A balance sheet as of December 31 for the previous three years, if available, or for any shorter period that is available, and as of the date of the most recent quarterly statement.

c. A copy of the Management's Discussion and Analysis that was filed as a supplement to the previous year's annual statement.

d. An explanation of the reason for the transfer.

(c) The notice of transfer shall include a preaddressed, postage-paid response card that the policyholder may return as the policyholder's written statement of acceptance or rejection of the transfer and novation.

(d) The notice of transfer shall be filed as part of the prior approval requirement set forth in subsection (e) of this section.

(e) Prior approval by the Commissioner is required for any transaction in which a domestic insurer assumes or transfers obligations or risks on policies under an assumption reinsurance agreement. No insurer licensed in this State shall transfer obligations or risks on policies issued to or owned by residents of this State to any insurer that is not licensed in this State. A domestic insurer shall not assume obligations or risks on policies issued to or owned by policyholders residing in any other state unless it is licensed in the other state, or the insurance regulator of that state has approved the assumption.

(f) Any licensed foreign insurer that enters into an assumption reinsurance agreement that transfers the obligations or risks on policies issued to or owned by residents of this State shall file with the Commissioner the assumption certificate, a copy of the notice of transfer, and an affidavit that the transaction is subject to substantially similar requirements in the states of domicile of both the transferring and assuming insurers. If those requirements do not exist in the state of domicile of either the transferring or assuming insurer, the requirements of subsection (g) of this section apply.

(g) Any licensed foreign insurer that enters into an assumption reinsurance agreement that transfers the obligations or risks on policies issued to or owned by residents of this State shall obtain prior approval of the Commissioner and be subject to all other requirements of this Part with respect to residents of this State, unless the transferring and assuming insurers are subject to assumption reinsurance requirements adopted by statute or administrative rule in the states of their domicile that are substantially similar to those contained in this Part and in any administrative rules adopted under this Part.

(h) The following factors, along with any other factors the Commissioner deems to be appropriate under the circumstances, shall be considered by the Commissioner in reviewing a request for approval:

(1) The financial condition of the transferring and assuming insurers and the effect the transaction will have on the financial condition of each company.

(2) The competence, experience, and integrity of those persons who control the operation of the assuming insurer.

(3) The plans or proposals the assuming insurer has with respect to the administration of the policies subject to the proposed transfer.

(4) Whether the transfer is fair and reasonable to the policyholders of both insurers.

(5) Whether the notice of transfer to be provided by the insurer is fair, adequate, and not misleading. (1995, c. 318, s. 1.)

§ 58-10-35. Policyholder rights.

(a) Policyholders may reject the transfer and novation of their policies by indicating on the response card that the assumption is rejected and returning the card to the transferring insurer.

(b) Payment of any premium to the assuming company during the 24-month period after the notice of transfer has been received indicates the policyholder's acceptance of the transfer to the assuming insurer; and a novation shall occur only if the premium notice clearly states that payment of the premium to the assuming insurer constitutes acceptance of the transfer. The premium notice shall also provide a method for the policyholder to pay the premium while reserving the right to reject the transfer. With respect to any home service business or any other business not using premium notices, the disclosures and procedural requirements of this subsection are to be set forth in the notice of transfer required by G.S. 58-10-30 and in the assumption certificate.

(c) After no fewer than 24 months after the mailing of the initial notice of transfer required under G.S. 58-10-30, if positive consent to, or rejection of, the transfer and assumption has not been received or consent has not been deemed to have occurred under subsection (b) of this section, the transferring insurer shall send to the policyholder a second and final notice of transfer as specified in G.S. 58-10-30. If the policyholder does not accept or reject the transfer during the one-month period immediately after the date on which the transferring insurer mailed the second and final notice of transfer, the policyholder's consent and novation of the contract will occur. With respect to the home service business, or any other business not using premium notices, the 24-month and one-month periods shall be measured from the date of delivery of the notice of transfer under G.S. 58-10-30.

(d) The transferring insurer shall be deemed to have received the response card on the date it is postmarked. A policyholder may also send the response card by facsimile, other electronic transmission, registered mail, express delivery, or courier service; in which case the response card shall be deemed to have been received by the transferring insurer on the date of actual receipt by the transferring insurer. (1995, c. 318, s. 1; 2007-298, s. 7.3; 2007-484, s. 43.5.)

§ 58-10-40. Effect of consent.

If a policyholder consents to the transfer under G.S. 58-10-35 or if the transfer is effected under G.S. 58-10-45, there shall be a novation of the policy, subject to the assumption reinsurance agreement, with the result that the transferring insurer is thereby relieved of all insurance obligations or risks transferred under the assumption reinsurance agreement and the assuming insurer is directly and solely liable to the policyholder for those insurance obligations or risks. (1995, c. 318, s. 1.)

§ 58-10-45. Commissioner's discretion.

If a domestic insurer or a foreign insurer from a state having a substantially similar law is deemed by its domiciliary insurance regulator to be in hazardous financial condition or a proceeding has been instituted against it for the purpose of reorganizing or conserving the insurer, and the transfer of the policies is in the best interest of the policyholders, as determined by the domiciliary insurance regulator, a transfer and novation may be effected notwithstanding the provisions of this Part. This may include a form of implied consent and adequate notification to the policyholders of the circumstances requiring the transfer as approved by the Commissioner. (1995, c. 318, s. 1.)

Part 3. Disclosure of Material Transactions.

§ 58-10-55. Report.

(a) This Part applies only to domestic insurers. Effective October 1, 1995, every insurer shall file a report with the Commissioner disclosing material acquisitions and dispositions of assets or material nonrenewals, cancellations, or revisions of ceded reinsurance agreements, unless the acquisitions and dispositions of assets or material nonrenewals, cancellations, or revisions of ceded reinsurance agreements have been submitted to the Commissioner for review, approval, or informational purposes under any other provisions of this Chapter or the North Carolina Administrative Code. This report is due within 15 days after the end of the calendar month in which any of these transactions occurred. A copy of the report, including any filed exhibits or other attachments, shall also be filed with the NAIC.

(b) All reports obtained by or disclosed to the Commissioner under this Part are confidential and are not subject to subpoena. No report shall be made public by the Commissioner, the NAIC, or any other person, except to insurance regulators of other states, without the prior written consent of the reporting insurer, unless the Commissioner, after giving the insurer notice and an opportunity to be heard, determines that the interest of policyholders, shareholders, or the public will be served by the publication of the report. In that event, the Commissioner may publish all or any part of the report in a manner the Commissioner considers appropriate. (1995, c. 318, s. 1.)

§ 58-10-60. Acquisitions and dispositions of assets.

(a) Insurers do not have to report acquisitions or dispositions under G.S. 58-10-55 if they are not material. For the purposes of this Part, a material acquisition or the aggregate of any series of related acquisitions during any 30-day period, or a material disposition or the aggregate of any series of related dispositions during any 30-day period, is one that is nonrecurring, not in the ordinary course of business, and involves more than five percent (5%) of the insurer's total admitted assets as reported in its most recent financial statement filed with the Department.

(b) Asset acquisitions subject to this Part include every purchase, lease, exchange, merger, consolidation, succession, or other acquisition, other than the construction or development of real property by or for the insurer or the acquisition of materials for that purpose. Asset dispositions subject to this Part include every sale, lease, exchange, merger, consolidation, mortgage, hypothecation, assignment for the benefit of creditors or otherwise, abandonment, destruction, or other disposition.

(c) The following information shall be disclosed in any report under this section:

(1) Date of the transaction.

(2) Manner of acquisition or disposition.

(3) Description of the assets involved.

(4) Nature and amount of the consideration given or received.

(5) Purpose of, or reason for, the transaction.

(6) Manner by which the amount of consideration was determined.

(7) Gain or loss recognized or realized as a result of the transaction.

(8) Name of each person from whom the assets were acquired or to whom they were disposed.

(d) Every insurer shall report material acquisitions and dispositions on a nonconsolidated basis unless the insurer is part of a consolidated group of insurers that uses a pooling arrangement or one hundred percent (100%) reinsurance agreement that affects the solvency and integrity of the insurer's reserves and the insurer ceded substantially all of its direct and assumed business to the pool. An insurer cedes substantially all of its direct and assumed business to a pool if the insurer has less than one million dollars ($1,000,000) total direct plus assumed written premiums during a calendar year that are not subject to a pooling arrangement and the net income of the business not subject to the pooling arrangement represents less than five percent (5%) of the insurer's capital and surplus. (1995, c. 318, s. 1.)

§ 58-10-65. Nonrenewals, cancellations, or revisions of ceded reinsurance agreements.

(a) Insurers do not have to report nonrenewals, cancellations, or revisions of ceded reinsurance agreements under G.S. 58-10-55 if they are not material. For the purposes of this Part, a nonrenewal, cancellation, or revision of a ceded reinsurance agreement is considered material and must be reported if:

(1) It is for property and casualty business, including accident and health business written by a property and casualty insurer and affects:

a. More than fifty percent (50%) of the insurer's total ceded written premium; or

b. More than fifty percent (50%) of the insurer's total ceded indemnity and loss adjustment reserves.

(2) It is for life, annuity, and accident and health business and affects more than fifty percent (50%) of the total reserve credit taken for business ceded, on an annualized basis, as indicated in the insurer's most recent annual statement.

(3) It is for either property and casualty, or life, annuity, and accident and health business, and:

a. An authorized reinsurer representing more than ten percent (10%) of a total cession is replaced by one or more unauthorized reinsurers; or

b. Previously established collateral requirements have been reduced or waived with respect to one or more unauthorized reinsurer's representing collectively more than ten percent (10%) of a total cession.

(b) No filing is required if:

(1) For property and casualty business, including accident and health business written by a property and casualty insurer, the insurer's total ceded written premium represents, on an annualized basis, less than ten percent (10%) of its total written premium for direct and assumed business.

(2) For life, annuity, and accident and health business, the total reserve credit taken for business ceded represents, on an annualized basis, less than ten percent (10%) of the statutory reserve requirement before any cession.

(c) The following information shall be disclosed in any report under this section:

(1) Effective date of the nonrenewal, cancellation, or revision.

(2) Description of the transaction, with an identification of the initiator of the transaction.

(3) Purpose of, or reason for, the transaction.

(4) If applicable, identity of the replacement reinsurers.

(d) Every insurer shall report all material nonrenewals, cancellations, or revisions of ceded reinsurance agreements on a nonconsolidated basis unless the insurer is part of a consolidated group of insurers that uses a pooling arrangement or one hundred percent (100%) reinsurance agreement that affects the solvency and integrity of the insurer's reserves and the insurer ceded substantially all of its direct and assumed business to the pool. An insurer cedes substantially all of its direct and assumed business to a pool if the insurer has less than one million dollars ($1,000,000) total direct plus assumed written premiums during a calendar year that are not subject to the pooling arrangement and the net income of the business not subject to the pooling arrangement represents less than five percent (5%) of the insurer's capital and surplus. (1995, c. 318, s. 1.)

Part 4. Protected Cell Companies.

§ 58-10-75. Purpose and legislative intent.

This Part provides a basis for the creation of protected cells by a domestic insurer as one means of accessing alternative sources of capital and achieving the benefits of insurance securitization. Investors in fully funded insurance securitization transactions provide funds that are available to pay the insurer's insurance obligations or to repay the investors or both. The creation of protected cells is intended to be a means to achieve more efficiencies in conducting insurance securitizations. (2001-223, s. 25.)

§ 58-10-80. Definitions.

As used in this Part, unless the context requires otherwise, the following terms have the following meanings:

(1) "Domestic insurer" means an insurer domiciled in the State of North Carolina.

(2) "Fair value" means the amount at which that asset (or liability) could be bought (or incurred) or sold (or settled) in a current transaction between willing parties, that is, other than in a forced or liquidation sale. Quoted marked prices in active markets are the best evidence of fair value and shall be used as the basis for the measurement, if available. If a quoted market price is available, the fair value is the product of the number of trading units times market price. If quoted market prices are not available, the estimate of fair value shall be based on the best information available. The estimate of fair value shall consider prices for similar assets and liabilities and the results of valuation techniques to the extent available in the circumstances. Examples of valuation techniques include the present value of estimated expected future cash flows using a discount rate commensurate with the risks involved, option-pricing models, matrix pricing, option-adjusted spread models, and fundamental analysis. Valuation techniques for measuring financial assets and liabilities and servicing assets and liabilities shall be consistent with the objective of measuring fair value. Those techniques shall incorporate assumptions that market participants would use in their estimates of values, future revenues, and future expenses, including assumptions about interest rates, default, prepayment, and volatility. In

measuring financial liabilities and servicing liabilities at fair value by discounting estimated future cash flows, an objective is to use discount rates at which those liabilities could be settled in an arm's-length transaction. Estimates of expected future cash flows, if used to estimate fair value, shall be the best estimate based on reasonable and supportable assumptions and projections. All available evidence shall be considered in developing estimates of expected future cash flows. The weight given to the evidence shall be commensurate with the extent to which the evidence can be verified objectively. If a range is estimated for either the amount or timing of possible cash flows, the likelihood of possible outcomes shall be considered in determining the best estimate of future cash flows.

(3)   "Fully funded" means that, with respect to any exposure attributed to a protected cell, the market value of the protected cell assets, on the date on which the insurance securitization is effected, equals or exceeds the maximum possible exposure attributable to the protected cell with respect to the exposures.

(4)   "General account" means the assets and liabilities of a protected cell company other than protected cell assets and protected cell liabilities.

(5)   "Indemnity trigger" means a transaction term by which relief of the issuer's obligation to repay investors is triggered by its incurring a specified level of losses under its insurance or reinsurance contracts.

(6)   "Nonindemnity trigger" means a transaction term by which relief of the issuer's obligation to repay investors is triggered solely by some event or condition other than the individual protected cell company incurring a specified level of losses under its insurance or reinsurance contracts.

(7)   "Protected cell" means an identified pool of assets and liabilities of a protected cell company segregated and insulated by means of this Chapter from the remainder of the protected cell company's assets and liabilities.

(8)   "Protected cell account" means a specifically identified bank or custodial account established by a protected cell company for the purpose of segregating the protected cell assets of one protected cell from the protected cell assets of other protected cells and from the assets of the protected cell company's general account.

(9) "Protected cell assets" means all assets, contract rights, and general intangibles, identified with and attributable to a specific protected cell of a protected cell company.

(10) "Protected cell company" means a domestic insurer that has one or more protected cells.

(11) "Protected cell company insurance securitization" means the issuance of debt instruments, the proceeds from which support the exposures attributed to the protected cell, by a protected cell company where repayment of principal or interest, or both, to investors under the transaction terms is contingent upon the occurrence or nonoccurrence of an event with respect to which the protected cell company is exposed to loss under insurance or reinsurance contracts it has issued.

(12) "Protected cell liabilities" means all liabilities and other obligations identified with and attributable to a specific protected cell of a protected cell company. (2001-223, s. 25.)

§ 58-10-85. Establishment of protected cells.

(a) A protected cell company may establish one or more protected cells with the prior written approval of the Commissioner of a plan of operation or amendments submitted by the protected cell company with respect to each protected cell in connection with an insurance securitization. Upon the Commissioner's written approval of the plan of operation, which plan shall include the specific business objectives and investment guidelines of the protected cell, the protected cell company, in accordance with the approved plan of operation, may attribute to the protected cell insurance obligations with respect to its insurance business and obligations relating to the insurance securitization and assets to fund the obligations. A protected cell shall have its own distinct name or designation, which shall include the words "protected cell." The protected cell company shall transfer all assets attributable to a protected cell to one or more separately established and identified protected cell accounts bearing the name or designation of that protected cell. Protected cell assets must be held in the protected cell accounts for the purpose of satisfying the obligations of that protected cell.

(b)   All attributions of assets and liabilities between a protected cell and the general account must be in accordance with the plan of operation approved by the Commissioner. A protected cell company may make no other attribution of assets or liabilities between the protected cell company's general account and its protected cells. Any attribution of assets and liabilities between the general account and a protected cell, or from investors in the form of principal on a debt instrument issued by a protected cell company in connection with a protected cell company securitization, must be in cash or in readily marketable securities with established market values.

(c)   The creation of a protected cell does not create, with respect to that protected cell, a legal person separate from the protected cell company. Amounts attributed to a protected cell under this Chapter, including assets transferred to a protected cell account, are owned by the protected cell company, and the protected cell company may not be, or may not hold itself out to be, a trustee with respect to those protected cell assets of that protected cell account. Notwithstanding the provisions of this subsection, the protected cell company may allow for a security interest to attach to protected cell assets or a protected cell account when in favor of a creditor of the protected cell and otherwise allowed under applicable law.

(d)   This Part does not prohibit the protected cell company from contracting with or arranging for an investment advisor, commodity trading advisor, or other third party to manage the protected cell assets of a protected cell, if all remuneration, expenses, and other compensation of the third-party advisor or manager are payable from the protected cell assets of that protected cell and not from the protected cell assets of other protected cells or the assets of the protected cell company's general account.

(e)   A protected cell company shall establish administrative and accounting procedures necessary to properly identify the one or more protected cells of the protected cell company and the protected cell assets and protected cell liabilities attributable to the protected cells. It shall be the duty of the directors of a protected cell company to keep protected cell assets and protected cell liabilities:

(1)   Separate and separately identifiable from the assets and liabilities of the protected cell company's general account; and

(2)   Attributable to one protected cell separate and separately identifiable from protected cell assets and protected cell liabilities attributable to other

protected cells. Notwithstanding the provisions of this subsection, if this subsection is violated, the remedy of tracing is applicable to protected cell assets when commingled with protected cell assets of other protected cells or the assets of the protected cell company's general account. The remedy of tracing is not an exclusive remedy.

(f) When establishing a protected cell, the protected cell company shall attribute to the protected cell assets a value at least equal to the reserves and other insurance liabilities attributed to that protected cell. (2001-223, s. 25.)

§ 58-10-90. Use and operation of protected cells.

(a) The protected cell assets of a protected cell may not be charged with liabilities arising out of any other business the protected cell company may conduct. All contracts or other documentation reflecting protected cell liabilities shall clearly indicate that only the protected cell assets are available for the satisfaction of those protected cell liabilities.

(b) The income, gains and losses, realized or unrealized, from protected cell assets and protected cell liabilities must be credited to or charged against the protected cell without regard to other income, gains or losses of the protected cell company, including income, gains or losses of other protected cells. Amounts attributed to any protected cell and accumulations on the attributed amounts may be invested and reinvested without regard to any requirements or limitations of this Chapter and the investments in a protected cell or cells may not be taken into account in applying the investment limitations otherwise applicable to the investments of the protected cell company.

(c) Assets attributed to a protected cell must be valued at their fair value on the date of valuation.

(d) A protected cell company, with respect to any of its protected cells, shall engage in fully funded indemnity triggered insurance securitization to support in full the protected cell exposures attributable to that protected cell. A protected cell company insurance securitization that is nonindemnity triggered shall qualify as an insurance securitization under the terms of this Chapter only after the Commissioner adopts rules addressing the methods of funding of the portion of this risk that is not indemnity based and addressing accounting, disclosure, risk-based capital treatment, and assessing risks associated with the securitizations.

A protected cell company insurance securitization that is not fully funded, whether indemnity triggered or nonindemnity triggered, is prohibited. Protected cell assets may be used to pay interest or other consideration on any outstanding debt or other obligation attributable to that protected cell, and nothing in this subsection may be construed or interpreted to prevent a protected cell company from entering into a swap agreement or other transaction for the account of the protected cell that has the effect of guaranteeing interest or other consideration.

(e)   In all protected cell company insurance securitizations, the contracts or other documentation effecting the transaction shall contain provisions identifying the protected cell to which the transaction will be attributed. In addition, the contracts or other documentation shall clearly disclose that the assets of that protected cell, and only those assets, are available to pay the obligations of that protected cell. Notwithstanding the provisions of this subsection and subject to the provisions of this Chapter and any other applicable law or rule, the failure to include such language in the contracts or other documentation may not be used as the sole basis by creditors, reinsurers, or other claimants to circumvent the provisions of this Part.

(f)   A protected cell company shall only be authorized to attribute to a protected cell account the insurance obligations relating to the protected cell company's general account. Under no circumstances may a protected cell be authorized to issue insurance or reinsurance contracts directly to policyholders or reinsureds or have any obligation to the policyholders or reinsureds of the protected cell company's general account.

(g)   At the cessation of business of a protected cell in accordance with the plan approved by the Commissioner, the protected cell company voluntarily shall close out the protected cell account. (2001-223, s. 25.)

§ 58-10-95. Reach of creditors and other claimants.

(a)   Protected cell assets shall only be available to the creditors of the protected cell company that are creditors with respect to that protected cell and, accordingly, are entitled, in conformity with this Chapter, to have recourse to the protected cell assets attributable to that protected cell and are absolutely protected from the creditors of the protected cell company that are not creditors with respect to that protected cell and who, accordingly, are not entitled to have recourse to the protected cell assets attributable to that protected cell. Creditors with respect to a protected cell are not entitled to have recourse against the protected cell assets of other protected cells or the assets or the protected cell company's general account. Protected cell assets are only available to creditors of a protected cell company after all protected cell liabilities have been extinguished or otherwise provided for in accordance with the plan of operation relating to that protected cell.

(b) When an obligation of a protected cell company to a person arises from a transaction, or is otherwise imposed, with respect to a protected cell:

(1) That obligation of the protected cell company extends only to the protected cell assets attributable to that protected cell, and the person, with respect to that obligation, is entitled to have recourse only to the protected cell assets attributable to that protected cell; and

(2) That obligation of the protected cell company does not extend to the protected cell assets of any other protected cell or the assets of the protected cell company's general account, and that person, with respect to that obligation, is not entitled to have recourse to the protected cell assets of any other protected cell or the assets of the protected cell company's general account.

(c) When an obligation of a protected cell company relates solely to the general account, the obligation of the protected cell company extends only to, and that creditor, with respect to that obligation, is entitled to have recourse only to the assets of the protected cell company's general account.

(d) The activities, assets, and obligations relating to a protected cell are not subject to the provisions of Articles 48 and 62 of this Chapter, and neither a protected cell nor a protected cell company may be assessed by, or otherwise be required to contribute to, any guaranty fund or guaranty association in this State with respect to the activities, assets, or obligations of a protected cell. Nothing in this subsection affects the activities or obligations of an insurer's general account.

(e) The establishment of one or more protected cells alone does not constitute a fraudulent conveyance, an intent by the protected cell company to defraud creditors, or the carrying out of business by the protected cell company for any other fraudulent purpose. (2001-223, s. 25.)

§ 58-10-100. Conservation, rehabilitation, or liquidation of protected cell companies.

(a) Notwithstanding any other provision of law or rule, upon an order of conservation, rehabilitation, or liquidation of a protected cell company, the receiver shall deal with the protected cell company's assets and liabilities, including protected cell assets and protected cell liabilities, in accordance with the requirements set forth in this Part.

(b) With respect to amounts recoverable under a protected cell company insurance securitization, the amount recoverable by the receiver may not be reduced or diminished as a result of the entry of an order of conservation, rehabilitation, or liquidation with respect to the protected cell company, notwithstanding any provisions to the contrary in the contracts or other documentation governing the protected cell company insurance securitization. (2001-223, s. 25.)

§ 58-10-105. No transaction of an insurance business.

A protected cell company insurance securitization may not be deemed to be an insurance or reinsurance contract. An investor in a protected cell company insurance securitization, by sole means of this investment, may not be deemed to be conducting an insurance business in this State. The underwriters or selling agents and their partners, directors, officers, members, managers, employees, agents, representatives, and advisors involved in a protected cell company insurance securitization may not be deemed to be conducting an insurance or reinsurance agency, brokerage, intermediary, advisory, or consulting business by virtue of their activities in connection with that business. (2001-223, s. 25.)

§ 58-10-110. Authority to adopt rules.

The Commissioner may adopt rules necessary to effectuate the purposes of this Part. (2001-223, s. 25.)

Part 5. Mortgage Guaranty Insurance.

§ 58-10-120. Definitions.

As used in this Part:

(1) "Mortgage guaranty insurers report of policyholders position" means the supplementary report required by the Commissioner.

(2) "Policyholders position" means the contingency reserve established under G.S. 58-10-135 and policyholders' surplus. "Minimum policyholders position" is calculated as described in G.S. 58-10-125.

(3) "Policyholders surplus" means an insurer's net worth; the difference between its assets and liabilities, as reported in its annual statement. (2001-223, s. 11; 2005-215, s. 11.)

§ 58-10-125. Policyholders position and capital and surplus requirements.

(a) For the purpose of complying with G.S. 58-7-75, a mortgage guaranty insurer shall maintain at all times a minimum policyholders position of not less than one twenty-fifth of the insurer's aggregate insured risk outstanding. The policyholders position shall be net of reinsurance ceded but shall include reinsurance assumed.

(b) Subject to the provisions of subsections (i) through (l) of this section, if a mortgage guaranty insurer does not have the minimum amount of policyholders position required by this section it shall cease transacting new business until the time that its policyholders position is in compliance with this section.

(c) A mortgage guaranty insurer shall at all times maintain capital and surplus in the greater of the amount required by G.S. 58-7-75 or subsection (a) of this section, unless a waiver is obtained by the mortgage guaranty insurer pursuant to subsection (i) of this section.

(d) through (h) Repealed by Session Laws 2007-127, s. 5, effective July 1, 2007.

(i) The Commissioner may waive the requirement found in subsection (a) of this section at the written request of a mortgage guaranty insurer upon a finding that the mortgage guaranty insurer's policyholders position is reasonable in relationship to the mortgage guaranty insurer's aggregate insured risk and adequate to its financial needs. The request must be made in writing at least 90 days in advance of the date that the mortgage guaranty insurer expects to exceed the requirement of subsection (a) of this section and shall, at a minimum, address the factors specified in subsection (j) of this section.

(j) In determining whether a mortgage guaranty insurer's policyholders position is reasonable in relation to the mortgage guaranty insurer's aggregate insured risk and adequate to its financial needs, all of the following factors, among others, shall be considered:

(1) The size of the mortgage guaranty insurer as measured by its assets, capital and surplus, reserves, premium writings, insurance in force, and other appropriate criteria.

(2) The extent to which the mortgage guaranty insurer's business is diversified across time, geography, credit quality, origination, and distribution channels.

(3) The nature and extent of the mortgage guaranty insurer's reinsurance program.

(4) The quality, diversification, and liquidity of the mortgage guaranty insurer's assets and its investment portfolio.

(5) The historical and forecasted trend in the size of the mortgage guaranty insurer's policyholders position.

(6) The policyholders position maintained by other comparable mortgage guaranty insurers in relation to the nature of their respective insured risks.

(7) The adequacy of the mortgage guaranty insurer's reserves.

(8) The quality and liquidity of investments in affiliates. The Commissioner may treat any such investment as a nonadmitted asset for purposes of determining the adequacy of surplus as regards policyholders.

(9) The quality of the mortgage guaranty insurer's earnings and the extent to which the reported earnings of the mortgage guaranty insurer include extraordinary items.

(10) An independent actuary's opinion as to the reasonableness and adequacy of the mortgage guaranty insurer's historical and projected policyholders position.

(11) The capital contributions which have been infused or are available for future infusion into the mortgage guaranty insurer.

(12) The historical and projected trends in the components of the mortgage guaranty insurer's aggregate insured risk, including, but not limited to, the quality and type of the risks included in the aggregate insured risk.

(k) The Commissioner may retain accountants, actuaries, or other experts to assist the Commissioner in the review of the mortgage guaranty insurer's request submitted pursuant to subsection (i) of this section. The mortgage guaranty insurer shall bear the Commissioner's cost of retaining those persons.

(l) Any waiver shall be (i) for a specified period of time not to exceed two years and (ii) subject to any terms and conditions that the Commissioner shall deem best suited to restoring the mortgage guaranty insurer's minimum policyholders position required by subsection (a) of this section. (2001-223, s. 11; 2007-127, s. 5; 2009-254, s. 1; 2010-40, ss. 1, 2; 2013-199, s. 3(a), (b).)

§ 58-10-130. Unearned premium reserve.

(a) The unearned premium reserve shall be computed as follows:

(1) The unearned premium reserve for premiums paid in advance annually shall be calculated on the monthly pro rata fractional basis.

(2) Premiums paid in advance for 10-year coverage shall be placed in the unearned premium reserve and shall be released from this reserve as follows:

a. 1st month - 1/132;

b. 2nd through 12th month - 2/132 each month;

c. 13th month - 3/264;

d. 14th through 120th month - 1/132 per month;

e. 121st month - 1/264

(3) Premiums paid in advance for periods in excess of 10 years. During the first 10 years of coverage the unearned portion of the premium shall be the premium collected minus an amount equal to the premium that would have been earned had the applicable premium for 10 years of coverage been received. The premium remaining after 10 years shall be released from the unearned premium reserve monthly pro rata over the remaining term of coverage.

(b) Repealed by Session Laws 2001-334, s. 16.1.

(c) The case basis method shall be used to determine the loss reserve which shall include a reserve for claims reported and unpaid and a reserve for claims incurred but not reported. (2001-223, s. 11; 2001-334, s. 16.1.)

§ 58-10-135. Contingency reserve for mortgage guaranty insurers.

(a) Subject to G.S. 58-7-21, a mortgage guaranty insurer shall make an annual contribution to the contingency reserve which in the aggregate shall be fifty percent (50%) of the net earned mortgage guaranty premium reported in the annual statement.

(b) Repealed by Session Laws 2007-127, s. 6, effective July 1, 2007.

(c) The contingency reserve established by this section shall be maintained for 120 months and reported in the financial statements as a liability. That portion of the contingency reserve established and maintained for more than 120 months shall be released and shall no longer constitute part of the contingency reserve.

(d) With the approval of the Commissioner, withdrawals may be made from the contingency reserve when incurred losses and incurred loss expenses exceed thirty-five percent (35%) of the net earned premium. On a quarterly basis, provisional withdrawals may be made from the contingency reserve in an amount not to exceed seventy-five percent (75%) of the withdrawal calculated in accordance with this subsection.

(e) With the approval of the Commissioner, a mortgage guaranty insurer may withdraw from the contingency reserve any amounts which are in excess of the minimum policyholders position as filed with the most recently filed annual statement. In reviewing a request for withdrawal pursuant to this subsection, the Commissioner may consider loss development and trends. If any portion of the contingency reserve for which withdrawal is requested pursuant to this subsection is maintained by a reinsurer, the Commissioner may also consider the financial condition of the reinsurer. If any portion of the contingency reserve for which withdrawal is requested pursuant to this subsection is maintained in a segregated account or segregated trust and such withdrawal would result in funds being removed from the segregated account or segregated trust, the Commissioner may also consider the financial condition of the reinsurer.

(f) Releases and withdrawals from the contingency reserve shall be accounted for on a first-in-first-out basis as prescribed by the Commissioner.

(g) The calculations to develop the contingency reserve shall be made in the following sequence:

(1) The additions required by subsection (a) of this section;

(2) The releases permitted by subsection (c) of this section;

(3) The withdrawals permitted by subsection (d) of this section; and

(4) The withdrawals permitted by subsection (e) of this section.

(h) Whenever the laws or regulations of another jurisdiction in which a mortgage guaranty insurer, subject to the requirements of this Part is licensed, require a larger unearned premium reserve or a larger contingency reserve in the aggregate than that set forth in this Part, the establishment and maintenance of the larger unearned premium reserve or contingency reserve shall be deemed to be in compliance with this Part. (2001-223, s. 11; 2001-334, ss. 16.2, 16.3; 2007-127, s. 6.)

§ 58-10-140. Report of policyholder's position.

Each mortgage guaranty insurance company doing business in this State must file on a form prescribed by the Commissioner a Mortgage Guaranty Insurers Report of Policyholders Position. The supplemental reports shall be filed with the annual and quarterly statements pursuant to G.S. 58-2-165. (2005-215, s. 12.)

§ 58-10-145. Monoline requirement for mortgage guaranty insurers.

A mortgage guaranty insurance company that transacts any kind of insurance other than mortgage guaranty insurance is not eligible to transact business in this State. Provided, however, that a mortgage guaranty insurance company may, until December 31, 2012, assume reinsurance for "credit insurance," as defined in G.S. 58-7-15(17). (2007-127, s. 7; 2008-124, s. 2.2.)

Part 6. Property and Casualty Actuarial Opinions.

§ 58-10-150. Statement of actuarial opinion.

Every property and casualty insurance company doing business in this State, unless otherwise exempted by the Commissioner, shall annually submit the opinion of an appointed actuary entitled, "statement of actuarial opinion." This opinion shall be filed in accordance with the appropriate NAIC Property and Casualty Annual Statement Instructions. (2007-127, s. 15.)

§ 58-10-155. Actuarial opinion summary.

(a) Every property and casualty insurance company domiciled in this State that is required to submit a statement of actuarial opinion shall annually submit an actuarial opinion summary, written by the company's appointed actuary. This actuarial opinion summary shall be filed in accordance with the appropriate NAIC Property and Casualty Annual Statement Instructions and shall be considered as a document supporting the statement of actuarial opinion required in G.S. 58-10-150.

(b) A company licensed but not domiciled in this State, and a company writing business in this State although not specifically licensed to do so or otherwise authorized, shall provide the actuarial opinion summary upon request. (2007-127, s. 15.)

§ 58-10-160. Actuarial report and work papers.

(a) An actuarial report and underlying work papers as required by the appropriate NAIC Property and Casualty Annual Statement Instructions shall be prepared to support each statement of actuarial opinion and actuarial opinion summary.

(b) If an insurance company fails to provide a supporting actuarial report or work papers at the request of the Commissioner or if the Commissioner determines that the supporting actuarial report or work papers provided by an insurance company are unsatisfactory to the Commissioner, the Commissioner may engage an independent, qualified actuary at the expense of the company to (i) review the opinion and the basis for the opinion and (ii) prepare an actuarial report or work papers. (2007-127, s. 15.)

§ 58-10-165. Monetary penalties for failure to provide documents.

A company that fails to provide a statement of actuarial opinion, actuarial opinion summary, actuarial report, or work papers within the time frame provided in the Commissioner's written request, is subject to the monetary penalties set forth in G.S. 58-2-70. (2007-127, s. 15.)

§ 58-10-170. Qualified immunity of appointed actuary.

The appointed actuary shall not be liable for damages to any person other than the insurance company or the Commissioner for any act, error, omission, decision, or conduct with respect to the appointed actuary's opinion, except in cases of fraud or willful misconduct by the appointed actuary. (2007-127, s. 15.)

§ 58-10-175. Confidentiality.

(a) The statement of actuarial opinion shall be treated as a public record.

(b) Documents, materials, or other information in the possession or control of the Department that are considered an actuarial opinion summary, actuarial report, or work papers provided in support of the opinion, and any other material provided by the company to the Commissioner in connection with the actuarial opinion summary, actuarial report, or work papers shall be confidential by law and privileged, in accord with G.S. 58-2-240, shall not be subject to G.S. 58-2-100, shall not be subject to subpoena, and shall not be subject to discovery or admissible as evidence in any private civil action.

(c) Subsection (b) of this section shall not be construed to limit the Commissioner's authority to release documents to the Actuarial Board for Counseling and Discipline if the documents are required for the purpose of professional disciplinary proceedings and if the Actuarial Board for Counseling and Discipline establishes procedures satisfactory to the Commissioner for preserving the confidentiality of the documents. In addition, this section shall not be construed to limit the Commissioner's authority to use any documents, materials, or other information in furtherance of any regulatory or legal action brought as part of the Commissioner's official duties.

(d) Neither the Commissioner nor any person who received documents, materials, or other information while acting under the authority of the Commissioner shall be permitted or required to testify in any private civil action concerning any confidential documents, materials, or information subject to subsection (b) of this section.

(e) In order to assist in the performance of the Commissioner's duties, the Commissioner:

(1) May share documents, materials, or other information, including the confidential and privileged documents, materials, or information subject to subsection (b) of this section with other state, federal, and international regulatory agencies, with the NAIC and its affiliates and subsidiaries, and with state, federal, and international law enforcement authorities, provided that the recipient agrees to maintain the confidentiality and privileged status of the document, material, or other information and has the legal authority to maintain confidentiality.

(2) May receive documents, materials, or information, including otherwise confidential and privileged documents, materials, or information, from the NAIC and its affiliates and subsidiaries, and from regulatory and law enforcement officials of other foreign or domestic jurisdictions, and shall maintain as confidential or privileged any document, material, or information received with notice or the understanding that it is confidential or privileged under the laws of the jurisdiction that is the source of the document, material, or information.

(3) May enter into agreements governing the sharing and use of information consistent with this section.

(f) No waiver of any applicable privilege or claim of confidentiality in the documents, materials, or information shall occur as a result of disclosure to the Commissioner under this section or as a result of sharing as authorized in subsection (e) of this section. (2007-127, s. 15.)

Part 7. Annual Financial Reporting.

§ 58-10-185. Purpose and scope.

(a) The purpose of this Part is to improve the Commissioner's ability to monitor the financial condition of insurers by requiring (i) an annual audit of financial statements reporting the financial position and the results of operations of insurers by independent certified public accountants, (ii) communication of internal control related matters noted in an audit, and (iii) management's report of internal control over financial reporting.

(b) Every insurer, as defined in G.S. 58-10-190, shall be subject to this Part. Insurers having direct premiums written in this State of less than one million dollars ($1,000,000) in any calendar year and fewer than 1,000 policyholders or certificate holders of direct written policies nationwide at the end of the calendar year shall be exempt from this Part for the year, unless the Commissioner makes a specific finding that compliance is necessary for the Commissioner to carry out statutory responsibilities, except that insurers having assumed premiums pursuant to contracts of reinsurance of one million dollars ($1,000,000) or more will not be exempt.

(c) Foreign or alien insurers filing the audited financial report in another state, pursuant to that state's requirement for filing of audited financial reports, which has been found by the Commissioner to be substantially similar to the requirements in this Part, are exempt from G.S. 58-10-195 through G.S. 58-10-240 if:

(1) A copy of the audited financial report, communication of internal control related matters noted in an audit, and the accountant's letter of qualifications that are filed with the other state are filed with the Commissioner in accordance with the filing dates specified in G.S. 58-10-195, 58-10-230, and 58-10-235, respectively. Canadian insurers may submit accountants' reports as filed with the Office of the Superintendent of Financial Institutions, Canada.

(2) A copy of any notification of adverse financial condition report filed with the other state is filed with the Commissioner within the time specified in G.S. 58-10-225.

(d) Foreign or alien insurers required to file management's report of internal control over financial reporting in another state are exempt from filing the report in this State provided the other state has substantially similar reporting requirements and the report is filed with the Commissioner of the other state within the time specified.

(e) This Part shall not prohibit, preclude, or in any way limit the Commissioner from ordering, conducting, or performing examinations of insurers in accordance with G.S. 58-2-131 through G.S. 58-2-134, known as the Examination Law. (2009-384, s. 1.)

§ 58-10-190. Definitions.

As used in this Part:

(1) "Accountant" or "independent certified public accountant" means an independent certified public accountant or accounting firm in good standing with the American Institute of Certified Public Accountants (AICPA) and in all states in which he or she is licensed to practice; for Canadian and British companies, it means a Canadian-chartered or British-chartered accountant.

(2) An "affiliate" of, or person "affiliated" with, a specific person has the same meaning set forth in G.S. 58-19-5.

(3) "Audit committee" means a committee, or equivalent body, established by the board of directors of an entity for the purpose of overseeing the accounting and financial reporting processes of an insurer or group of insurers and audits of financial statements of the insurer or group of insurers. The audit committee of any entity that controls a group of insurers may be deemed to be the audit committee for one or more of these controlled insurers at the election of the controlling person as provided in G.S. 58-10-245(f). If an audit committee is not designated by the insurer, the insurer's entire board of directors shall constitute the audit committee.

(4) "Audited financial report" means and includes those items specified in G.S. 58-10-200.

(5) "Controlling person" has the same meaning set forth in G.S. 58-19-5.

(6) "Group of insurers" means those licensed insurers included in the reporting requirements of Article 19 of this Chapter, or a set of insurers as identified by management, for the purpose of assessing the effectiveness of internal control over financial reporting.

(7) "Indemnification" means an agreement of indemnity or a release from liability where the intent or effect is to shift or limit in any manner the potential liability of the person or firm for failure to adhere to applicable auditing or professional standards, whether or not resulting from other known misrepresentations made by the insurer or its representatives.

(8) "Insurer" means any insurance entity as identified in Articles 7, 8, 11, 15, 17, 23, 24, 25, 26, 65, and 67 of this Chapter and regulated by the Commissioner.

(9) "Internal control over financial reporting" means a process effected by an entity's board of directors, management, and other personnel designed to provide reasonable assurance regarding the reliability of the financial statements, that is, those items specified in G.S. 58-10-200(b)(2) through G.S. 58-10-200(b)(6) and includes those policies and procedures that meet all of the following criteria:

a. Pertain to the maintenance of records that, in reasonable detail, accurately and fairly reflect the transactions and dispositions of assets.

b. Provide reasonable assurance that transactions are recorded as necessary to permit preparation of the financial statements, that is, those items specified in G.S. 58-10-200(b)(2) through G.S. 58-10-200(b)(6) and that receipts and expenditures are being made only in accordance with authorizations of management and directors.

c. Provide reasonable assurance regarding prevention or timely detection of unauthorized acquisition, use, or disposition of assets that could have a material effect on the financial statements, including those items specified in G.S. 58-10-200(b)(2) through G.S. 58-10-200(b)(6).

(10) "SEC" means the United States Securities and Exchange Commission, or any successor agency.

(11) "Section 404" means Section 404 of the Sarbanes-Oxley Act of 2002 and the SEC's rules and regulations promulgated under that act.

(12) "Section 404 report" means management's report on "internal control over financial reporting" as defined by the SEC and the related attestation report of the independent certified public accountant as described in Section 3A of the Sarbanes-Oxley Act of 2002.

(13) "SOX-compliant entity" means an entity that either is required to be compliant with, or voluntarily is compliant with, all of the following provisions of the Sarbanes-Oxley Act of 2002: (i) Section 202. Preapproval requirements of Title II, Auditor Independence; (ii) Section 301. Audit Committees independence requirements of Title III, Corporate Responsibility; and (iii) Section 404. Management assessment of internal controls requirements of Title IV, Enhanced Financial Disclosures. (2009-384, s. 1.)

§ 58-10-195. General requirements related to filing and extensions for filing of annual audited financial reports and audit committee appointment.

(a) All insurers shall have an annual audit by an independent certified public accountant and shall file an audited financial report with the Commissioner on or before June 1 for the year ended December 31 immediately preceding. The

Commissioner may require an insurer to file an audited financial report earlier than June 1 with 90 days' advance notice to the insurer.

(b)   Extensions of the June 1 filing date may be granted by the Commissioner for 30-day periods upon a showing by the insurer and its independent certified public accountant of the reasons for requesting an extension and determination by the Commissioner of good cause for an extension. The request for extension must be received in writing not less than 10 days before the due date and in sufficient detail to permit the Commissioner to make an informed decision with respect to the requested extension.

(c)   If an extension is granted in accordance with the provisions in subsection (b) of this section, a similar extension of 30 days is granted to the filing of management's report of internal control over financial reporting.

(d)   Every insurer required to file an annual audited financial report pursuant to this Part shall designate a group of individuals as constituting its audit committee, as defined in G.S. 58-10-190. The audit committee of an entity that controls an insurer may be deemed to be the insurer's audit committee at the election of the controlling person. (2009-384, s. 1.)

§ 58-10-200. Contents of annual audited financial report.

(a)   The annual audited financial report shall report the financial position of the insurer as of the end of the most recent calendar year and the results of its operations, cash flows, and changes in capital and surplus for the year then ended in conformity with G.S. 58-2-165(c). The financial statements included in the audited financial report shall be prepared in a form and using language and groupings substantially the same as the relevant sections of the annual statement of the insurer filed with the Commissioner, and the financial statement shall be comparative, presenting the amounts as of December 31 of the current year and the amounts as of the immediately preceding December 31. However, in the first year in which an insurer is required to file an audited financial report, the comparative data may be omitted.

(b)   The annual audited financial report shall include the following:

(1)   Report of independent certified public accountant.

(2) Balance sheet reporting admitted assets, liabilities, capital, and surplus.

(3) Statement of operations.

(4) Statement of cash flows.

(5) Statement of changes in capital and surplus.

(6) Notes to financial statements, which shall be those required by the appropriate NAIC Annual Statement Instructions and the NAIC Accounting Practices and Procedures Manual. The notes shall include a reconciliation of differences, if any, between the audited statutory financial statements and the annual statement filed pursuant to G.S. 58-2-165(c) with a written description of the nature of these differences. (2009-384, s. 1.)

§ 58-10-205. Designation of independent certified public accountant.

(a) Each insurer required by this Part to file an annual audited financial report must, within 60 days after becoming subject to the requirement, register with the Commissioner in writing the name and address of the independent certified public accountant or accounting firm retained to conduct the annual audit. Insurers not retaining an independent certified public accountant on July 31, 2009, shall register the name and address of their retained independent certified public accountant not less than six months before the date when the first audited financial report is to be filed.

(b) The insurer shall obtain a letter from the accountant and file a copy with the Commissioner stating that the accountant is aware of the provisions of the insurance laws and the regulations of the State of North Carolina that relate to accounting and financial matters and affirming that the accountant will express his or her opinion on the financial statement in terms of its conformity to the statutory accounting practices prescribed or otherwise permitted by the Commissioner, specifying such exceptions as he or she may believe appropriate.

(c) If an accountant for the immediately preceding filed audited financial report is dismissed or resigns, the insurer shall within five business days notify the Commissioner of this event. The insurer shall also furnish the Commissioner with a separate letter within 10 business days after the notification stating whether in the 24 months preceding such event there were any disagreements with the former accountant on any matter of accounting principles or practices, financial statement disclosure, or auditing scope or procedure; which disagreements, if not resolved to the satisfaction of the former accountant, would have caused him or her to make reference to the subject matter of the disagreement in connection with his or her opinion. The disagreements required to be reported in response to this section include both those resolved to the former accountant's satisfaction and those not resolved to the former accountant's satisfaction. Disagreements contemplated by this section could include, but are not limited to, disagreements between personnel of the insurer responsible for presentation of its financial statements and personnel of the accounting firm responsible for rendering its report. The insurer shall also in writing request the former accountant to furnish a letter addressed to the insurer stating whether the accountant agrees with the statements contained in the insurer's letter and, if not, stating the reasons for which he or she does not agree; and the insurer shall furnish the responsive letter from the former accountant to the Commissioner together with its own. (2009-384, s. 1.)

§ 58-10-210. Qualifications of independent certified public accountant.

(a) The Commissioner shall not recognize a person or firm as a qualified independent certified public accountant if the person or firm:

(1) Is not in good standing with the North Carolina State Board of Certified Public Accountant Examiners and in all other states in which the accountant is licensed to practice, or, for a Canadian or British company, that is not a chartered accountant; or

(2) Has either directly or indirectly entered into an agreement of indemnity or release from liability, collectively referred to as indemnification, with respect to the audit of the insurer.

(b) Except as otherwise provided in this Part, the Commissioner shall recognize an independent certified public accountant as qualified as long as he or she conforms to the standards of his or her profession, as contained in the Code of Professional Ethics of the AICPA and Rules and Regulations and Code of Ethics and Rules of Professional Conduct of the North Carolina State Board of Certified Public Accountant Examiners or similar code.

(c)   A qualified independent certified public accountant may enter into an agreement with an insurer to have disputes relating to an audit resolved by mediation or arbitration. However, in the event of a delinquency proceeding commenced against the insurer under Article 30 of this Chapter, the mediation or arbitration provisions shall operate at the option of the statutory successor.

(d)   Lead Audit Partner Rotation Required.

(1)   The lead or coordinating audit partner, having primary responsibility for the audit, may not act in that capacity for more than five consecutive years. The person shall be disqualified from acting in that or a similar capacity for the same company or its insurance subsidiaries or affiliates for a period of five consecutive years. An insurer may apply to the Commissioner for relief from the rotation requirement on the basis of unusual circumstances. This application shall be made at least 30 days before the end of the calendar year. The Commissioner may consider any of the following factors in determining if the relief should be granted:

a.   The number of partners, expertise of the partners, or the number of insurance clients in the currently registered firm.

b.   The premium volume of the insurer.

c.   The number of jurisdictions in which the insurer transacts business.

(2)   The insurer shall file, with its annual statement filing, the approval for relief granted pursuant to subdivision (1) of this subsection with the states in which it is licensed or doing business and with the NAIC. If the nondomestic state accepts electronic filing with the NAIC, the insurer shall file the approval in an electronic format.

(e)   The Commissioner shall neither recognize as a qualified independent certified public accountant, nor accept an annual audited financial report prepared, in whole or in part, by a natural person who meets any of the following criteria:

(1)   The person has been convicted of fraud, bribery, a violation of the Racketeer Influenced and Corrupt Organizations Act, 18 U.S.C. §§ 1961 to 1968k, or any dishonest conduct or practices under federal or state law.

(2) The person has been found to have violated the insurance laws of this State with respect to any previous reports submitted under this Part.

(3) The person has demonstrated a pattern or practice of failing to detect or disclose material information in previous reports filed under the provisions of this Part.

(f) The Commissioner may, as provided in G.S. 58-2-50, hold a hearing to determine whether an independent certified public accountant is qualified and, considering the evidence presented, may rule that the accountant is not qualified for purposes of expressing his or her opinion on the financial statements in the annual audited financial report made pursuant to this Part and require the insurer to replace the accountant with another whose relationship with the insurer is qualified within the meaning of this Part.

(g) Independence of Services.

(1) The Commissioner shall not recognize as a qualified independent certified public accountant nor accept an annual audited financial report prepared, in whole or in part, by an accountant who provides to an insurer, contemporaneously with the audit, any of the following nonaudit services:

a. Bookkeeping or other services related to the accounting records or financial statements of the insurer.

b. Financial information systems design and implementation.

c. Appraisal or valuation services, fairness opinions, or contribution-in-kind reports.

d. Actuarially oriented advisory services involving the determination of amounts recorded in the financial statements. The accountant may assist an insurer in understanding the methods, assumptions, and inputs used in the determination of amounts recorded in the financial statement only if it is reasonable to conclude that the services provided will not be subject to audit procedures during an audit of the insurer's financial statements. An accountant's actuary may also issue an actuarial opinion or certification on an insurer's reserves if all of the following conditions have been met:

1. Neither the accountant nor the accountant's actuary has performed any management functions or made any management decisions.

2. The insurer has competent personnel, or engages a third-party actuary to estimate the reserves for which management takes responsibility.

3. The accountant's actuary tests the reasonableness of the reserves after the insurer's management has determined the amount of the reserves.

e. Internal audit outsourcing services.

f. Management functions or human resources.

g. Broker or dealer, investment adviser, or investment banking services.

h. Legal services or expert services unrelated to the audit.

i. Any other services that the Commissioner determines, by administrative rule, are impermissible.

(2) In general, the principles of independence with respect to services provided by the qualified independent certified public accountant are largely predicated on three basic principles, violations of which would impair the accountant's independence. The principles are that the accountant cannot function in the role of management, cannot audit his or her own work, and cannot serve in an advocacy role for the insurer.

(h) Insurers having direct written and assumed premiums of less than one hundred million dollars ($100,000,000) in any calendar year may request an exemption from subdivision (1) of subsection (g) of this section. The insurer shall file with the Commissioner a written statement discussing the reasons why the insurer should be exempt from these provisions. If the Commissioner finds, upon review of this statement, that compliance with this Part would constitute a financial or organizational hardship upon the insurer, an exemption may be granted.

(i) A qualified independent certified public accountant who performs the audit may engage in other nonaudit services, including tax services, that are not described in subdivision (1) of subsection (g) of this section or that do not conflict with the principles set forth in subdivision (2) of subsection (g) of this section, only if the activity is approved in advance by the audit committee, in accordance with subsection (j) of this section.

(j) All auditing services and nonaudit services provided to an insurer by the qualified independent certified public accountant of the insurer shall be preapproved by the audit committee. The preapproval requirement is waived with respect to nonaudit services if the insurer is a SOX-compliant entity or is a direct or indirect wholly owned subsidiary of a SOX-compliant entity or all of the following apply:

(1) The aggregate amount of all such nonaudit services provided to the insurer constitutes not more than five percent (5%) of the total amount of fees paid by the insurer to its qualified independent certified public accountant during the fiscal year in which the nonaudit services are provided.

(2) The services were not recognized by the insurer at the time of the engagement to be nonaudit services.

(3) The services are promptly brought to the attention of the audit committee and approved before the completion of the audit by the audit committee or by one or more members of the audit committee who are the members of the board of directors to whom authority to grant such approvals has been delegated by the audit committee.

(k) The audit committee may delegate to one or more designated members of the audit committee the authority to grant the preapprovals required by subsection (j) of this section. The decisions of any member to whom this authority is delegated shall be presented to the full audit committee at each of its scheduled meetings.

(l) Cooling-Off Period.

(1) The Commissioner shall not recognize an independent certified public accountant as qualified for a particular insurer if a member of the board, president, chief executive officer, controller, chief financial officer, chief accounting officer, or any person serving in an equivalent position for that insurer was employed by the independent certified public accountant and participated in the audit of that insurer during the one-year period preceding the date that the most current statutory opinion is due. This section shall only apply to partners and senior managers involved in the audit. An insurer may apply to the Commissioner for relief from this requirement on the basis of unusual circumstances.

(2) The insurer shall file, with its annual statement filing, the approval for relief granted pursuant to subdivision (1) of this subsection with the states in which it is licensed or doing business and the NAIC. If the nondomestic state accepts electronic filing with the NAIC, the insurer shall file the approval in an electronic format. (2009-384, s. 1.)

§ 58-10-215. Consolidated or combined audits.

An insurer may make written application to the Commissioner for approval to file audited consolidated or combined financial statements in lieu of separate annual audited financial statements if the insurer is part of a group of insurance companies that utilizes a pooling or one hundred percent (100%) reinsurance agreement that affects the solvency of the insurer and affects the integrity of the insurer's reserves and the insurer cedes all of its direct and assumed business to the pool. In such cases, a columnar consolidating or combining worksheet that meets all of the following criteria shall be filed with the report:

(1) Amounts shown on the consolidated or combined audited financial report shall be shown on the worksheet.

(2) Amounts for each insurer subject to this section shall be stated separately.

(3) Noninsurance operations may be shown on the worksheet on a combined or individual basis.

(4) Explanations of consolidating and eliminating entries shall be included.

(5) A reconciliation shall be included of any differences between the amounts shown in the individual insurer columns of the worksheet and comparable amounts shown on the annual statements of the insurers. (2009-384, s. 1.)

§ 58-10-220. Scope of audit and report of independent certified public accountant.

Financial statements furnished pursuant to G.S. 58-10-200 shall be examined by the independent certified public accountant. The audit of the insurer's financial statements shall be conducted in accordance with generally accepted auditing standards. In accordance with AU Section 319 of the Professional Standards of the AICPA, Consideration of Internal Control in a Financial Statement Audit, the independent certified public accountant should obtain an understanding of internal control sufficient to plan the audit. To the extent required by AU Section 319, for those insurers required to file a management's report of internal control over financial reporting pursuant to G.S. 58-10-255, the independent certified public accountant should consider, as that term is defined in "Statement on Auditing Standards No. 102 of the AICPA Professional Standards, Defining Professional Requirements in Statements on Auditing Standards" or its replacement, the most recently available report in planning and performing the audit of the statutory financial statements. Consideration shall be given to the procedures illustrated in the Financial Condition Examiners Handbook promulgated by the NAIC as the independent certified public accountant deems necessary. (2009-384, s. 1.)

§ 58-10-225. Notification of adverse financial condition.

(a)   The insurer required to furnish the annual audited financial report shall require the independent certified public accountant to report, in writing, within five business days to the board of directors or its audit committee any determination by the independent certified public accountant that the insurer has materially misstated its financial condition as reported to the Commissioner as of the balance sheet date currently under audit or that the insurer does not meet the minimum capital and surplus requirement of G.S. 58-7-75 as of that date. An insurer that has received a report pursuant to this subsection shall forward a copy of the report to the Commissioner within five business days after receipt of the report and shall provide the independent certified public accountant making the report with evidence of the report being furnished to the Commissioner. If the independent certified public accountant fails to receive the evidence within the required five-business-day period, the independent certified public accountant shall furnish to the Commissioner a copy of its report within the next five business days.

(b)   No independent certified public accountant shall be liable in any manner to any person for any statement made in connection with subsection (a) of this section if the statement is made in good faith in compliance with that subsection.

(c)   If the accountant, subsequent to the date of the audited financial report filed pursuant to this Part, becomes aware of facts that might have affected his or her report, the Commissioner notes the obligation of the accountant to take such action as prescribed in Volume 1, Section AU 561 of the Professional Standards of the AICPA. (2009-384, s. 1.)

§ 58-10-230. Communication of internal control related matters noted in an audit.

(a)   In addition to the annual audited financial report, each insurer shall furnish the Commissioner with a written communication as to any unremediated material weaknesses in its internal control over financial reporting noted during the audit. Such communication shall be prepared by the accountant within 60 days after the filing of the annual audited financial report and shall contain a description of any unremediated material weakness, as the term "material weakness" is defined by "Statement on Auditing Standards No. 112 of the AICPA Professional Standards, Communication of Internal Control Related Matters Noted in an Audit," or its replacement, as of December 31 immediately preceding, so as to coincide with the audited financial report described in G.S. 58-10-195(a) in the insurer's internal control over financial reporting noted by the accountant during the course of their audit of the financial statements. If no unremediated material weaknesses are noted, the communication should so state.

(b)   The insurer shall provide a description of remedial actions taken or proposed to correct unremediated material weaknesses, if the actions are not described in the accountant's communication. (2009-384, s. 1.)

§ 58-10-235. Accountant's letter of qualifications.

The accountant shall furnish the insurer, in connection with, and for inclusion in, the filing of the annual audited financial report, a letter stating all of the following:

(1)   That the accountant is independent with respect to the insurer and conforms to the standards of his or her profession as contained in the Code of Professional Ethics and pronouncements of the AICPA and the Rules of

Professional Conduct of the North Carolina State Board of Certified Public Accountant Examiners Board of Public Accountancy, or similar code.

(2) The background and experience in general and the experience in audits of insurers of the staff assigned to the engagement and whether each is an independent certified public accountant. Nothing within this Part shall be construed as prohibiting the accountant from utilizing such staff as he or she deems appropriate where their use is consistent with the standards prescribed by generally accepted auditing standards.

(3) That the accountant understands the annual audited financial report and his opinion thereon will be filed in compliance with this Part and that the Commissioner will be relying on this information in the monitoring and regulation of the financial position of insurers.

(4) That the accountant consents to the requirements of G.S. 58-10-240 and that the accountant consents and agrees to make available for review by the Commissioner, or the Commissioner's designee or appointed agent, the work papers, as described in G.S. 58-10-240.

(5) A representation that the accountant is properly licensed by an appropriate state licensing authority and is a member in good standing in the AICPA.

(6) A representation that the accountant is in compliance with the requirements of G.S. 58-10-210. (2009-384, s. 1.)

§ 58-10-240. Definition, availability, and maintenance of independent certified public accountants' work papers.

(a) Work papers are the records kept by the independent certified public accountant of the procedures followed, the tests performed, the information obtained, and the conclusions reached pertinent to the accountant's audit of the financial statements of an insurer. Work papers, accordingly, may include audit planning documentation, work programs, analyses, memoranda, letters of confirmation and representation, abstracts of company documents, and schedules or commentaries prepared or obtained by the independent certified public accountant in the course of his or her audit of the financial statements of an insurer and which support the accountant's opinion.

(b) Every insurer required to file an audited financial report pursuant to this Part shall require the accountant to make available for review by the Commissioner all work papers prepared in the conduct of the accountant's audit and any communications related to the audit between the accountant and the insurer at the offices of the insurer, at the offices of the Commissioner, or at any other reasonable place designated by the Commissioner. The insurer shall require that the accountant retain the audit work papers and communications until the Commissioner has filed a report on examination covering the period of the audit but no longer than seven years after the date of the audit report.

(c) In the conduct of the periodic review by the Commissioner's examiners in subsection (b) of this section, copies of pertinent audit work papers may be made and retained by the Commissioner. Such reviews by the Commissioner's examiners shall be considered investigations, and all working papers and communications obtained during the course of such investigations shall be confidential. (2009-384, s. 1.)

§ 58-10-245. Requirements for audit committees.

(a) This section shall not apply to foreign or alien insurers licensed in this State or an insurer that is a SOX-compliant entity or a direct or indirect wholly owned subsidiary of a SOX-compliant entity.

(b) The audit committee shall be directly responsible for the appointment, compensation, and oversight of the work of any accountant, including resolution of disagreements between management and the accountant regarding financial reporting, for the purpose of preparing or issuing the audited financial report or related work. Each accountant shall report directly to the audit committee.

(c) Each member of the audit committee shall be a member of the board of directors of the insurer or a member of the board of directors of an entity elected pursuant to subsection (f) of this section and G.S. 58-10-190(3).

(d) In order to be considered independent for purposes of this section, a member of the audit committee shall not, other than in his or her capacity as a member of the audit committee, the board of directors, or any other board committee, accept any consulting, advisory, or other compensatory fee from the entity or be an affiliated person of the entity or any subsidiary of the entity.

However, if North Carolina law requires board participation by otherwise nonindependent members, that law shall prevail and such members may participate in the audit committee and be designated as independent for audit committee purposes, unless they are an officer or employee of the insurer or one of its affiliates.

(e) If a member of the audit committee ceases to be independent for reasons outside the member's reasonable control, that person, with notice by the responsible entity to the Commissioner, may remain an audit committee member of the responsible entity until the earlier of the next annual meeting of the responsible entity or one year from the occurrence of the event that caused the member to be no longer independent.

(f) To exercise the election of the controlling person to designate the audit committee, the ultimate controlling person shall provide written notice of the affected insurers to the Commissioner. Notification shall be made timely before the issuance of the statutory audit report and include a description of the basis for the election. The election can be changed through notice to the Commissioner by the insurer, which shall include a description of the basis for the change. The election shall remain in effect for perpetuity, until rescinded.

(g) Reports From Accountant.

(1) The audit committee shall require the accountant that performs for an insurer any audit required by this Part to timely report to the audit committee in accordance with the requirements of "Statement on Auditing Standards No. 61 of the AICPA Professional Standards, Communication with Audit Committees," or its replacement, including all of the following:

a. All significant accounting policies and material permitted practices.

b. All material alternative treatments of financial information within statutory accounting principles that have been discussed with management officials of the insurer, ramifications of the use of the alternative disclosures and treatments, and the treatment preferred by the accountant.

c. Other material written communications between the accountant and the management of the insurer, such as any management letter or schedule of unadjusted differences.

(2)   If an insurer is a member of an insurance holding company system, the reports required by subdivision (1) of subsection (g) of this section may be provided to the audit committee on an aggregate basis for insurers in the holding company system, provided that any substantial differences among insurers in the system are identified to the audit committee.

(h)   The proportion of independent audit committee members shall meet or exceed the following criteria:

Prior Calendar Year Direct Written and Assumed Premiums

$0 - $300,000,000	Over $300,000,000 - $500,000,000	Over $500,000,000
No minimum of members requirements.	Majority (50% or more) of members shall be independent.	Supermajority (75% or more) shall be independent.

The Commissioner shall require the entity's board to enact improvements to the independence of the audit committee membership if the insurer is in a risk-based capital action level event, meets one or more of the standards of an insurer deemed to be in hazardous financial condition, or otherwise exhibits qualities of a troubled insurer. The Commissioner may order any insurer with less than five hundred million dollars ($500,000,000) in prior year direct written and assumed premiums to structure its audit committee with at least a supermajority of independent audit committee members. Prior calendar year direct written and assumed premiums shall be the combined total of direct premiums and assumed premiums from nonaffiliates for the reporting entities.

(i)   An insurer with direct written and assumed premiums, excluding premiums reinsured with the Federal Crop Insurance Corporation and Federal

Flood Program, of less than five hundred million dollars ($500,000,000) may apply to the Commissioner for a waiver from the requirements in this section based upon hardship. The insurer shall file, with its annual statement filing, the approval for relief from this section with the states in which it is licensed or doing business and with the NAIC. If the nondomestic state accepts electronic filing with the NAIC, the insurer shall file the approval in an electronic format. (2009-384, s. 1.)

§ 58-10-250. Conduct of insurer in connection with the preparation of required reports and documents.

(a) No director or officer of an insurer shall, directly or indirectly, do any of the following:

(1) Make or cause to be made a materially false or misleading statement to an accountant in connection with any audit, review, or communication required under this Part.

(2) Omit to state, or cause another person to omit to state, any material fact necessary in order to make statements made, in light of the circumstances under which the statements were made, not misleading to an accountant in connection with any audit, review, or communication required under this Part.

(b) No officer or director of an insurer, or any other person acting under the direction thereof, shall directly or indirectly take any action to coerce, manipulate, mislead, or fraudulently influence any accountant engaged in the performance of an audit pursuant to this Part if that person knew or should have known that the action, if successful, could result in rendering the insurer's financial statements materially misleading.

(c) For purposes of subsection (b) of this section, actions that, "if successful, could result in rendering the insurer's financial statements materially misleading" include, but are not limited to, actions taken at anytime with respect to the professional engagement period to coerce, manipulate, mislead, or fraudulently influence an accountant to do any of the following:

(1) Issue or reissue a report on an insurer's financial statements that is not warranted in the circumstances, due to material violations of statutory

accounting principles prescribed by the Commissioner, generally accepted auditing standards, or other professional or regulatory standards.

(2)	Not perform audit, review, or other procedures required by generally accepted auditing standards or other professional standards.

(3)	Not withdraw an issued report.

(4)	Not communicate matters to an insurer's audit committee. (2009-384, s. 1.)

§ 58-10-255. Management's report of internal control over financial reporting.

(a)	Every insurer required to file an audited financial report pursuant to this Part that has annual direct written and assumed premiums, excluding premiums reinsured with the Federal Crop Insurance Corporation and Federal Flood Program, of five hundred million dollars ($500,000,000) or more shall prepare a report of the insurer's or group of insurers' internal control over financial reporting, as these terms are defined in G.S. 58-10-190. The report shall be filed with the Commissioner along with the communication of internal control related matters noted in an audit described under G.S. 58-10-230. Management's report of internal control over financial reporting shall be as of December 31 immediately preceding.

(b)	Notwithstanding the premium threshold in subsection (a) of this section, the Commissioner may require an insurer to file management's report of internal control over financial reporting if the insurer is in any risk-based capital level event, or meets any one or more of the standards of an insurer deemed to be in hazardous financial condition as defined in G.S. 58-30-60(b).

(c)	An insurer or a group of insurers that is:

(1)	Directly subject to Section 404;

(2)	Part of a holding company system whose parent is directly subject to Section 404;

(3)	Not directly subject to Section 404 but is a SOX-compliant entity; or

(4) A member of a holding company system whose parent is not directly subject to Section 404 but is a SOX-compliant entity may file its or its parent's Section 404 report and an addendum in satisfaction of this subsection's requirement provided that those internal controls of the insurer or group of insurers having a material impact on the preparation of the insurer's or group of insurers' audited statutory financial statements for items included in G.S. 58-10-200(b)(2) through G.S. 58-10-200(b)(6) were included in the scope of the Section 404 report. The addendum shall be a positive statement by management that there are no material processes with respect to the preparation of the insurer's or group of insurers' audited statutory financial statements for items included in G.S. 58-10-200(b)(2) through G.S. 58-10-200(b)(6) that were excluded from the Section 404 report. If there are internal controls of the insurer or group of insurers that have a material impact on the preparation of the insurer's or group of insurers' audited statutory financial statements and those internal controls were not included in the scope of the Section 404 report, the insurer or group of insurers may either file (i) a G.S. 58-10-255 report, or (ii) the Section 404 report and a G.S. 58-10-255 report for those internal controls that have a material impact on the preparation of the insurer's or group of insurers' audited statutory financial statements not covered by the Section 404 report.

(d) Management's report of internal control over financial reporting shall include all of the following:

(1) A statement that management is responsible for establishing and maintaining adequate internal control over financial reporting.

(2) A statement that management has established internal control over financial reporting and an assertion, to the best of management's knowledge and belief, after diligent inquiry, as to whether its internal control over financial reporting is effective to provide reasonable assurance regarding the reliability of financial statements in accordance with statutory accounting principles.

(3) A statement that briefly describes the approach or processes by which management evaluated the effectiveness of its internal control over financial reporting.

(4) A statement that briefly describes the scope of work that is included and whether any internal controls were excluded.

(5) Disclosure of any unremediated material weaknesses in the internal control over financial reporting identified by management as of December 31 immediately preceding. Management is not permitted to conclude that the internal control over financial reporting is effective to provide reasonable assurance regarding the reliability of financial statements in accordance with statutory accounting principles if there are one or more unremediated material weaknesses in its internal control over financial reporting.

(6) A statement regarding the inherent limitations of internal control systems.

(7) Signatures of the chief executive officer and the chief financial officer, or equivalent positionitle.

(e) Management shall document and make available upon a financial condition examination the basis upon which its assertions, required in subsection (d) of this section, are made. Management may base its assertions, in part, upon its review, monitoring, and testing of internal controls undertaken in the normal course of its activities. Management shall have discretion as to the nature of the internal control framework used, and the nature and extent of documentation, in order to make its assertion in a cost-effective manner and, as such, may include assembly of or reference to existing documentation. Management's report on internal control over financial reporting, required by subsection (a) of this section, and any documentation provided in support thereof during the course of a financial condition examination, shall be kept confidential by the Commissioner. (2009-384, s. 1.)

§ 58-10-260. Exemptions and effective dates.

(a) Upon written application of any insurer, the Commissioner may grant an exemption from compliance with any and all provisions of this Part if the Commissioner finds, upon review of the application, that compliance with this Part would constitute a financial or organizational hardship upon the insurer. An exemption may be granted at anytime and from time to time for a specified period or periods. Within 10 days after a denial of an insurer's written request for an exemption, the insurer may request in writing a hearing on its application for an exemption. The hearing shall be held in accordance with Article 3A of Chapter 150B of the General Statutes.

(b) Domestic insurers retaining a certified public accountant on July 31, 2009, who qualify as independent shall comply with this Part for the year ending December 31, 2010, and each year thereafter unless the Commissioner permits otherwise.

(c) Foreign insurers shall comply with this Part for the year ending December 31, 2010, and each year thereafter unless the Commissioner permits otherwise.

(d) The requirements of G.S. 58-10-210(d) shall become effective for audits of the year beginning January 1, 2010, and each year thereafter.

(e) The requirements of G.S. 58-10-245 shall become effective on January 1, 2010. An insurer or group of insurers that is not required to have independent audit committee members or only a majority of independent audit committee members, as opposed to a supermajority, because the total written and assumed premium is below the threshold and subsequently becomes subject to one of the independence requirements due to changes in premium shall have one year following the year the threshold is exceeded, but not earlier than January 1, 2010, to comply with the independence requirements. Likewise, an insurer that becomes subject to one of the independence requirements as a result of a business combination shall have one calendar year following the date of acquisition or combination to comply with the independence requirements.

(f) The requirements of G.S. 58-10-255 become effective beginning with the reporting period ending December 31, 2010, and each year thereafter. An insurer or group of insurers that is not required to file a report because the total written premium is below the threshold and subsequently becomes subject to the reporting requirements shall have two years following the year the threshold is exceeded, but not earlier than December 31, 2010, to file a report. An insurer acquired in a business combination shall have two calendar years after the date of acquisition or combination to comply with the reporting requirements. (2009-384, s. 1.)

§ 58-10-265. Canadian and British companies.

(a) In the case of Canadian and British insurers, the annual audited financial report shall be defined as the annual statement of total business on the form filed by such companies with their supervision authority duly audited by an independent chartered accountant.

(b) For such insurers, the letter required in G.S. 58-10-205(b) shall state that the accountant is aware of the requirements relating to the annual audited financial report filed with the Commissioner pursuant to G.S. 58-10-195 and shall affirm that the opinion expressed is in conformity with those requirements. (2009-384, s. 1.)

Part 8. Mutual Insurance Holding Companies.

§ 58-10-275. Definitions.

The following definitions apply in this Part:

(1) Affiliated. - Defined in G.S. 58-19-5.

(2) Control. - Defined in G.S. 58-19-5.

(3) Domestic mutual insurance company. - An insurance company organized on a mutual plan and incorporated under the laws of North Carolina.

(4) Interested person. - With respect to another person, includes any of the following:

a. Any affiliated person.

b. Any member of the immediate family of any natural person who is an affiliated person of such company.

c. Any person or partner or employee of any person who at any time since the beginning of the last two completed fiscal years of such company has acted as legal counsel for such company.

d. Any natural person whom the Commissioner by order shall have determined to be an interested person by reason of having had, at any time since the beginning of the last two completed fiscal years of such company, a material business or professional relationship with such company or with the principal executive officer of such company.

(5) Intermediate holding company. - A holding company that is a subsidiary of a mutual insurance holding company or part of a holding company system controlled by a mutual insurance holding company subject to the terms and conditions of Article 19 of this Chapter and that either directly or through a subsidiary intermediate holding company has one or more subsidiary reorganized insurance companies of which a majority of the voting shares of the capital stock would otherwise have been required by this section to be at all times owned by the mutual insurance holding company.

(6) Limited application. - An application by a domestic mutual insurance company for reorganization to a mutual insurance holding company which will hold, at all times, one hundred percent (100%) of the stock of its insurance subsidiaries.

(7) Majority of the voting shares of the capital stock of the reorganized insurance company. - Shares of the capital stock of a reorganized insurance company which carry the right to cast a majority of the votes entitled to be cast by all of the outstanding shares of the capital stock of the reorganized insurance company for the election of directors and on all other matters submitted to a vote of the shareholders of the reorganized insurance company.

(8) Member of the immediate family. - Any parent, spouse of a parent, child, spouse of a child, spouse, brother, or sister, including step and adoptive relationships.

(9) Mutual insurance holding company. - A holding company organized on a mutual plan and incorporated under the laws of North Carolina, resulting from the reorganization of a domestic mutual insurance company pursuant to this Part, with one or more stock insurance holding company subsidiaries or stock insurance company subsidiaries.

(10) Plan of reorganization. - A plan to reorganize a domestic mutual insurance company by forming a mutual insurance holding company.

(11) Standard application. - An application by a domestic mutual insurance company for reorganization to a mutual insurance holding company which may sell interests in its subsidiaries to third parties.

(12) Stock. - Any security evidencing an equity interest in the issuing entity.

(13) Stock offering. - Any proposed sale, exchange, transfer, or other change of ownership of stock or of securities convertible into or exchangeable or exercisable for stock. For the purposes of this Article, "stock offering" shall not include any of the following:

a. An offering of preferred stock which is not convertible or exchangeable into common stock and which has no ordinary voting rights.

b. A transfer of stock among any of the following:

1. A mutual insurance holding company.

2. An insurance company subsidiary of a mutual insurance holding company.

3. An intermediate holding company subsidiary of a mutual insurance holding company.

4. An insurance company subsidiary of an intermediate holding company subsidiary to a mutual insurance holding company.

(14) Subsidiary. - Defined in G.S. 58-19-5. (2012-161, s. 1.)

§ 58-10-280. General provisions.

(a) A domestic mutual insurance company, upon approval of the Commissioner, may reorganize by forming an insurance holding company based upon a mutual plan and by continuing the corporate existence of the reorganizing insurance company as a stock insurance company. If the Commissioner, after a public comment period as provided in G.S. 58-10-285, or, if applicable, a public hearing, is satisfied that the interests of the policyholders are properly protected and that the plan of reorganization is fair and equitable to the policyholders, the Commissioner may approve the proposed plan of reorganization and may require as a condition of approval such modifications of the proposed plan of reorganization as the Commissioner finds necessary for the protection of the policyholders' interests. The Commissioner may retain consultants as provided in G.S. 58-10-285 to assist in the review of the proposed plan. The Commissioner shall retain jurisdiction over a mutual insurance holding company organized under this Part to assure that policyholder interests are protected. All of the initial shares of the capital stock of the reorganized insurance company shall be issued to the mutual insurance holding company. The membership interests of the policyholders of the reorganized insurance company shall become membership interests in the mutual insurance holding company, pursuant to the terms and conditions of the plan of reorganization approved by the Commissioner. Policyholders of the reorganized insurance company shall be members of the mutual insurance holding company in accordance with the articles of incorporation and bylaws of the mutual insurance holding company. The mutual insurance holding company shall at all times own a majority of the voting shares of the capital stock of the reorganized insurance company.

(b)   A domestic mutual insurance company, after approval by the Commissioner, may reorganize by merging its policyholders' membership interests into a mutual insurance holding company formed under subsection (a) of this section and continuing the corporate existence of the reorganizing insurance company as a stock insurance company subsidiary of the mutual insurance holding company. If the Commissioner is satisfied that the interests of the policyholders are properly protected and that the merger of interests is fair and equitable to the policyholders, the Commissioner may approve the proposed merger of interests and may require as a condition of approval such modifications of the proposed merger of interests as the Commissioner finds necessary for the protection of the policyholders' interests. The Commissioner may retain consultants as provided in G.S. 58-10-285. The Commissioner has jurisdiction over the mutual insurance holding company organized under this Part to assure that policyholder interests are protected. All of the initial shares of the capital stock of the reorganized insurance company shall be issued to the mutual insurance holding company. The membership interests of the policyholders of the reorganized insurance company shall, pursuant to the terms and conditions of the plan of reorganization approved by the Commissioner, become membership interests in the mutual insurance holding company. Policyholders of the reorganized insurance company shall be members of the mutual insurance holding company in accordance with subsection (a) of this section and the articles of incorporation and bylaws of the mutual insurance holding company. The mutual insurance holding company shall at all times own a majority of the voting shares of the capital stock of the reorganized insurance company.

(c)   A mutual insurance holding company resulting from the reorganization of a domestic mutual insurance company that was organized under Articles 7 and 8 and other applicable provisions of this Chapter shall be incorporated under this Chapter. The articles of incorporation and any amendments to such articles of the mutual insurance holding company shall be subject to approval of the Commissioner in the same manner as those of a mutual insurance company.

(d)   A mutual insurance holding company is an insurer subject to Article 30 of this Chapter and shall automatically be a party to any proceeding under Article 30 of this Chapter involving an insurance company which, as a result of a reorganization under subsection (a) or (b) of this section, is a subsidiary of the mutual insurance holding company. In any proceeding under Article 30 of this Chapter involving the reorganized insurance company, the assets of the mutual insurance holding company are deemed to be assets of the estate of the reorganized insurance company for purposes of satisfying the claims of the reorganized insurance company's policyholders. A mutual insurance holding company shall not dissolve or liquidate without the approval of the Commissioner or as ordered by the court pursuant to Article 30 of this Chapter.

(e)   G.S. 58-10-10 and G.S. 58-10-12 are not applicable to a reorganization or merger of interests under this Part. G.S. 58-10-10 and G.S. 58-10-12 are applicable to demutualization of a mutual insurance holding company that resulted from the reorganization of a domestic mutual insurance company organized under this Chapter as if the mutual insurance holding company was a mutual insurance company.

(f)   A membership interest in a domestic mutual insurance holding company shall not constitute a security as defined in Chapter 78A of the General Statutes.

(g)   The majority of the voting shares of the capital stock of the reorganized insurance company, which is required by this section to be at all times owned by a mutual insurance holding company, shall not be conveyed, transferred, assigned, pledged, subjected to a security interest or lien, encumbered, or otherwise hypothecated or alienated by the mutual insurance holding company or intermediate holding company. Any conveyance, transfer, assignment, pledge, security interest, lien, encumbrance, or hypothecation or alienation of, in, or on the majority of the voting shares of the reorganized insurance company is a violation of this section and shall be void in inverse chronological order of the date of such conveyance, transfer, assignment, pledge, security interest, lien, encumbrance, or hypothecation or alienation, as to the shares necessary to constitute a majority of such voting shares. The majority of the voting shares of the capital stock of the reorganized insurance company shall not be subject to execution and levy as provided in Chapter 1 of the General Statutes. The shares of the capital stock of the surviving or new company resulting from a merger or consolidation of two or more reorganized insurance companies or two or more intermediate holding companies that were subsidiaries of the same mutual insurance holding company are subject to the same requirements, restrictions, and limitations to which the shares of the merging or consolidating reorganized insurance companies or intermediate holding companies were subject by this section prior to the merger or consolidation. The ownership of a majority of the voting shares of the capital stock of the reorganized insurance company that are required by this section to be at all times owned by a parent mutual insurance holding company includes indirect ownership through one or more intermediate holding companies in a corporate structure approved by the Commissioner. However, indirect ownership through one or more intermediate holding companies shall not result in the mutual insurance holding company owning less than the equivalent of a majority of the voting shares of the capital stock of the reorganized insurance company. The Commissioner shall have jurisdiction over an intermediate holding company as if it were a mutual insurance holding company.

(h) The applicant's articles of incorporation or bylaws, as appropriate, shall require a policyholder vote of approval of the reorganization by a two-thirds majority of the domestic mutual insurance company's policyholders voting on it in person, by proxy, or by mail at a meeting called for the purpose of voting on the reorganization. (2012-161, s. 1.)

§ 58-10-285. Application; contents; process.

(a) An application shall be designated as either a limited application or a standard application. The filing of a limited application shall not preclude the subsequent filing of an application for approval of an initial sale of stock as provided in G.S. 58-10-315.

(b) The application shall be filed in triplicate with the Commissioner and shall include the following items:

(1) Designation as a limited or standard application.

(2) A plan of reorganization as set forth in G.S. 58-10-290.

(3) A plan to obtain the approval of the policyholders in accordance with this Part and the applicant's articles of incorporation and bylaws.

(4) A copy of the mutual insurance holding company's proposed articles of incorporation and bylaws specifying all membership rights.

(5) The names, addresses, and occupational information of all corporate officers and members of the initial mutual insurance holding company board of directors.

(6) Information sufficient to demonstrate that the financial condition of the applicant will not be diminished upon reorganization.

(7) A copy of the proposed articles of incorporation and bylaws for any insurance company subsidiary or intermediate holding company subsidiary.

(8) A "Form A" filing as described in Chapter 11 of Title 11 of the North Carolina Administrative Code.

(9) A statement that the application is in compliance with all pertinent North Carolina General Statutes and Administrative Rules and that the requirements for a plan of reorganization have been fulfilled.

(10) An index demonstrating wherein the application information supplied in compliance with this subsection is found.

(11) The applicable fee required by subsection (f) of this section.

(12) Any other information requested by the Commissioner at any time during the course of proceedings.

(c) Upon receipt and review by the Commissioner of all information provided pursuant to subsection (b) of this section, the Commissioner may establish a period during which the Department will receive and consider public comments on the proposed reorganization. The Commissioner may inform the public of the limited or standard application in a manner deemed appropriate by the Commissioner and may hold a public hearing concerning the application.

(d) The Commissioner may contract, at the expense of the person filing the application, with any attorneys, actuaries, economists, accountants, consultants, or other professional advisors not otherwise a part of the Commissioner's staff to assist the Commissioner in reviewing the application. These contracts are personal professional service contracts exempt from Articles 3 and 3C of Chapter 143 of the General Statutes.

(e) The expenses of mailing any notices and other materials required by this section shall be borne by the person filing the application.

(f) An applicant filing a limited application under this section shall submit with the application under subsection (b) of this section an application fee of two hundred fifty dollars ($250.00). An applicant filing a standard application under this section shall submit with the application under subsection (b) of this section an application fee of five hundred dollars ($500.00). (2012-161, s. 1.)

§ 58-10-290. Plan of reorganization.

(a) A limited application plan of reorganization shall include the following provisions:

(1) Establishing a mutual insurance holding company with at least one stock insurance company subsidiary or one intermediary stock holding company with a stock insurance company subsidiary, the shares of which shall be held exclusively by the mutual insurance holding company.

(2) Protecting the interests of existing policyholders.

(3) Ensuring immediate membership in the mutual insurance holding company of all existing policyholders of the reorganizing domestic mutual insurance company.

(4) Describing a plan providing for membership interests of future policyholders.

(5) Describing the number of members of the board of directors of the mutual insurance holding company required to be policyholders.

(6) Demonstrating that, in the event of proceedings under Article 30 of this Chapter involving a stock insurance company subsidiary of the mutual insurance holding company which resulted from the reorganization of a domestic mutual insurance company, the assets of the mutual insurance holding

company will be available to satisfy the policyholder obligations of the stock insurance company.

(7) Describing how any accumulation or prospective accumulation of earnings by the mutual insurance holding company in excess of that determined by the board of directors of the mutual insurance holding company to be necessary shall inure to the exclusive benefit of the policyholders of its insurance company subsidiaries who are members.

(8) Describing the nature and content of the annual report and financial statement to be sent to each member.

(9) Describing any other relevant matters the applicant deems appropriate.

(b) A standard application plan of reorganization shall include the following provisions:

(1) Establishing a mutual insurance holding company with at least one stock insurance company subsidiary or one wholly owned intermediate stock holding company with a stock insurance company subsidiary, the shares of which shall be held exclusively by the wholly owned intermediate holding company.

(2) Protecting the interests of existing policyholders.

(3) Ensuring immediate membership in the mutual insurance holding company of all existing policyholders of the reorganizing domestic mutual insurance company.

(4) Providing for membership interests of future policyholders.

(5) Describing the number of members of the board of directors of the mutual insurance holding company required to be policyholders.

(6) Demonstrating that, in the event of proceedings under Article 30 of this Chapter involving a stock insurance company subsidiary of the mutual insurance holding company which resulted from the reorganization of a domestic mutual insurance company, the assets of the mutual insurance holding company will be available to satisfy the policyholder obligations of the stock insurance company.

(7) Describing how any accumulation or prospective accumulation of earnings by the mutual insurance holding company in excess of that determined by the board of directors of the mutual insurance holding company to be necessary shall inure to the exclusive benefit of the policyholders of its insurance company subsidiaries who are members.

(8) Describing the nature and content of the annual report and financial statement to be sent to each member.

(9) Describing the applicant's plan for a stock offering in accordance with the provisions of G.S. 58-10-315.

(10) Describing any other relevant matters the applicant deems appropriate.

(c) With regard to either a limited or standard application, the plan of reorganization submitted to the Commissioner shall demonstrate the following:

(1) Policyholder interests are properly preserved and protected.

(2) The plan is fair and equitable to policyholders.

(3) The financial condition of the applicant will not be diminished. (2012-161, s. 1.)

§ 58-10-295. Powers of the Commissioner.

(a) The Commissioner shall at all times retain jurisdiction over the mutual insurance holding company, its intermediate holding company subsidiaries with stock insurance company subsidiaries, and its stock insurance company subsidiaries.

(b) Following any public comment period or hearing pursuant to G.S. 58-10-285, the Commissioner by order shall approve, conditionally approve, or deny an application. The Commissioner may require, as a condition of approval of the proposed reorganization, modifications of the proposed plan of reorganization that the Commissioner finds necessary. The applicant shall accept the required modifications by filing appropriate amendments to the proposed plan of reorganization with the Commissioner within 30 days of the date of the Commissioner's order requiring the modifications. If the applicant does not accept the required modifications by failing to file the required amendments to the proposed plan of reorganization within 30 days, the proposed reorganization shall be deemed denied.

(c) An approval or conditional approval of a plan of reorganization shall expire if the reorganization is not completed within 210 days after the approval or conditional approval unless the time period is extended by the Commissioner upon a showing of good cause.

(d) The Commissioner may revoke approval or conditional approval of an applicant's plan of reorganization in the event the Commissioner finds the applicant has failed to comply with the plan of reorganization. The Commissioner may compel completion of a plan of reorganization unless the plan is abandoned in its entirety, in accordance with the applicant's provisions for governance.

(e) Upon completion of all elements of a plan of reorganization, the applicant shall provide a notice of completion to the Commissioner. (2012-161, s. 1.)

§ 58-10-300. Special financial requirements.

(a) Mutual insurance holding companies and their insurance company subsidiaries and affiliates shall comply with the provisions of Article 19 of this Chapter except as expressly provided in this Part. Mutual insurance holding companies' investments in subsidiaries, including intermediate holding companies, shall not be subject to any of the restrictions on investment activities set forth in G.S. 58-19-10.

(b) When a mutual insurance holding company acquires or plans to acquire more than fifty percent (50%) of a stock insurance company, the mutual insurance holding company shall submit to the Commissioner a plan describing any membership interests of policyholders.

(c) Each mutual insurance holding company shall supply to the Commissioner, by April 1 of each year, an annual statement consisting of the following:

(1) An income statement.

(2) A balance sheet.

(3) A cash flow statement.

(4) Complete information on the status of any closed block formed as a part of a plan of reorganization.

(5) An investment plan covering all assets.

(6) A statement disclosing any intention to pledge, borrow against, alienate, hypothecate, or in any way encumber the assets of the mutual insurance holding company.

(d) At least fifty percent (50%) of the net worth of the mutual insurance holding company, based upon generally accepted accounting practices, shall be invested in insurance company subsidiaries. The Commissioner may waive the fifty percent (50%) limitation upon a showing of good cause.

(e) No policyholder who is a member of a mutual insurance holding company shall receive on account of such membership interest any payment of a policy credit, dividend, or other distribution unless the payment has been approved by the Commissioner. The Commissioner, if satisfied the proposed payment is fair and equitable to policyholders who are members, may approve the proposed payment and may require as a condition of the approval modification of the proposed payment that the Commissioner finds necessary for the protection of the policyholders.

(f) Mutual insurance holding companies shall comply with Part 3 of this Article and shall be considered a domestic insurer for the purposes of compliance with Part 3 of this Article. (2012-161, s. 1.)

§ 58-10-305. Reorganization of domestic mutual insurer with mutual insurance holding company.

A domestic mutual insurance company may apply to reorganize by merging its policyholders' membership interests into a mutual insurance holding company by filing with the Commissioner a joint application with the mutual insurance holding company complying with the provisions of G.S. 58-10-285. (2012-161, s. 1.)

§ 58-10-310. Mergers of mutual insurance holding companies.

A mutual insurance holding company may apply to merge with another mutual insurance holding company by filing with the Commissioner a plan of merger and complying with the provisions of Article 19 of this Chapter. (2012-161, s. 1.)

§ 58-10-315. Stock offerings.

(a) No stock offering by a mutual insurance holding company, an insurance company subsidiary of a mutual insurance holding company, an intermediate holding company subsidiary of a mutual insurance holding company, or an insurance company subsidiary of an intermediate holding company subsidiary to a mutual insurance holding company shall occur without the prior approval of the Commissioner.

(b) Every application for approval of a stock offering shall contain the following information:

(1) A description of the stock intended to be offered by the applicant, including a description of all shareholder rights.

(2) The total number of shares authorized to be issued, the estimated number the applicant requests permission to offer, and the intended date or range of dates for the offer.

(3) A justification for a uniform planned offering price or a justification of the method by which the offering price will be determined.

(4) The name or names of any underwriter, syndicate member, or placement agent involved and, if known, the name or names of each entity, person, or group of persons to whom the stock offering is to be made who will control five percent (5%) of the total outstanding class of shares, and the manner in which the offer is to be tendered. If any such entity or person is a corporation or business organization, the name of each member of its board of

directors or equivalent management team shall be provided along with the name of each member of the board of directors of the offeror. Copies of any filings with the United States Securities and Exchange Commission disclosing intended acquisitions of the stock shall be included in the application.

(5) A description of stock subscription rights to be afforded members of the mutual insurance holding company in conjunction with the stock offering.

(6) A detailed description of all expenses to be incurred in conjunction with the stock offering.

(7) An explanation of how funds raised by the stock offering are to be used.

(8) Any other information requested by the Commissioner.

(c) No application regarding a planned stock offering shall be approved unless the plan contains the following provisions:

(1) Prohibiting officers, directors, and insiders of the mutual insurance holding company and its subsidiaries and affiliates from purchase or ownership of shares of the stock offering, or issuance of stock options to or for the benefit of such officers, directors, and insiders, in excess of five percent (5%) of the stock offering. The Commissioner may waive this requirement upon a showing of good cause. This subdivision does not limit the rights of officers, directors, and insiders from exercising subscription rights that are generally accorded members of the mutual insurance holding company. However, pursuant to those subscription rights, the officers, directors, and insiders of the mutual insurance holding company and its subsidiaries and affiliates may not purchase or own, in the aggregate, more than five percent (5%) of the stock offering.

(2) Requiring that, after the initial stock offering, a majority of the board of directors of the mutual insurance holding company be persons who are not interested persons of the mutual insurance holding company or of an affiliated person of the company. For purposes of this subdivision, a member of the mutual insurance holding company or a policyholder of any of its insurance company subsidiaries shall not be considered an "interested person" or an "affiliated person." The Commissioner may waive this requirement upon a showing of good cause.

(3) For the mutual insurance holding company to adopt articles of incorporation prohibiting any waiver of dividends from stock subsidiaries except

under conditions specified in its articles of incorporation and after approval of the waiver by the board of directors of the mutual insurance holding company and the Commissioner.

(4)   Requiring that, after the initial stock offering by an insurance company subsidiary of a mutual insurance holding company, an intermediate holding company subsidiary of a mutual insurance holding company, or an insurance company subsidiary of an intermediate holding company subsidiary of a mutual insurance holding company, the boards of directors of each insurance company or intermediate holding company include at least three directors who are not interested persons of the mutual insurance holding company. The Commissioner may waive this requirement upon a showing of good cause.

(5)   Establishing, within the board of directors of the corporation offering stock, a pricing committee consisting exclusively of directors who are not members of management of the insurance company subsidiary whose responsibility is to evaluate and approve the price of any stock offering.

(d)   An insurance company subsidiary of a mutual insurance holding company, an intermediate holding company subsidiary of a mutual insurance holding company, or an insurance company subsidiary of an intermediate holding company subsidiary to a mutual insurance holding company may issue more than one class of stock, provided, however, that the issuer complies with all of the following requirements:

(1)   At all times a majority of the voting stock is held by the mutual insurance holding company or its subsidiary.

(2)   No class of common stock may possess greater dividend or other rights than the class held by the mutual insurance holding company or its subsidiary.

(e)   The Commissioner may retain, at the expense of the person filing the application, any attorneys, actuaries, economists, accountants, consultants, or other professional advisors not otherwise a part of the Commissioner's staff to assist the Commissioner in reviewing the application. These contracts are personal professional service contracts exempt from Articles 3 and 3C of Chapter 143 of the General Statutes.

(f)   The expenses of mailing any notices and other materials required by this section shall be borne by the person filing the application.

(g) Upon receipt and review by the Commissioner of all information provided under this section, the Commissioner may establish a period during which the Department will receive and consider public comments about the proposed offering. The Commissioner shall inform the public of the offering by posting information about the application in a manner deemed appropriate by the Commissioner. The Commissioner may hold a public hearing concerning the application or the proposed offering. Following any public comment period or hearing, if applicable, the Commissioner may approve, conditionally approve, or deny the application. The Commissioner may approve the application if the following apply:

(1) The offering complies with this Part and other provisions of law.

(2) The method for establishing the price of a stock offering is consistent with generally accepted market or industry practices for establishing stock offering prices in similar transactions.

(3) The plan and offering will not unfairly impact the interests of members of the mutual insurance holding company.

Nothing in this subsection shall be deemed to prohibit the filing of a registration statement with the United States Securities and Exchange Commission before or concurrently with the giving of notice to members.

(h) Notwithstanding the provisions of subsections (a) through (g) of this section, stock offerings which are not an initial stock offering, and which are proposed by entities with a class of securities regularly traded on the New York Stock Exchange, the American Stock Exchange, or another exchange approved by the Commissioner, or designated on the National Association of Securities Dealers Automated Quotations national market system (NASDAQ), may be sold in accordance with the following procedure: if a mutual insurance holding company, an insurance company subsidiary of a mutual insurance holding company, an intermediate holding company, or an insurance company subsidiary of an intermediate holding company intends to make a stock offering which would be governed by the provisions of this subsection, that entity shall deliver to the Commissioner, not less than 60 days prior to the offering, a notice of the planned stock offering and all of the following information:

(1) The total number of shares intended to be offered.

(2) The intended date of sale.

(3) Evidence the stock is regularly traded on one of the public exchanges specified in this subsection.

(4) A record of the trading price and trading volume of the stock during the prior 52 weeks.

The Commissioner shall be deemed to have approved the sale unless, within 60 days following receipt of such notice, the Commissioner issues an objection to the sale. If the Commissioner issues an objection to the sale, the application process set forth in subsections (a) through (g) of this section shall be followed to determine whether the Commissioner approves of the proposed sale.

(i) Approval of a stock offering obtained under either subsection (g) or (h) of this section shall expire 120 days following the date of the approval or deemed approval, except as otherwise provided by order of the Commissioner.

(j) No prospectus, information, sales material, or sales presentation by the applicant, or by any representative, agent, or affiliate of the applicant, shall contain a representation that the Commissioner has endorsed the price, price range, or any other information relating to the stock.

(k) No company making a stock offering under this section shall engage in any of the following practices:

(1) Borrow funds from the mutual insurance holding company, or its subsidiaries and affiliates, to finance the purchase of any portion of a stock offering.

(2) Pay any commissions, "special fees," or any other special payments or extraordinary compensation to officers, directors, interested persons, and affiliates for arranging, promoting, aiding, or assisting in reorganization to a mutual insurance holding company or for arranging, promoting, aiding, assisting, or participating in the structuring and placement of a stock offering.

(3) Enter into an understanding or agreement transferring legal or beneficial ownership of stock to another person to avoid the requirements of this Part. (2012-161, s. 1.)

§ 58-10-320. Regulation of holding company system.

(a) All material transactions, as that term is defined under Part 3 of this Article, between or among subsidiaries and affiliates of the mutual insurance holding company, must, after review and exercise of director duties by the directors of the mutual insurance holding company, be approved by a majority of the directors of the mutual insurance holding company as being fair and reasonable.

(b) If the Commissioner determines that activities within a mutual insurance holding company system have violated provisions of the General Statutes of North Carolina or the North Carolina Administrative Code or acted to circumvent requirements or prohibitions contained in the General Statutes or Administrative Code, the Commissioner may prohibit or order rescission of any transaction relating to those activities. (2012-161, s. 1.)

§ 58-10-325. Reporting of stock ownership and transactions.

(a) Any director or officer of a mutual insurance holding company, its subsidiary, or affiliate, who acquires directly or indirectly the beneficial ownership of any security issued by any intermediate holding company or any insurance company subsidiary of an intermediate holding company or mutual insurance holding company shall, within 15 days following the transaction, file with the Commissioner a statement of the transaction on the form prescribed by the Commissioner.

(b) A mutual insurance holding company, and its subsidiaries and affiliates, shall file with the Commissioner, within 15 days of receipt, copies of Form 3, Form 4, and Schedule 13D, or any equivalent filings, such filings made under the federal Securities Exchange Act of 1934, as amended. (2012-161, s. 1.)

Part 9. Captive Insurance Companies.

Subpart 1. General Provisions.

§ 58-10-335. Purpose.

(a) This Part shall be known and may be cited as the "North Carolina Captive Insurance Act."

(b) The purpose of this Part is to establish the procedures for the organization and regulation of the operations of captive insurance companies transacting insurance business within this State and thereby promote the general welfare of the people of this State. (2013-116, s. 1.)

§ 58-10-340. Definitions.

The following definitions apply in this Part:

(1) Affiliated company. - Any company in the same corporate system as a parent, an industrial insured, or a member organization by virtue of common ownership, control, operation, or management.

(2) Alien. - An alien company as defined in G.S. 58-1-5.

(3) Alien captive insurance company. - Any insurance company formed to write insurance business for its parents and affiliates and licensed pursuant to the laws of an alien jurisdiction which imposes statutory or regulatory standards in a form acceptable to the Commissioner on companies transacting the business of insurance in such jurisdiction.

(4) Association. - Any legal association of individuals, corporations, limited liability companies, partnerships, associations, or other entities that meets the criteria set forth in either sub-subdivision a. or b. of this subdivision:

a. The member organizations of the association or the association itself, either alone or in conjunction with some or all of the member organizations, are described by any of the following:

1. Owning, controlling, or holding with power to vote all of the outstanding voting securities of an association captive insurance company incorporated as a stock insurer.

2. Having complete voting control over an association captive insurance company incorporated as a mutual insurer.

3. Constituting all of the subscribers of an association captive insurance company formed as a reciprocal insurer.

4. Having complete voting control over an association captive insurance company formed as a limited liability company.

b. Each member organization of the association is one of the following:

1. A not-for-profit corporation, nonprofit association, or similar nonprofit organization.

2. An entity or organization exempt from taxation under Section 501(c) of the Internal Revenue Code, 26 U.S.C. § 501(c).

3. A municipality, metropolitan government, county, authority, utility district, or other public body generally classified as a governmental body or governmental entity, whether organized by local act or public act of the General Assembly, or any agency, board, or commission of any municipality, metropolitan government, county, authority, utility district or other public body generally classified as a governmental body or governmental entity. This sub-sub-subdivision shall be liberally construed.

(5) Association captive insurance company. - Any company that insures risks of the member organizations of an association, and that also may insure the risks of affiliated companies of the member organizations and the risks of the association itself.

(6) Branch business. - Any insurance business transacted by a branch captive insurance company in this State.

(7) Branch captive insurance company. - Any alien captive insurance company licensed by the Commissioner to transact the business of insurance in this State through a business unit with a principal place of business in this State. A branch captive insurance company is a pure captive insurance company with respect to operations in this State, unless otherwise permitted by the Commissioner.

(8) Branch operations. - Any business operations of a branch captive insurance company in this State.

(9) Captive insurance company. - Any pure captive insurance company, association captive insurance company, industrial insured captive insurance company, risk retention group, protected cell captive insurance company, incorporated cell captive insurance company, or special purpose financial captive insurance company formed or licensed under this Part.

(10) Commissioner. - Defined in G.S. 58-1-5.

(11) Control, controlling, controlled by, or under common control with. - The possession, direct or indirect, of the power to direct or cause the direction of the management and policies of a person, whether through the ownership of voting securities, by contract other than a commercial contract for goods or nonmanagement services, or otherwise; provided that such power is not the result of an official position or corporate office held by the person. Control shall be presumed to exist if a person, directly or indirectly, owns, controls, holds with the power to vote, or holds proxies representing ten percent (10%) or more of the voting securities of another person. This presumption may be rebutted by a showing that control does not exist. Notwithstanding this definition, for purposes of this Part, the fact that an SPFC exclusively provides reinsurance to a ceding insurer under an SPFC contract is not by itself sufficient grounds for a finding that the SPFC and ceding insurer are under common control.

(12) Controlled unaffiliated business. - A person meeting all of the following:

a. The person is not in the corporate system of a parent and its affiliated companies in the case of a pure captive insurance company or is not in the corporate system of an industrial insured and its affiliated companies in the case of an industrial insured captive insurance company.

b. The person has an existing contractual relationship with a parent or one of its affiliated companies in the case of a pure captive insurance company or with an industrial insured or one of its affiliated companies in the case of an industrial insured captive insurance company.

c. The person's risks are managed by a pure captive insurance company or an industrial insured captive insurance company, as applicable, in accordance with G.S. 58-10-470.

(13) Counterparty. - An SPFC's parent or affiliated company or a ceding insurer to the SPFC contract. A nonaffiliated company may be designated a

counterparty, but that designation is subject to the prior approval of the Commissioner.

(14)	Court. - Defined in G.S. 58-30-10.

(15)	Department. - Defined in G.S. 58-1-5.

(16)	General account. - All assets and liabilities of a protected cell captive insurance company not attributable to a protected cell.

(17)	Incorporated cell. - A protected cell of an incorporated cell captive insurance company that is organized as a corporation or other legal entity separate from the incorporated cell captive insurance company.

(18)	Incorporated cell captive insurance company. - A protected cell captive insurance company that is established as a corporation or other legal entity separate from its incorporated cells that are also organized as separate legal entities.

(19)	Industrial insured. - An insured that meets all of the following:

a.	It procures the insurance of any risk or risks by use of the services of a full-time employee acting as an insurance manager or buyer.

b.	Its aggregate annual premiums for insurance on all risks total at least twenty-five thousand dollars ($25,000).

c.	It has at least 25 full-time employees.

(20)	Industrial insured captive insurance company. - Any company that insures risks of the industrial insureds that comprise the industrial insured group and that may insure the risks of the affiliated companies of the industrial insureds and the risks of the controlled unaffiliated business of an industrial insured or its affiliated companies.

(21)	Industrial insured group. - Any group of industrial insureds that collectively are described by any of the following:

a.	Own, control, or hold with power to vote all of the outstanding voting securities of an industrial insured captive insurance company incorporated as a stock insurer.

b. Have complete voting control over an industrial insured captive insurance company incorporated as a mutual insurer.

c. Constitute all of the subscribers of an industrial insured captive insurance company formed as a reciprocal insurer.

d. Have complete voting control over an industrial insured captive insurance company formed as a limited liability company.

(22) Insurance securitization or securitization. - A transaction or a group of related transactions which meet the requirements of sub-subdivisions a. and b. of this subdivision:

a. The transactions include capital market offerings that are effected through related risk transfer instruments and facilitating administrative agreements where all or part of the result of such transactions is used to fund the SPFC's obligations under a reinsurance contract with a ceding insurer and by which one of the following occur:

1. Proceeds are obtained by a SPFC, directly or indirectly, through the issuance of securities by the SPFC or any other person.

2. All of the following occur: (i) a person provides one or more letters of credit or other assets for the benefit of the SPFC; (ii) the Commissioner authorizes the SPFC to treat such letters of credit or other assets as admitted assets for purposes of the SPFC's annual report; and (iii) all or any part of such proceeds, letters of credit, or assets, as applicable, are used to fund the SPFC's obligations under a reinsurance contract with a ceding insurer.

b. The transactions do not include the issuance of a letter of credit for the benefit of the Commissioner to satisfy all or part of the SPFC's capital and surplus requirements under G.S. 58-10-575.

(23) Member organization. - Any individual, corporation, limited liability company, partnership, association, or other entity that belongs to an association.

(24) Mutual corporation. - A corporation organized without stockholders and includes a nonprofit corporation with members.

(25) Mutual insurer. - A company owned by its policyholders where no stock is available for purchase on the stock exchanges.

(26) NAIC. - Defined in G.S. 58-1-5.

(27) Organizational documents. - The documents that must be submitted pursuant to North Carolina law in order to legally form a business in this State or to obtain a certificate of authority to transact business in this State.

(28) Parent. - An individual, corporation, limited liability company, partnership, association, or other entity, or individual that directly or indirectly owns, controls, or holds with power to vote more than fifty percent (50%) of the outstanding voting of any of the following interests:

a. Securities of a pure captive insurance company organized as a stock corporation.

b. Membership interests of a pure captive insurance company organized as a nonprofit corporation.

c. Membership interests of a pure captive insurance company organized as a limited liability company.

d. Securities of an SPFC.

(29) Participant. - A person or an entity authorized to be a participant by G.S. 58-10-515, and any affiliate of a participant, that is insured by a protected cell captive insurance company, if the losses of the participant are limited through a participant contract.

(30) Participant contract. - A contract by which a protected cell captive insurance company insures the risks of a participant and limits the losses of each such participant to its pro rata share of the assets of one or more protected cells identified in such participant contract.

(31) Person. - Defined in G.S. 58-1-5.

(32) Protected cell. - Either of the following:

a. A separate account established by a protected cell captive insurance company formed or licensed under this Part, in which an identified pool of assets and liabilities is segregated and insulated by means of this Part from the remainder of the protected cell captive insurance company's assets and liabilities, in accordance with the terms of one or more participant contracts to fund the liability of the protected cell captive insurance company, with respect to the participants as set forth in the participant contracts.

b. A separate account established and maintained by an SPFC for one SPFC contract and the accompanying insurance securitization with a counterparty.

(33) Protected cell assets. - All assets, contract rights, and general intangibles identified with and attributable to a specific protected cell of a protected cell captive insurance company.

(34) Protected cell captive insurance company. - Any captive insurance company meeting all of the following:

a. The minimum capital and surplus required by this Part are provided by one or more sponsors.

b. The company is formed or licensed under this Part.

c. The company insures the risks of separate participants through participant contracts.

d. The company funds its liability to each participant through one or more protected cells and segregates the assets of each protected cell from the assets of other protected cells and from the assets of the protected cell captive insurance company's general account.

(35) Protected cell liabilities. - All liabilities and other obligations identified with and attributed to a specific protected cell of a protected cell captive insurance company.

(36) Pure captive insurance company. - Any company that insures risks of its parent and affiliated companies or a controlled unaffiliated business or businesses.

(37) Risk retention group. - A captive insurance company organized under the laws of this State pursuant to the Liability Risk Retention Act of 1986, 15 U.S.C. § 3901, et seq., as amended, as a stock or mutual corporation or as a

reciprocal or other limited liability entity. Risk retention groups formed under this Part are subject to all applicable insurance laws including, but not limited to, any applicable provisions in Articles 1, 2, 3, 7, 19, 22, 33, and 34 of this Chapter.

(38) Securities. - Those different types of debt obligations, equity, surplus certificates, surplus notes, funding agreements, derivatives, and other legal forms of financial instruments.

(39) SPFC or Special Purpose Financial Captive. - A captive insurance company that has received a certificate of authority from the Commissioner for the limited purposes provided for in this Part.

(40) SPFC contract. - A contract between the SPFC and the counterparty pursuant to which the SPFC agrees to provide insurance or reinsurance protection to the counterparty for risks associated with the counterparty's insurance or reinsurance business.

(41) SPFC securities. - The securities issued by an SPFC.

(42) Sponsor. - Any person or entity that is approved by the Commissioner to provide all or part of the capital and surplus required by this Part and to organize and operate a protected cell captive insurance company.

(43) Surplus note. - An unsecured subordinated debt obligation deemed to be a surplus certificate under this Part and otherwise possessing characteristics consistent with paragraph 3 of the NAIC's Statement of Statutory Accounting Principles No. 41, as amended. (2013-116, s. 1.)

§ 58-10-345. Licensing; authority; confidentiality.

(a) Any captive insurance company, when permitted by its organizational documents, may apply to the Commissioner for a license to do any and all insurance comprised in G.S. 58-7-15; provided, however, that:

(1) No pure captive insurance company shall insure any risks other than those of its parent and affiliated companies or a controlled unaffiliated business or businesses.

(2) No association captive insurance company shall insure any risks other than those of its association, those of the member organizations of its association, and those of a member organization's affiliated companies.

(3) No industrial insured captive insurance company shall insure any risks other than those of the industrial insureds that comprise the industrial insured group, those of their affiliated companies, and those of the controlled unaffiliated business of an industrial insured or its affiliated companies.

(4) No risk retention group shall insure any risks other than those of its members and owners.

(5) No captive insurance company shall provide personal motor vehicle or homeowner's insurance coverage or any component thereof.

(6) No captive insurance company shall accept or cede reinsurance except as provided in G.S. 58-10-445 and G.S. 58-10-605.

(7) No captive insurance company shall provide accident and health insurance on a direct basis.

(8) No captive insurance company shall provide workers' compensation and employer's liability insurance on a direct basis.

(9) No captive insurance company shall provide life insurance or annuities on a direct basis.

(b) No captive insurance company shall transact any insurance business in this State unless:

(1) It obtains a license from the Commissioner pursuant to subsection (c) of this section authorizing it to do insurance business in this State.

(2) Its board of directors or committee of managers or, in the case of a reciprocal insurer, its subscribers' advisory committee holds at least one meeting each year in this State.

(3) It maintains its principal place of business in this State.

(4) It appoints a registered agent to accept service of process and to otherwise act on its behalf in this State, provided that whenever such registered

agent cannot with reasonable diligence be found at the registered office of the captive insurance company, the Commissioner shall be an agent of such captive insurance company upon whom any process, notice, or demand may be served and such service shall be done in accordance with G.S. 58-16-30.

(c) In order to receive a license to issue policies of insurance as a captive insurance company in this State, an applicant business entity shall meet all of the following requirements:

(1) The applicant business entity shall submit its organizational documents to the Commissioner. If the Commissioner approves the organizational documents, then the Commissioner shall issue a letter to the applicant certifying the Commissioner's approval. The applicant business entity shall submit the organizational documents, along with a copy of the approval letter issued by the Commissioner, and the required filing fees for organizational documents prescribed by North Carolina law to the Secretary of State for filing. Upon filing the organizational documents, the Secretary of State shall issue a certificate of filing to the applicant. The applicant business entity shall submit a copy of the certificate of filing relative to the applicant's organizational documents issued by the Secretary of State to the Commissioner.

(2) The applicant business entity shall file a statement under oath of its president and secretary showing its financial condition.

(3) The applicant business entity shall file its plan of operation.

(4) The applicant business entity shall file other documents as required by the Commissioner.

(5) The applicant business entity shall also file with the Commissioner evidence of all of the following:

a. The amount and liquidity of its assets relative to the risks to be assumed.

b. The adequacy of the expertise, experience, and character of the person or persons who will manage it.

c. The overall soundness of its plan of operation.

d. The adequacy of the loss prevention programs of its insureds.

e. Such other factors deemed relevant by the Commissioner in ascertaining whether the applicant business entity will be able to meet its policy obligations.

(6) No less than the amount required by G.S. 58-10-370 shall be paid in by the applicant business entity and deposited with the Commissioner. In the alternative, an irrevocable letter of credit in that amount and acceptable to the Commissioner shall be filed with the Commissioner.

(7) The applicant business entity shall submit to the Commissioner for approval a description of the coverages, deductibles, coverage limits, and rates, together with such additional information as the Commissioner may require.

(d) Whenever a captive insurance company desires to amend the organizational documents submitted pursuant to subdivision (c)(1) of this section, the company shall submit the amended organizational documents to the Commissioner. If the Commissioner approves the amendment, then the Commissioner shall issue a letter to the applicant certifying the Commissioner's approval. The applicant business entity shall submit the organizational documents, along with a copy of the approval letter issued by the Commissioner, and the required filing fees for organizational documents prescribed in North Carolina law to the Secretary of State for filing. Upon filing the organizational documents, the Secretary of State shall issue a certificate of filing to the applicant. The applicant shall submit a copy of the certificate of filing relative to the applicant's organizational documents issued by the Secretary of State to the Commissioner.

(e) If a captive insurance company makes any subsequent material change to any item in the description submitted pursuant to subdivision (c)(7) of this section, then the captive insurance company shall submit an appropriate revision to the Commissioner for approval and shall not offer any additional kinds of insurance until a revision of such description is approved by the Commissioner. The captive insurance company shall inform the Commissioner of any material change in rates within 30 days of the adoption of such change.

(f) Information submitted pursuant to this subsection is confidential and may be made public by the Commissioner or the Commissioner's designee only upon an order of a court of competent jurisdiction except:

(1) This subdivision shall not apply to any risk retention group.

(2) The Commissioner shall have the discretion to disclose such information to a public official having jurisdiction over the regulation of insurance in another state, provided that:

a. The public official agrees in writing to maintain the confidentiality of such information; and

b. The laws of the state in which the public official serves require the information to be and to remain confidential.

(3) Organizational documents filed with the Secretary of State shall continue to be nonconfidential public records in the Secretary of State's office.

(g) The Commissioner is authorized to retain legal, financial, and examination services from outside the Department, the costs of which shall be reimbursed by the applicant. G.S. 58-2-160 shall apply to examinations, investigations, and processing conducted under the authority of this section.

(h) If the Commissioner is satisfied that the documents and statements filed by an applicant captive insurance company comply with this section, then the Commissioner shall grant a license authorizing it to do insurance business in this State. (2013-116, s. 1.)

§ 58-10-350. Commissioner use of consultants and other professionals.

The Commissioner may contract with consultants and other professionals to expedite and complete the application process, examinations, and other regulatory activities required pursuant to this Part. Such contracts for financial, legal, examination, and other services shall not be subject to any of the following:

(1) G.S. 114-2.3.

(2) G.S. 147-17.

(3) Articles 3, 3C, and 8 of Chapter 143 of the General Statutes, together with rules and procedures adopted under those Articles concerning procurement, contracting, and contract review. (2013-116, s. 1.)

§ 58-10-355. Organizational examination.

In addition to the processing of the application, an organizational investigation or examination may be performed before an applicant is licensed. Such investigation or examination shall consist of a general survey of the applicant's corporate records, including charters, bylaws, and minute books; verification of capital and surplus; verification of principal place of business; determination of assets and liabilities; and a review of such other factors as the Commissioner deems necessary. (2013-116, s. 1.)

§ 58-10-360. Designation of captive manager.

Before licensing, captive insurance companies shall report in writing to the Commissioner the name and address of the manager designated to manage the captive insurance company. The Commissioner shall approve the captive manager and may require the submission of additional information regarding the proposed captive manager in a form and manner as the Commissioner may designate. (2013-116, s. 1.)

§ 58-10-365. Names of companies.

No captive insurance company shall adopt a name that is the same, deceptively similar, or likely to be confused with or mistaken for any other existing business name registered in this State nor any name likely to mislead the public. Any name adopted by a captive insurance company shall comply with the requirements of State law. (2013-116, s. 1.)

§ 58-10-370. Capital and surplus requirements.

(a) No captive insurance company shall be issued a license unless it possesses and maintains unimpaired paid-in capital and surplus of:

(1) In the case of a pure captive insurance company, not less than two hundred fifty thousand dollars ($250,000) or such other amount determined by the Commissioner.

(2) In the case of an association captive insurance company, not less than five hundred thousand dollars ($500,000).

(3) In the case of an industrial insured captive insurance company, not less than five hundred thousand dollars ($500,000).

(4) In the case of a risk retention group, not less than one million dollars ($1,000,000).

(5) In the case of a protected cell captive insurance company, not less than two hundred fifty thousand dollars ($250,000).

(b) The Commissioner may prescribe additional capital and surplus based upon the type, volume, and nature of insurance business to be transacted.

(c) Capital and surplus shall be in the form of cash or an irrevocable letter of credit issued by a bank approved by the Commissioner. (2013-116, s. 1.)

§ 58-10-375. Dividends and distributions.

No captive insurance company shall pay a dividend or other distribution from capital or surplus without the prior approval of the Commissioner. Approval of an ongoing plan for the payment of dividends or other distributions shall be conditioned upon the retention, at the time of each payment, of capital or surplus in excess of amounts specified by or determined in accordance with formulas approved by the Commissioner. A captive insurance company may otherwise make such distributions as are in conformity with its purposes and approved by the Commissioner. (2013-116, s. 1.)

§ 58-10-380. Formation of captive insurance companies.

(a) A pure captive insurance company may be incorporated as a stock insurer with its capital divided into shares and held by the stockholders, as a nonprofit corporation with one or more members, or as a manager-managed limited liability company.

(b) An association captive insurance company, an industrial insured captive insurance company, or a risk retention group may be any of the following:

(1) Incorporated as a stock insurer with its capital divided into shares and held by the stockholders.

(2) Incorporated as a mutual corporation.

(3) Organized as a reciprocal insurer in accordance with Article 15 of this Chapter.

(4) Organized as a manager-managed limited liability company.

(c) A captive insurance company incorporated or organized in this State shall have not less than three incorporators or three organizers of whom not less than one shall be a resident of this State.

(d) The capital stock of a captive insurance company incorporated as a stock insurer may be authorized with no par value.

(e) In the case of a captive insurance company formed as a corporation, at least one of the members of the board of directors shall be a resident of this State. In the case of a captive insurance company formed as a reciprocal insurer, at least one of the members of the subscribers' advisory committee shall be a resident of this State. In the case of a captive insurance company formed as a limited liability company, at least one of the managers shall be a resident of this State.

(f) Captive insurance companies formed as corporations, limited liability companies, partnerships, or as nonprofit corporations under this Part shall have the privileges provided in and be subject to all State statutes and laws, as applicable, provided that this Part shall control in the event of a conflict.

(g) Mergers, consolidations, conversions, mutualizations, acquisitions, redomestications, or other similar transactions of captive insurance companies shall be subject to the same provisions of this Chapter applicable to traditional insurance companies, except:

(1) The Commissioner may, upon request of an insurer party to a merger authorized under this subsection, waive such applicable requirements.

(2) The Commissioner may waive or modify the requirements for public notice and hearing.

(3) An alien insurer may be a party to a merger authorized under this subsection, provided that the requirements for a merger between a captive insurance company and a foreign insurer under this Chapter shall apply to a merger between a captive insurance company and an alien insurer under this subsection. For the purposes of this subdivision, an alien insurer shall be treated as a foreign insurer under this Chapter, and the domicile of the alien shall be the equivalent to that of another state.

(h) Captive insurance companies formed as reciprocal insurers under this Part shall have the privileges provided in and be subject to Article 15 of this Chapter in addition to this Part, provided that this Part shall control in the event of a conflict. To the extent a reciprocal insurer is made subject to other provisions of this Chapter pursuant to Article 15 of this Chapter, such provisions shall not be applicable to a reciprocal insurer formed under this Part unless such provisions are expressly made applicable to captive insurance companies under this Part.

(i) The articles of incorporation or bylaws of a captive insurance company formed as a corporation may authorize a quorum of its board of directors to consist of no fewer than one-third of the fixed or prescribed number of directors.

(j) The subscribers' agreement or other organizing document of a captive insurance company formed as a reciprocal insurer may authorize a quorum of its subscribers' advisory committee to consist of no fewer than one-third of the number of its members.

(k) With the Commissioner's approval, a captive insurance company organized as a stock insurer may convert to a nonprofit corporation with one or more members by filing with the Secretary of State an election for such conversion, provided that:

(1) The election shall certify that, at the time of the company's original organization and at all times thereafter, the company has conducted its business in a manner not inconsistent with a nonprofit purpose.

(2) At the time of the filing of its election, the company shall file with both the Commissioner and the Secretary of State articles of conversion, including articles of incorporation consistent with this Part and with all other applicable State statutes and laws.

(l) In the case of a captive insurance company formed as a limited liability company, a reciprocal insurance company, or mutual insurance company, any proxy executed by the members, subscribers, and policyholders of each shall be valid if executed and transmitted in compliance with all applicable State statutes and laws. (2013-116, s. 1.)

§ 58-10-385. Directors.

(a) Every captive insurance company shall report to the Commissioner within 30 days after any change in its executive officers or directors, including in its report a biographical affidavit for each new officer or director.

(b) No director, officer, or employee of a captive insurance company shall, except on behalf of the captive insurance company, accept or be the beneficiary of, any fee, brokerage, gift, or other compensation because of any investment, loan, deposit, purchase, sale, payment, or exchange made by or for the captive insurance company, but such person may receive reasonable compensation for necessary services rendered to the captive insurance company in his or her usual private, professional, or business capacity.

(c) Any profit or gain received by or on behalf of any person in violation of this section shall inure to and be recoverable by the captive insurance company. (2013-116, s. 1.)

§ 58-10-390. Conflict of interest.

(a) Each captive insurance company chartered in this State is required to adopt a conflict of interest statement for officers, directors, and key employees. Such statement shall disclose that the individual has no outside commitments, personal or otherwise, that would divert him or her from his or her duty to further the interests of the captive insurance company he or she represents, but this shall not preclude such person from being a director or officer in more than one insurance company.

(b) Each officer, director, and key employee shall file such disclosure with the Board of Directors yearly. (2013-116, s. 1.)

§ 58-10-395. Change of business.

(a) Any material change in a captive insurance company's business plan that was filed with the Commissioner at the time of initial application and any subsequent amendment of the plan requires prior approval from the Commissioner.

(b) Any change in any other information filed with the application must be filed with the Commissioner within 60 days but does not require prior approval. (2013-116, s. 1.)

§ 58-10-400. Insurance manager and intermediaries.

No person shall act in or from this State as a managing general agent, producer, or reinsurance intermediary for captive business without the authorization of the Commissioner. Application for such authorization must be on a form prescribed by the Commissioner. (2013-116, s. 1.)

§ 58-10-405. Annual reports.

(a) No captive insurance companies shall be required to make any annual report to the Commissioner except as provided in this Part.

(b) Prior to March 1 of each year, and prior to March 15 of each year in the case of pure captive insurance companies or industrial insured captive insurance companies, each captive insurance company shall submit to the Commissioner a report of its financial condition, verified by oath of two of its executive officers. Each captive insurance company shall report using generally accepted accounting principles, unless the Commissioner requires, approves, or accepts the use of statutory accounting principles or other comprehensive basis of accounting. The Commissioner may require, approve, or accept any appropriate or necessary modifications of the statutory accounting principles or other comprehensive basis of accounting for the type of insurance and kinds of insurers to be reported upon. The Commissioner may require additional information to supplement such report. Except as otherwise provided, each risk retention group and association captive insurance company shall file its report in the form required by G.S. 58-2-165, and each risk retention group and association captive insurance company shall comply with the requirements set forth in G.S. 58-4-5. All other captive insurance companies shall report on forms adopted by the Commissioner. G.S. 58-10-345(f) shall apply to each report filed pursuant to this section. Branch captive insurance companies shall file the report required by this section unless otherwise required by G.S. 58-10-545. Special Purpose Financial Captive insurance companies shall report in accordance with G.S. 58-10-625.

(c)   A pure captive insurance company or an industrial insured captive insurance company may make written application to the Commissioner for filing the required report on an alternative reporting date based on the company's fiscal year-end. If an alternative reporting date is granted by the Commissioner, then:

(1)   The annual report is due 75 days after the fiscal year-end.

(2)   In order to provide sufficient detail to support the premium tax return, the pure captive insurance company or industrial insured captive insurance company shall file, prior to March 15 of each year for each calendar year-end, pages 1, 2, 3, and 5 of the "Captive Annual Statement; Pure or Industrial Insured," verified by oath of two of its executive officers. (2013-116, s. 1.)

§ 58-10-410: Reserved for future codification purposes.

§ 58-10-415. Annual audit and actuarial certification.

(a)   All captive insurance companies shall have an annual audit by an independent certified public accountant and shall file such audited financial report with the Commissioner on or before June 30 for the prior calendar year.

(b) Captive insurance companies that have received approval to report on other than a calendar year basis pursuant to G.S. 58-10-405 shall file such statements within 180 days after the end of their fiscal year.

(c) Captive insurance companies with less than one million two hundred thousand dollars ($1,200,000) in written premium may make a written request for exemption from the annual audit requirement. Such request must be made at least 90 days prior to the captive insurance company's fiscal year-end or as otherwise required by the Commissioner. Requests will be considered on a case-by-case basis and may be subject to the Commissioner receiving an annual audit of the captive insurance company's parent company in lieu of the annual audit of the captive insurance company.

(d) The annual audit report shall be considered part of the captive insurance company's annual report of financial condition except with respect to the date by which it must be filed with the Commissioner. The annual audit shall consist of the following:

(1) Opinion of independent certified public accountant. - Financial statements furnished pursuant to this section shall be audited by independent certified public accountants in accordance with generally accepted auditing standards as determined by the American Institute of Certified Public Accountants or statutory accounting principles in accordance with the NAIC Accounting Practices and Procedures Manual in effect for the period covered by the report. The opinion of the independent certified public accountant shall cover all years presented. The opinion shall be addressed to the captive insurance company on stationery of the accountant showing the address of issuance and shall be signed and dated.

(2) Report of evaluation of internal controls. - This report shall include an evaluation of the internal controls of the captive insurance company relating to the methods and procedures used in the securing of assets and the reliability of the financial records, including, but not limited to, such controls as the system of authorization and approval and the separation of duties. The review shall be conducted in accordance with generally accepted auditing standards or statutory accounting principles and the report filed with the Commissioner. An exemption from this evaluation may be granted on a case-by-case basis upon written request to the Commissioner.

(3) Accountant's letter of qualifications. - The accountant shall furnish the captive insurance company, for inclusion in the filing of the audited annual report, a letter stating:

a. That the accountant is independent with respect to the captive insurance company and conforms to the standards of the profession as contained in the Code of Professional Ethics, pronouncements of the American Institute of Certified Public Accountants, and pronouncements of the Financial Accounting Standards Board.

b. The general background and experience of the staff engaged in the audit, including the experience in auditing captives or other insurance companies.

c. That the accountant understands that the audited annual report and the accountant's opinions thereon will be filed in compliance with this section with the Commissioner.

d. That the accountant consents to the requirements of G.S. 58-10-420(b) and (c) and that the accountant consents and agrees to make available for review by the Commissioner, the Commissioner's appointed agent, or other designee the work papers as defined in G.S. 58-10-420(c).

e. That the accountant is properly licensed by an appropriate state licensing authority and that he or she is a member in good standing of the American Institute of Certified Public Accountants.

(4) Financial statements. - Statements required shall be as follows:

a. Balance sheets reporting assets, liabilities, capital, and surplus.

b. Statements of operations.

c. Statements of cash flow.

d. Statements of changes in capital and surplus.

e. Notes to financial statements. The notes to financial statements shall be those required by generally accepted accounting principles, or as required by any other comprehensive basis of accounting in use by the captive insurance company and approved by the Commissioner, and shall include:

1. A reconciliation of differences, if any, between the audited financial report and the report of its financial condition filed with the Commissioner in accordance with G.S. 58-10-405(b).

2. A summary of ownership and relationship of the captive insurance company and all affiliated corporations or companies insured by the captive insurance company.

3. A narrative explanation of all material transactions and balances with the captive insurance company.

(5) Certification of loss reserves and loss expense reserves. - The annual audit shall be filed with a Statement of Actuarial Opinion evaluating the captive insurance company's loss reserves and loss expense reserves. The individual who prepares the Statement of Actuarial Opinion shall be a Fellow of the Casualty Actuarial Society, a member in good standing of the American Academy of Actuaries, or an individual who has demonstrated competence in loss reserve evaluation to the Commissioner. Certification shall be in such form as the Commissioner deems appropriate. (2013-116, s. 1.)

§ 58-10-420. Independent certified public accountants.

(a) A captive insurance company, after becoming subject to this Part, shall within 60 days report to the Commissioner in writing, the name and address of the independent certified public accountant retained to conduct the annual audit set forth in G.S. 58-10-415.

(b) A captive insurance company shall require its independent certified public accountant to immediately notify in writing an officer and all members of the board of directors of the captive insurance company of any determination by the independent certified public accountant that the captive insurance company has materially misstated its financial condition in its report to the Commissioner as required in G.S. 58-10-405. The independent certified public accountant shall furnish such notification to the Commissioner within five working days of notifying the captive insurance company.

(c) A captive insurance company shall require its independent certified public accountant to make available for review by the Commissioner or his or her appointed agent the work papers prepared in the conduct of the audit of the captive insurance company. The captive insurance company shall require that the independent certified public accountant retain the audit work papers for a period of not less than five years after the period reported upon. The aforementioned review by the Commissioner shall be considered an examination, and all working papers obtained during the course of such examination shall be confidential. The captive insurance company shall require that the independent certified public accountant provide copies, in such form as the Commissioner deems appropriate, of any of the working papers which the Commissioner considers relevant. Such working papers may be retained by the Commissioner. "Work papers" as referred to in this section include, but are not necessarily limited to, schedules, analyses, reconciliations, abstracts, memoranda, narratives, flow charts, copies of captive insurance company records, or other documents prepared or obtained by the independent certified public accountant and the independent certified public accountant's employees in the conduct of their audit of the captive insurance company.

(d) The lead audit partner may not act in that capacity for more than five consecutive years. For purposes of this subsection, lead audit partner means the partner having primary responsibility for the audit. The person shall be disqualified from acting in that or similar capacity for the captive insurance company for a period of five consecutive years. A captive insurance company may make application to the Commissioner for relief from the above rotation requirement on the basis of unusual circumstances. This application should be made at least 30 days before the end of the calendar year. The Commissioner may consider the following factors in determining if the relief should be granted:

(1) Number of partners, expertise of the partners, or the number of insurance clients in the firm;

(2) Premium volume of the captive insurance company; or

(3) Number of jurisdictions in which the insurer transacts business. (2013-116, s. 1.)

§ 58-10-425. Deposit requirement.

(a) Whenever the Commissioner deems that the financial condition of a captive insurance company warrants additional security beyond that required pursuant to G.S. 58-10-345(c)(6), the Commissioner may require a captive insurance company to deposit with the Commissioner additional cash or securities approved by the Commissioner or, alternatively, to furnish the Commissioner a clean irrevocable letter of credit issued by a bank chartered by the State or by a member bank of the Federal Reserve System and approved by the Commissioner.

(b)   A captive insurance company may receive interest or dividends from deposits held by the Commissioner or exchange the deposits for others of equal value with the approval of the Commissioner.

(c)   If a captive insurance company discontinues business, the Commissioner shall return deposits held by the Commissioner only after being satisfied that all obligations of the captive insurance company have been discharged. (2013-116, s. 1.)

§ 58-10-430. Examinations.

(a)   Whenever the Commissioner determines it to be prudent, the Commissioner shall visit a captive insurance company and inspect and examine its affairs to ascertain its financial condition, its ability to fulfill its obligations, and whether it has complied with this Part. The expenses and charges of the examination shall be paid by the captive insurance company.

(b)   G.S. 58-2-160 shall apply to examinations conducted under this section.

(c)   All examination reports, preliminary examination reports or results, working papers, recorded information, documents, and copies thereof produced by, obtained by, or disclosed to the Commissioner or any other person in the course of an examination made under this section are confidential, are not subject to subpoena, and may not be made public by the Commissioner or an employee or agent of the Commissioner. Nothing in this subsection shall prevent the Commissioner from using such information in furtherance of the Commissioner's regulatory authority under this Chapter. The Commissioner shall have the discretion to grant access to such information to public officials having jurisdiction over the regulation of insurance in any other state or country or to law enforcement officers of this State or any other state or agency of the federal government at any time only if the officials receiving the information agree in writing to maintain the confidentiality of the information in a manner consistent with this subsection. (2013-116, s. 1.)

§ 58-10-435. License suspension or revocation.

(a) The license of a captive insurance company may be suspended or revoked if the Commissioner finds, upon examination, hearing, or other evidence, that a captive insurance company has committed the violations described in subdivisions (1) through (7) of this subsection, or met the criteria in subdivisions (8) through (10) of this subsection, and that the suspension or revocation is in the best interest of the public and the policyholders of such captive insurance company, notwithstanding any other provision of this Chapter:

(1) Insolvency or impairment of capital or surplus.

(2) Failure to meet the requirements of G.S. 58-10-370.

(3) Refusal or failure to submit an annual report, as required by this Part, or any other report or statement required by law or by lawful order of the Commissioner.

(4) Failure to comply with its own charter, bylaws, or other organizational document.

(5) Failure to submit to or pay the cost of an examination or any legal obligation relative to an examination, as required by this Part.

(6) Use of methods that, although not otherwise specifically prohibited by law, nevertheless render its operation detrimental or its condition unsound with respect to the public or to its policyholders.

(7) Failure otherwise to comply with the laws of this State.

(8) Failure to commence business according to its plan of operation within two years of being licensed.

(9) Failure to carry on insurance business in or from this State.

(10) By request of the captive insurance company.

(b) Before the Commissioner suspends or revokes the license of a captive insurance company under subdivisions (a)(7) or (a)(8) of this section, the Commissioner shall give the captive insurance company notice in writing of the grounds on which the Commissioner proposes to suspend or revoke the license and shall afford the captive insurance company an opportunity to make objection in writing within the period of 30 days after receipt of notice. The Commissioner shall take into consideration any objection received by the Commissioner within that period and, if the Commissioner decides to suspend or revoke the license, cause the order of suspension or revocation to be served on the captive insurance company. (2013-116, s. 1.)

§ 58-10-440. Investment requirements.

(a) Except as may be otherwise authorized by the Commissioner, association captive insurance companies and risk retention groups shall comply with the investment requirements contained in G.S. 58-7-167, 58-7-170, 58-7-172, 58-7-173, 58-7-178, 58-7-179, 58-7-180, 58-7-183, 58-7-185, 58-7-187, 58-7-188, 58-7-192, 58-7-193, 58-7-197, 58-7-200, and 58-7-205, as applicable. Notwithstanding any other provision of this Chapter, the Commissioner may approve the use of alternative reliable methods of valuation and rating.

(b) No pure captive insurance company, industrial insured captive insurance company, protected cell captive insurance company, incorporated cell captive insurance company, or special purpose financial captive insurance company shall be subject to any restrictions on allowable investments, provided that the Commissioner may prohibit or limit any investment that threatens the solvency or liquidity of any such company.

(c) No pure captive insurance company shall make a loan to or an investment in its parent company or affiliates without prior written approval of the Commissioner, and any such loan or investment shall be evidenced by documentation approved by the Commissioner. Loans of minimum capital and surplus funds required by G.S. 58-10-370 are prohibited.

(d) Notwithstanding this section or G.S. 58-7-167, 58-7-170, 58-7-172, 58-7-173, 58-7-178, 58-7-179, 58-7-180, 58-7-183, 58-7-185, 58-7-187, 58-7-188, 58-7-192, 58-7-193, 58-7-197, 58-7-200, and 58-7-205, an association captive insurance company of an association described in G.S. 58-10-340(4)(b) may hold any interest in qualified headquarters property, and the qualified headquarters property shall be admitted assets and authorized investments of the association captive insurance company. The net book value of the qualified headquarters property deemed admitted and authorized under this subsection may not exceed two million five hundred thousand dollars ($2,500,000), and an association captive insurance company holding qualified headquarters property pursuant to this subsection shall at all times maintain total surplus, without regard to the qualified headquarters property, of at least the sum of (i) fifty percent (50%) of the net book value of the qualified headquarters property and (ii) the minimum capital and surplus requirements. For purposes of this subsection, "qualified headquarters property" includes the real property and the building in which the principal office of the association captive insurance company is located and also includes any improved and unimproved real property of the association captive insurance company that is located within 1,500 feet of the company's principal office. (2013-116, s. 1.)

§ 58-10-445. Reinsurance.

(a)   Any captive insurance company may provide reinsurance as authorized by this Chapter on risks ceded by any other insurer.

(b)   Any captive insurance company may take credit for the reinsurance of risks or portions of risks ceded to reinsurers complying with this Chapter. If the reinsurer is licensed as a risk retention group, then the ceding risk retention group or its members must qualify for membership with the reinsurer. The Commissioner shall have the discretion to allow a captive insurance company to take credit for the reinsurance of risks or portions of risks ceded to an unauthorized reinsurer, after review, on a case-by-case basis. The Commissioner may require any documents, financial information, or other evidence that such an unauthorized reinsurer will be able to demonstrate adequate security for its financial obligations.

(c)   In addition to reinsurers authorized by this Chapter, a captive insurance company may take credit for the reinsurance of risks or portions of risks ceded to a pool, exchange, or association to the extent authorized by the Commissioner. The Commissioner may require any documents, financial information, or other evidence that such a pool, exchange, or association will be able to provide adequate security for its financial obligations. The Commissioner may deny authorization or impose any limitations on the activities of a reinsurance pool, exchange, or association that in the Commissioner's judgment are necessary and proper to provide adequate security for the ceding captive insurance company and for the protection and consequent benefit of the public at large.

(d)   Insurance by a captive insurance company of any workers' compensation or accident and health-qualified self-insured plan shall only be in the form of reinsurance.

(e)   No credit shall be allowed for reinsurance where the reinsurance contract does not result in the complete transfer of the risk or liability to the reinsurer.

(f)   No credit shall be allowed, as an asset or a deduction from liability, to any ceding insurer for reinsurance unless the reinsurance is payable by the assuming insurer on the basis of the liability of the ceding insurer under the contract reinsured without diminution because of the insolvency of the ceding insurer.

(g)   Reinsurance under this section shall be effected through a written agreement of reinsurance setting forth the terms, provisions, and conditions governing such reinsurance. The Commissioner may require that complete copies of all reinsurance treaties and contracts be filed and approved by the Commissioner. (2013-116, s. 1.)

§ 58-10-450. Membership in rating organizations; exemption from compulsory associations.

(a)   No captive insurance company shall be required to join a rating organization.

(b)   No captive insurance company shall be permitted to join or contribute financially to any plan, pool, association, or guaranty or insolvency fund in this State, nor shall any such captive insurance company, or any insured or affiliate thereof, receive any benefit from any such plan, pool, association, or guaranty or insolvency fund for claims arising out of the operations of such captive insurance company. (2013-116, s. 1.)

§ 58-10-455. Taxation.

A captive insurance company is taxed in accordance with Article 8B of Chapter 105 of the General Statutes. (2013-116, s. 1.)

§ 58-10-460. Adoption and amendment of rules by Commissioner.

The Commissioner may adopt and, from time to time, amend such rules relating to captive insurance companies as are necessary to enable the Commissioner to carry out the provisions of this Part. (2013-116, s. 1.)

§ 58-10-465. Applicable provisions.

No provisions of this Chapter, other than those contained in this Part or as expressly provided in this Part, shall apply to captive insurance companies. Risk retention groups shall have the privileges and be subject to Article 22 of this Chapter in addition to the applicable provisions of this Part. (2013-116, s. 1.)

§ 58-10-470. Establishment of standards regarding risk management.

The Commissioner may adopt rules establishing standards to ensure that a parent or its affiliated company, or an industrial insured or its affiliated company, is able to exercise control of the risk management function of any controlled unaffiliated business to be insured by a pure captive insurance company or an industrial insured captive insurance company, respectively; provided, however, that until such time as rules under this section are adopted, the Commissioner may approve the coverage of such risks by a pure captive insurance company or an industrial insured captive insurance company. (2013-116, s. 1.)

§ 58-10-475. Supervision; rehabilitation; liquidation.

Except as otherwise provided in this Part, the terms and conditions set forth in Article 30 of this Chapter shall apply in full to captive insurance companies formed or licensed under this Part. (2013-116, s. 1.)

§ 58-10-480. Authority for expenditure of public funds.

Any municipality, county, authority, utility district, or other public body generally classified as a governmental body or governmental entity whether chartered or organized by local act or public act of the General Assembly, or otherwise, or any agency, board, or commission of any municipality, metropolitan government, county, authority, utility district, or other public body generally classified as a governmental body or governmental entity may expend public funds for the purchase of capital stock in a captive insurance company or to provide guaranty capital in a mutual captive insurance company, provided that at the time of authorization of expenditure of public funds adequate insurance markets in the United States are not available to cover the risks, hazards, and liabilities of the public body or that the needed coverage is only available at excessive rates or with unreasonable deductibles. (2013-116, s. 1.)

§ 58-10-485. Violations and penalties.

(a)   If, after providing the opportunity for a contested case hearing held in accordance with the provisions of Article 3A of Chapter 150B of the General Statutes, the Commissioner finds that any insurer, person, or entity required to be licensed, permitted, or authorized to transact the business of insurance under this Part has violated any provision of this Part or any rule or regulation authorized by this Part, the Commissioner may order:

(1)   The insurer, person, or entity to cease and desist from engaging in the act or practice giving rise to the violation.

(2)   Payment of a monetary penalty pursuant to G.S. 58-2-70.

(3)   The suspension or revocation of the insurer's, person's, or entity's license.

(b) Whenever the Commissioner has evidence that any person has violated or is violating any provisions of this Part, or has violated or is violating any order or requirement of the Commissioner issued by the Commissioner under this Part, and that the interests of policyholders, creditors, or the public may be irreparably harmed by delay, the Commissioner may issue an emergency cease and desist order that shall become effective on the date specified in the order. The emergency cease and desist order shall also include a notice of hearing, which shall be conducted as provided under Article 3A of Chapter 150B of the General Statutes. However, the person ordered to cease and desist under this subsection may request and shall be granted an expedited review of the order. The emergency order shall remain in effect prior to and during the proceedings, unless modified by the Commissioner. (2013-116, s. 1.)

§ 58-10-490: Reserved for future codification purposes.

§ 58-10-495. Captive insurance companies reinsuring life insurance policies.

(a) A captive insurance company that reinsures life insurance policies, including term, universal, and variable life policies, and related guarantees and riders, shall maintain reserves that are actuarially sufficient to support the liabilities incurred by the captive insurance company in reinsuring life insurance policies.

(b) For purposes of the annual report required pursuant to G.S. 58-10-405, a captive insurance company described by subsection (a) of this section shall comply with the following requirements:

(1) If the company uses statutory accounting principles, it shall submit the annual report in the form of the annual statement approved by the NAIC for life insurers, as modified or supplemented by the Commissioner, unless the Commissioner requires or approves a different form of annual report.

(2) If the company uses generally accepted accounting principles, including any appropriate modifications or adaptations thereto approved by the Commissioner, it shall submit the annual report in a form approved by the Commissioner. (2013-116, s. 1.)

Subpart 2. Protected Cell Captive Insurance Companies.

§ 58-10-500. Forming a protected cell captive insurance company.

(a) One or more sponsors may form a protected cell captive insurance company under this Subpart.

(b) A protected cell captive insurance company shall be incorporated as a stock insurer with its capital divided into shares and held by the stockholders, as a mutual corporation, as a nonprofit corporation with one or more members, or as a manager-managed limited liability company. (2013-116, s. 1.)

§ 58-10-505. Additional filing requirements for applicant protected cell captive insurance companies.

In addition to the information required by G.S. 58-10-345(c), each applicant protected cell captive insurance company shall file with the Commissioner all of the following:

(1) Materials demonstrating how the applicant will account for the loss and expense experience of each protected cell at a level of detail found to be sufficient by the Commissioner, and how it will report such experience to the Commissioner.

(2) A statement acknowledging that all records of the applicant, including records pertaining to any protected cells, shall be made available for inspection or examination by the Commissioner or the Commissioner's designated agent.

(3) All contracts or sample contracts between the applicant and any participants.

(4) Evidence that expenses shall be allocated to each protected cell in a fair and equitable manner. (2013-116, s. 1.)

§ 58-10-510. Establishment of protected cells.

(a) A protected cell captive insurance company formed or licensed under this Part may establish and maintain one or more incorporated or unincorporated protected cells, to insure risks of one or more participants, subject to the following conditions:

(1) A protected cell captive insurance company may establish one or more protected cells if the Commissioner has approved in writing a plan of operation or amendments to a plan of operation submitted by the protected cell captive insurance company with respect to each protected cell. A plan of operation shall include, but is not limited to, the specific business objectives and investment guidelines of the protected cell, provided that the Commissioner may require additional information in the plan of operation.

(2) Upon the Commissioner's written approval of the plan of operation, the protected cell captive insurance company may attribute insurance obligations with respect to its insurance business to the protected cell in accordance with the approved plan of operation.

(3) A protected cell shall have its own distinct name or designation that shall include the words "protected cell" or "incorporated cell."

(4) The protected cell captive insurance company shall transfer all assets attributable to a protected cell to one or more separately established and identified protected cell accounts bearing the name or designation of that protected cell. Protected cell assets must be held in the protected cell accounts for the purpose of satisfying the obligations of that protected cell.

(5) An incorporated protected cell may be organized and operated in any form of business organization authorized by the Commissioner. Each incorporated protected cell of a protected cell captive insurer shall be treated as a captive insurer for purposes of this Part. Unless otherwise permitted by the organizational documents of a protected cell captive insurer, each incorporated protected cell of the protected cell captive insurer must have the same directors, secretary, and registered office as the protected cell captive insurer.

(6) All attributions of assets and liabilities between a protected cell and the general account shall be in accordance with the plan of operation and participant contracts approved by the Commissioner. No other attribution of assets or liabilities shall be made by a protected cell captive insurance company between the protected cell captive insurance company's general account and its

protected cells. Any attribution of assets and liabilities between the general account and a protected cell shall be in cash or in readily marketable securities with established market values.

(b) The creation of a protected cell does not create, with respect to that protected cell, a legal person separate from the protected cell captive insurance company, unless the protected cell is an incorporated cell. Amounts attributed to a protected cell under this Part, including assets transferred to a protected cell account, are owned by the protected cell. No protected cell captive insurance company shall be, or hold itself out to be, a trustee with respect to those protected cell assets of that protected cell account. Notwithstanding this subsection, the protected cell captive insurance company may allow for a security interest to attach to protected cell assets or a protected cell account when the security interest is in favor of a creditor of the protected cell and otherwise allowed under applicable law.

(c) This Part shall not be construed to prohibit the protected cell captive insurance company from contracting with or arranging for an investment advisor, commodity trading advisor, or other third party to manage the protected cell assets of a protected cell, if all remuneration, expenses, and other compensation of the third-party advisor or manager are payable from the protected cell assets of that protected cell and not from the protected cell assets of other protected cells or the assets of the protected cell captive insurance company's general account.

(d) A protected cell captive insurance company shall establish administrative and accounting procedures necessary to properly identify (i) the one or more protected cells of the protected cell captive insurance company and (ii) the assets and liabilities attributable to each protected cell. The directors of a protected cell captive insurance company shall keep protected cell assets and liabilities:

(1) Separate and separately identifiable from the assets and liabilities of the protected cell captive insurance company's general account.

(2) Attributable to one protected cell separate and separately identifiable from protected cell assets and protected cell liabilities attributable to other protected cells.

If this subsection is violated, then the remedy of tracing is applicable to protected cell assets when commingled with protected cell assets of other protected cells or the assets of the protected cell captive insurance company's general account. The remedy of tracing shall not be construed as an exclusive remedy.

(e)   When establishing a protected cell, the protected cell captive insurance company shall attribute to the protected cell assets a value at least equal to the reserves and other insurance liabilities attributed to that protected cell.

(f)   Each protected cell shall be accounted for separately on the books and records of the protected cell captive insurance company to reflect (i) the financial condition and results of operations of such protected cell, (ii) net income or loss, (iii) dividends or other distributions to participants, and (iv) such other factors as may be provided in the participant contract or required by the Commissioner.

(g)   No asset of a protected cell shall be chargeable with liabilities arising out of any other insurance business the protected cell captive insurance company may conduct.

(h)   No sale, exchange, or other transfer of assets shall be made by such protected cell captive insurance company between or among any of its protected cells without the consent of such protected cells.

(i)   No sale, exchange, transfer of assets, dividend, or distribution shall be made from a protected cell to a protected cell captive insurance company or participant without the Commissioner's approval. In no event shall the Commissioner's approval be given if the sale, exchange, transfer, dividend, or distribution would result in the insolvency or impairment of a protected cell.

(j)   All attributions of assets and liabilities to the protected cells and the general account shall be in accordance with the plan of operation approved by the Commissioner. No other attribution of assets or liabilities shall be made by a protected cell captive insurance company between its general account and any protected cell, or between any protected cells. The protected cell captive insurance company shall attribute all insurance obligations, assets, and liabilities relating to a reinsurance contract entered into with respect to a protected cell to such protected cell. The performance under such reinsurance contract and any tax benefits, losses, refunds, or credits allocated pursuant to a tax allocation agreement to which the protected cell captive insurance company is a party, including any payments made by or due to be made to the protected cell captive insurance company pursuant to the terms of such agreement, shall reflect the insurance obligations, assets, and liabilities relating to the reinsurance contract that are attributed to such protected cell.

(k) In connection with the conservation, rehabilitation, or liquidation of a protected cell captive insurance company, the assets and liabilities of a protected cell shall, to the extent the Commissioner determines they are separable, at all times be kept separate from and shall not be commingled with those of other protected cells and the protected cell captive insurance company.

(l) Each protected cell captive insurance company shall annually file with the Commissioner such financial reports as required by the Commissioner. Any such financial report shall include without limitation accounting statements detailing the financial experience of each protected cell.

(m) Each protected cell captive insurance company shall notify the Commissioner in writing within 10 business days of any protected cell that is insolvent or otherwise unable to meet its claim or expense obligations.

(n) No participant contract shall take effect without the Commissioner's prior written approval. The addition of each new protected cell, the withdrawal of any participant, or the termination of any existing protected cell shall constitute a change in the plan of operation requiring the Commissioner's prior written approval.

(o) The business written by a protected cell captive insurance company, with respect to each protected cell, must be secured by one of the following methods:

(1) Fronted by an insurance company licensed under the laws of any state.

(2) Reinsured by a reinsurer authorized or approved by this State.

(3) Secured by a trust fund in the United States for the benefit of policyholders and claimants, funded by an irrevocable letter of credit, or other arrangement that is acceptable to the Commissioner. The amount of security provided shall be no less than the reserves associated with those liabilities which are neither fronted nor reinsured, including reserves for losses, allocated loss adjustment expenses, incurred but not reported losses, and unearned premiums for business written through the participant's protected cell. The Commissioner may require the protected cell captive insurance company to increase the funding of any security arrangement established under this

subdivision. If the form of security is a letter of credit, the letter of credit shall be issued or confirmed by a bank approved by the Commissioner. A trust maintained pursuant to this subdivision shall be established in a form and upon such terms approved by the Commissioner.

(p)   Notwithstanding this Chapter or other laws of this State, and in addition to G.S. 58-10-525, in the event of an insolvency of a protected cell captive insurance company where the Commissioner determines that one or more protected cells remain solvent, the Commissioner may separate such cells from the protected cell captive insurance company and may allow, on application of the protected cell captive insurance company, for the conversion of such protected cells into one or more new or existing protected cell captive insurance companies, or one or more other captive insurance companies, pursuant to such plan of operation as the Commissioner deems acceptable. (2013-116, s. 1.)

§ 58-10-515. Participation in a protected cell captive insurance company.

(a)   Associations, corporations, limited liability companies, partnerships, trusts, and other business entities may be participants in any protected cell captive insurance company formed or licensed under this Part.

(b)   A sponsor may be a participant in a protected cell captive insurance company.

(c)   A participant need not be a shareholder of the protected cell captive insurance company or any affiliate thereof.

(d)   A participant shall insure only its own risks through a protected cell captive insurance company. (2013-116, s. 1.)

§ 58-10-520. Combining assets of protected cells.

Notwithstanding G.S. 58-10-510, the assets of two or more protected cells may be combined for purposes of investment and such combination shall not be construed as defeating the segregation of such assets for accounting or other purposes. Protected cell captive insurance companies shall comply with the investment requirements contained in G.S. 58-7-167, 58-7-170, 58-7-172, 58-7-173, 58-7-178, 58-7-179, 58-7-180, 58-7-183, 58-7-185, 58-7-187, 58-7-188, 58-7-192, 58-7-193, 58-7-197, 58-7-200, and 58-7-205, as applicable; provided that compliance with such investment requirements shall be waived for protected cell captive insurance companies to the extent that credit for reinsurance ceded to reinsurers is allowed pursuant to G.S. 58-10-445 or to the extent otherwise deemed reasonable and appropriate by the Commissioner. Notwithstanding any other provision of this Chapter, the Commissioner may approve the use of alternative reliable methods of valuation and rating. (2013-116, s. 1.)

§ 58-10-525. Application of supervision, rehabilitation, and liquidation provisions to protected cell captive insurance companies.

(a) Except as otherwise provided in this Part, Article 30 of this Chapter shall apply to a protected cell captive insurance company.

(b) Upon any order of supervision, rehabilitation, or liquidation of a protected cell captive insurance company, the Commissioner or receiver shall manage the assets and liabilities of the protected cell captive insurance company pursuant to this Part.

(c) Notwithstanding Article 30 of this Chapter:

(1) No assets of a protected cell shall be used to pay any expenses or claims other than those attributable to such protected cell.

(2) A protected cell captive insurance company's capital and surplus shall at all times be available to pay any expenses of, or claims against, the protected cell captive insurance company. (2013-116, s. 1.)

Subpart 3. Branch Captive Insurance Companies.

§ 58-10-530. Establishment of branch captive insurance companies.

(a) A branch captive insurance company may be established in this State, in accordance with this Subpart, to write in this State any insurance or reinsurance of the employee benefit business of its parent and affiliated companies that is subject to the Employee Retirement Income Security Act of 1974, as amended, or any insurance or reinsurance permitted to be written by captive insurance companies pursuant to this Part.

(b) No branch captive insurance company shall do any insurance business in this State unless it maintains the principal place of business for its branch operations in this State. (2013-116, s. 1.)

§ 58-10-535. Security for payment of branch captive insurance company liabilities.

(a) No branch captive insurance company shall be issued a license by the Commissioner unless it possesses and maintains as security for the payment of liabilities attributable to the branch operations:

(1) An amount equal to the amount set forth in G.S. 58-10-370 as the minimum capital requirement for a pure captive insurance company.

(2) Reserves on such insurance policies or such reinsurance contracts as may be issued or assumed by the branch captive insurance company through its branch operations, including reserves for losses, allocated loss adjustment expenses, incurred but not reported losses, and unearned premiums with regard to business written through the branch operations; provided, however, that the Commissioner may permit a branch captive insurance company to credit against any such reserve requirement any security for loss reserves that the branch captive insurance company may post with a ceding insurer or that may be posted by a reinsurer with the branch captive insurance company, and in either case if such security remains posted.

(b) Subject to the prior approval of the Commissioner, the amounts required in subsection (a) of this section may be held in the form of:

(1) A trust formed under a trust agreement and funded by assets acceptable to the Commissioner.

(2) An irrevocable letter of credit issued or confirmed by a bank approved by the Commissioner.

(3) With respect to the amounts required in subdivision (a)(1) of this section only, cash on deposit with the Commissioner.

(4) Any combination of subdivisions (b)(1) through (3) of this section. (2013-116, s. 1.)

§ 58-10-540. Petition for certificate of authority.

In the case of an alien captive insurance company seeking to become licensed as a branch captive insurance company, the alien captive insurance company shall petition the Commissioner to issue a certificate setting forth the Commissioner's finding that, after considering the character, reputation, financial responsibility, insurance experience, and business qualifications of the officers and directors of the alien captive insurance company, the licensing and maintenance of the branch operations will promote the general good of the State. After the Commissioner issues a certificate of authorization, the alien captive insurance company shall comply with all other applicable State statutes or common law. (2013-116, s. 1.)

§ 58-10-545. Filing of reports and statements.

Prior to March 1 of each year, or with the approval of the Commissioner within 60 days after its fiscal year-end, a branch captive insurance company shall file with the Commissioner a copy of all reports and statements required to be filed under the laws of the jurisdiction in which the alien captive insurance company is formed, verified by oath of two of its executive officers. If the Commissioner is satisfied that the annual report filed by the alien captive insurance company in its domiciliary jurisdiction provides adequate information concerning the financial condition of the alien captive insurance company, the Commissioner may waive the requirement for completion of the captive annual statement for business written in the alien jurisdiction. (2013-116, s. 1.)

§ 58-10-550. Examination of a branch captive insurance company.

(a) Any examination of a branch captive insurance company pursuant to G.S. 58-10-430 shall be of branch business and branch operations only so long as the branch captive insurance company files annually with the Commissioner a certificate of compliance, or its equivalent, issued by or filed with the licensing authority of the jurisdiction in which the branch captive insurance company is formed, and demonstrates to the Commissioner's satisfaction that it is operating in sound financial condition in accordance with all applicable laws and regulations of such jurisdiction.

(b) As a condition of licensure, an alien captive insurance company shall grant authority to the Commissioner for examination of the affairs of the alien captive insurance company in the jurisdiction in which the alien captive insurance company is formed. (2013-116, s. 1.)

Subpart 4. Special Purpose Financial Captives.

§ 58-10-555. Creation of special purpose financial captives.

Special purpose financial captives (SPFCs) are provided by this Subpart exclusively to facilitate the securitization of one or more risks as a means of accessing alternative sources of capital and achieving the benefits of securitization. SPFCs are created for the limited purpose of entering into SPFC contracts and insurance securitization transactions and into related agreements to facilitate the accomplishment and execution of those transactions. The creation of SPFCs is intended to achieve greater efficiencies in structuring and executing insurance securitizations, to diversify and broaden sources of capital for insurers, to facilitate access for many insurers to insurance securitization and capital markets financing technology, and to further the economic development and expand the interest of this State through its captive insurance program. (2013-116, s. 1.)

§ 58-10-560. Controlling provisions when conflict exists; exemptions.

(a) No provisions of this Chapter, other than those expressly provided in this Part, shall apply to an SPFC. If any conflict occurs in this Part related to an SPFC, the provisions of this Subpart shall control.

(b)   The Commissioner, by rule, regulation, or order, may exempt an SPFC or its protected cells, on a case-by-case basis, from this Part if the Commissioner determines regulation under this Part to be inappropriate given the nature of the risks to be insured. (2013-116, s. 1.)

§ 58-10-565. Application requirements.

(a)   An SPFC, when permitted by its organizational documents, may apply to the Commissioner for a certificate of authority to transact insurance or reinsurance business as authorized by this Part. An SPFC shall only insure or reinsure the risks of its counterparty. Notwithstanding any other provision of this Part, an SPFC may purchase reinsurance to cede the risks assumed under the SPFC contract as approved by the Commissioner.

(b)   To transact business in this State, an SPFC shall:

(1)   Comply with the procedures established in G.S. 58-10-345(c).

(2)   Obtain from the Commissioner a certificate of authority authorizing it to conduct insurance or reinsurance business, or both, in this State.

(3)   Hold at least one management meeting each year in this State. For the purposes of this section, management is defined as the board of directors, managing board, or other individual or individuals vested with overall responsibility for the management of the affairs of the SPFC, including the election and appointment of officers or other of those agents to act on behalf of the SPFC.

(4)   Maintain its principal place of business in this State.

(5)   Appoint a resident registered agent to accept service of process and to otherwise act on its behalf in this State. If the registered agent, with reasonable diligence, is not found at the registered office of the SPFC, the Commissioner shall be an agent of the SPFC upon whom any process, notice, or demand may be served.

(6)   Provide such documentation of the insurance securitization as requested by the Commissioner immediately upon closing of the transaction, including:

a. An opinion of a duly licensed North Carolina legal counsel with respect to compliance with this Part and any other applicable laws as of the effective date of the transaction.

b. A statement under oath of its president and secretary demonstrating its financial condition.

(7) Provide a complete set of the documentation of the insurance securitization to the Commissioner immediately following closing of the transaction.

(c) A complete SPFC application shall include the following:

(1) A certified copy of the SPFC's organizational documents.

(2) Evidence of:

a. The amount and liquidity of its assets relative to the risks to be assumed.

b. The adequacy of the expertise, experience, and character of the person or persons who manage the SPFC.

c. The overall soundness of the SPFC's plan of operation.

d. Other factors considered relevant by the Commissioner in ascertaining whether the proposed SPFC is able to meet its policy obligations.

e. The applicant SPFC's financial condition, including the source and form of the minimum capital to be contributed to the SPFC.

(3) A plan of operation consisting of a description of or statement of intent with respect to the contemplated insurance securitization, the SPFC contract, and related transactions, which shall include:

a. Draft documentation or, at the discretion of the Commissioner, a written summary of all material agreements that are entered into to effectuate the SPFC contract and, before the effectuation of the SPFC contract, the insurance securitization, to include the names of the counterparty, the nature of the risks being assumed, the proposed use of protected cells, if any, and the maximum amounts, purpose, and nature and the interrelationships of the various transactions required to effectuate the insurance securitization.

b. The source and form of additional capital to be contributed to the SPFC.

c. The proposed investment strategy of the SPFC.

d. A description of the underwriting, reporting, and claims payment methods by which losses covered by the SPFC contract are reported, accounted for, and settled.

e. A pro forma balance sheet and income statement illustrating various stress case scenarios for the performance of the SPFC under the SPFC contract.

(4) Biographical affidavits in NAIC format of all of the prospective SPFC's officers and directors, providing the officers' and directors' legal names, any names under which they have or are conducting their affairs, and any other biographical information as the Commissioner may request.

(5) An affidavit from the applicant SPFC verifying:

a. The applicant SPFC complies with this Part.

b. The applicant SPFC operates only pursuant to this Part.

c. The applicant SPFC's investment strategy reflects and takes into account the liquidity of assets and the reasonable preservation, administration, and asset management of such assets relative to the risks associated with the SPFC contract and the insurance securitization transaction.

d. The securities proposed to be issued, if any, are valid legal obligations that are either properly registered with the Commissioner or constitute an exempt security or form part of an exempt transaction.

(6) Any other statements or documents required by the Commissioner to evaluate and complete the licensing of the SPFC.

(d) In addition to the information required by subsection (c) of this section and by G.S. 58-10-585, when a protected cell is used, an applicant SPFC shall file with the Commissioner:

(1) A business plan demonstrating how the applicant SPFC accounts for the loss and expense experience of each protected cell at a level of detail found to be sufficient by the Commissioner and how the applicant will report the experience to the Commissioner.

(2) A statement acknowledging that all records of the SPFC, including records pertaining to any protected cells, must be made available for inspection or examination by the Commissioner.

(3) All contracts or sample contracts between the SPFC and any counterparty related to each protected cell.

(4) A description of the expenses allocated to each protected cell.

(e) Information submitted pursuant to this section shall be and remain confidential, and shall not be made public by the Commissioner or the Commissioner's designee unless disclosure is ordered by a court of competent jurisdiction. In addition, the Commissioner shall have the discretion to disclose such information to a public official having jurisdiction over the regulation of insurance in another state, provided that:

(1) Such public official shall agree in writing to maintain the confidentiality of such information.

(2) The laws of the state in which such public official serves require such information to be and to remain confidential.

(f) G.S. 58-10-430 applies to SPFCs.

(g) SPFCs are subject to any rules or regulations promulgated pursuant to G.S. 58-10-460.

(h) The Commissioner may retain legal, financial, and examination services from outside the Department to examine and investigate the application, the cost of which may be charged against the applicant. The Commissioner also may use internal resources to examine and investigate the application based upon an hourly rate for the services performed or the usual and customary fee charged by the financial services industry for similar work subject to a minimum fee of twelve thousand dollars ($12,000), six thousand dollars ($6,000) of which is payable upon filing of the application and the remainder upon licensure.

(i) An SPFC shall be subject to payment of premium taxes as required by G.S. 58-10-455.

(j) The Commissioner shall grant a certificate of authority authorizing the SPFC to transact insurance or reinsurance business as an SPFC in this State, upon a finding by the Commissioner that:

(1) The SPFC's proposed plan of operation provides a reasonable and expected successful operation.

(2) The terms of the SPFC contract and related transactions comply with this Part.

(3) The proposed plan of operation is not hazardous to any counterparty.

(4) To the extent required by law or regulation, the Commissioner or an equivalent regulatory authority of the state of domicile of each counterparty has notified the Commissioner in writing or otherwise provided assurance satisfactory to the Commissioner that it has approved or not disapproved the transaction.

(5) The certificate of authority authorizing the SPFC to transact business is limited only to the insurance or reinsurance activities that the SPFC is authorized to conduct pursuant to this Part.

(k) In evaluating the expectation of a successful operation, factors the Commissioner shall consider include whether the proposed SPFC and its management are of known good character and reasonably believed not to be affiliated, directly or indirectly, through ownership, control, management, reinsurance transactions, or other insurance or business relations, with a person known to have been involved in the improper manipulation of assets, accounts, or reinsurance.

(l) To ensure the proposed plan of operation is not hazardous to any counterparty, the Commissioner may require reasonable safeguards in the SPFC's plan of operation where applicable and appropriate in the circumstance, including, without limitation, that certain assets of the SPFC be held in a trust to secure the obligations of the SPFC to a counterparty under an SPFC contract.

(m) A foreign or alien corporation or limited liability company, upon approval of the Commissioner, may become a domestic SPFC after complying with G.S. 58-10-345(c)(1). After such documents are successfully filed, the foreign or alien corporation or limited liability company is entitled to the necessary or appropriate certificates or licenses to transact business as an SPFC in this State and is subject to the authority and jurisdiction of this State. In connection with this redomestication, the Commissioner may waive any requirements for public hearings. It is not necessary for a corporation or limited liability company redomesticating into this State to merge, consolidate, transfer assets, or otherwise engage in another reorganization, other than as specified in this section. (2013-116, s. 1.)

§ 58-10-570. Organization of an SPFC.

(a) An SPFC may be established as a stock corporation, limited liability company, mutual, partnership, or other form of organization approved by the Commissioner.

(b) The SPFC's organizational documents shall limit the SPFC's authority to transact the business of insurance or reinsurance to those activities the SPFC conducts to accomplish its purpose as expressed in this Part.

(c) The SPFC shall not adopt a name that is the same as, deceptively similar to, or likely to be confused with or mistaken for another existing business name registered in this State. Any name adopted by an SPFC shall comply with State law.

(d) An SPFC shall have at least three incorporators or organizers, of whom at least two shall be residents of this State.

(e) At least one of the members of the management of the SPFC shall be a resident of this State.

(f) An SPFC formed pursuant to this Part has the privileges of and is subject to all other requirements of this State's law applicable to its formation, as well as the applicable provisions contained in this Part, provided that this Part controls if a conflict exists in this State's law. (2013-116, s. 1.)

§ 58-10-575. Minimum capital.

(a) An SPFC shall initially possess and maintain minimum capital of not less than two hundred and fifty thousand dollars ($250,000). All of the minimum initial capitalization shall be in cash. All other funds of the SPFC in excess of its minimum initial capitalization shall be in the form of cash, cash equivalent, or securities invested as approved by the Commissioner.

(b) Additional capitalization for the SPFC shall be determined, if so required, by the Commissioner after giving due consideration to the SPFC's plan of operation, feasibility study, pro formas, and the nature of the risks being insured or reinsured, which may be prescribed in formulas approved by the Commissioner. (2013-116, s. 1.)

§ 58-10-580. Authorized activities.

(a) An SPFC shall only insure the risks of a counterparty.

(b) No SPFC shall issue a contract for assumption of risk or indemnification of loss other than an SPFC contract. However, the SPFC may cede risks assumed through an SPFC contract to third-party reinsurers through the purchase of reinsurance or retrocession protection on terms approved by the Commissioner.

(c) An SPFC may enter into contracts and conduct other commercial activities related or incidental to and necessary to fulfill the purposes of the SPFC contract, insurance securitization, and this Part. Those activities may include, but are not limited to:

(1) Entering into SPFC contracts.

(2) Issuing SPFC securities in accordance with applicable securities law.

(3) Complying with the terms of such contracts or securities.

(4) Entering into trust, guaranteed investment contract, letter of credit, swap, tax, administration, reimbursement, or fiscal agent transactions.

(5) Complying with trust indenture, reinsurance, or retrocession, and agreements necessary or incidental to effectuate an insurance securitization in compliance with this Part or the plan of operation approved by the Commissioner.

(d) An SPFC shall do all of the following:

(1) Discount its reserves at discount rates as approved by the Commissioner.

(2) Maintain reserves that are actuarially sufficient to support the liabilities incurred by an SPFC in reinsuring life insurance policies.

(3) File annually with the Commissioner an actuarial opinion on reserves provided by an approved independent actuary. (2013-116, s. 1.)

§ 58-10-585. Establishment of protected cell accounts.

(a) This section and G.S. 58-10-590 provide a basis for the creation and use of protected cells by an SPFC as a means of accessing alternative sources of capital, lowering formation and administrative expenses, and generally making insurance securitizations more efficient. If a conflict exists between other provisions of this Part and either this section or G.S. 58-10-590, then this section or G.S. 58-10-515 shall control as applicable.

(b) An SPFC may establish and maintain one or more protected cells with prior written approval of the Commissioner and subject to compliance with the applicable provisions of this Part and all of the following conditions:

(1) A protected cell shall be established only for the purpose of insuring or reinsuring risks of one or more SPFC contracts with a counterparty with the intent of facilitating an insurance securitization.

(2) Each protected cell shall be accounted for separately on the books and records of the SPFC to reflect the financial condition and results of operations of the protected cell, net income or loss, dividends, or other distributions to the counterparty for the SPFC contract with each cell, and other factors as may be provided in the SPFC contract, insurance securitization transaction documents, plan of operation, or business plan, or as required by the Commissioner.

(3) Amounts attributed to a protected cell under this Part, including assets transferred to a protected cell account, are owned by the SPFC, and no SPFC shall be or hold itself out to be a trustee with respect to those protected cell assets of that protected cell account.

(4) All attributions of assets and liabilities between a protected cell and the general account shall be in accordance with the plan of operation approved by the Commissioner, and no other attribution of assets or liabilities by an SPFC between the SPFC's general account and its protected cell or cells is permitted. The SPFC shall attribute all insurance obligations, assets, and liabilities relating to an SPFC contract and the related insurance securitization transaction, including any securities issued by the SPFC as part of the insurance securitization, to a particular protected cell. The insurance obligations, assets, and liabilities relating to the SPFC contract and the insurance securitization transaction that are attributed to a particular protected cell shall be consistent with:

a. The rights, benefits, obligations, and liabilities of any securities attributable to that protected cell.

b. The performance under an SPFC contract and the related securitization transaction and any tax benefits, losses, refunds, or credits allocated, at any point in time pursuant to a tax allocation agreement between the SPFC and the SPFC's counterparty, parent, or company or group company, or any of them, in common control with them, as the case may be, including any payments made by or due to be made to the SPFC pursuant to the terms of the agreement.

(5) No assets of a protected cell shall be chargeable with liabilities arising out of an SPFC contract related to or associated with another protected cell. However, one or more SPFC contracts may be attributed to a protected cell only if the SPFC contracts are intended to be and ultimately are part of a single securitization transaction.

(6) No sale, exchange, or other transfer of assets shall be made by the SPFC between or among any of the SPFC's protected cells without the consent of the Commissioner, counterparty, and each protected cell.

(7) Except as otherwise contemplated in the SPFC contract or related insurance securitization transaction documents, or both, no sale, exchange, transfer of assets, dividend, or distribution shall be made from a protected cell to

a counterparty or parent without the Commissioner's approval and the sale, exchange, transfer, dividend, or distribution shall not be approved if the sale, exchange, transfer, dividend, or distribution would result in a protected cell's insolvency or impairment.

(8) An SPFC may pay interest or repay principal, or both, and make distributions or repayments with respect to any securities attributed to a particular protected cell from assets or cash flows relating to or emerging from the SPFC contract and the insurance securitization transactions that are attributable to that particular protected cell in accordance with this Part, or as otherwise approved by the Commissioner.

(c) No SPFC contract with or attributable to a protected cell shall take effect without the Commissioner's prior written approval, and the addition of each new protected cell constitutes a change in the business plan requiring the Commissioner's prior written approval. The Commissioner may retain legal, financial, and examination services from outside the Department to examine and investigate the application for a protected cell, the cost of which may be charged against the applicant, or the Commissioner may use internal resources to examine and investigate the application, the cost of which may be charged against the applicant, or both.

(d) An SPFC utilizing protected cells shall possess and maintain minimum capitalization separate and apart from the capitalization of its protected cell or cells in an amount determined by the Commissioner after giving due consideration of the SPFC's business plan, feasibility study, and pro formas, including the nature of the risks to be insured or reinsured. For purposes of determining the capitalization of each protected cell, an SPFC shall initially capitalize and maintain capitalization in each protected cell in the amount and manner required for an SPFC in G.S. 58-10-575.

(e) The establishment of one or more protected cells alone shall not constitute and shall not be deemed to be a fraudulent conveyance, an intent by the SPFC to defraud creditors, or the carrying out of business by the SPFC for any other fraudulent purpose. (2013-116, s. 1.)

§ 58-10-590. Protected cell accounts.

(a) All of the following shall apply to a protected cell:

(1) The creation of a protected cell shall not create, with respect to that protected cell, a legal person separate from the SPFC.

(2) Notwithstanding subdivision (a)(1) of this subsection, a protected cell shall have its own distinct name or designation that includes the words "protected cell." The SPFC shall transfer all assets attributable to the protected cell to one or more separately established and identified protected cell accounts bearing the name or designation of that protected cell.

(3) Although a protected cell is not a separate legal person, the property of an SPFC in a protected cell is subject to orders of the court by name as the property would have been if the protected cell were a separate legal person.

(4) The property of an SPFC in a protected cell shall be served with process in its own name in all civil actions or proceedings involving or relating to the activities of that protected cell or a breach by the SPFC of a duty to the protected cell or to a counterparty to a transaction linked or attributed to it by serving the SPFC.

(5) A protected cell exists only at the pleasure of the SPFC. At the cessation of business of a protected cell in accordance with the plan approved by the Commissioner, the SPFC shall close out the protected cell account.

(b) Nothing in this section shall be construed to prohibit an SPFC from contracting with or arranging for an investment advisor, commodity trading advisor, or other third party to manage the assets of a protected cell, if all remuneration, expenses, and other compensation of the third-party advisor or manager are payable from the assets of that protected cell and not from the assets of other protected cells or the assets of the SPFC's general account, unless approved by the Commissioner.

(c) Creditors with respect to a protected cell are not entitled to have recourse against the protected cell assets of other protected cells or the assets of the SPFC's general account. If an obligation of an SPFC relates only to the general account, the obligation of the SPFC extends only to that creditor with respect to that obligation, and the creditor is entitled to have recourse only to the assets of the SPFC's general account.

(d) The assets of the protected cell shall not be used to pay expenses or claims other than those attributable to the protected cell. Protected cell assets are available only to the SPFC contract counterparty and other creditors of the SPFC that are creditors only with respect to that protected cell and, accordingly, are entitled in conformity with this Part, to have recourse to the protected cell assets attributable to that protected cell. The assets of the protected cell are protected from the creditors of the SPFC that are not creditors with respect to that protected cell and who, accordingly, are not entitled to have recourse to the protected cell assets attributable to that protected cell. If an obligation of an SPFC to a person or counterparty arises from an SPFC contract or related insurance securitization transaction, or is otherwise incurred with respect to a protected cell, then the obligation shall:

(1)   Extend only to the protected cell assets attributable to that protected cell, and the person or counterparty, with respect to that obligation, is entitled to have recourse only to the protected cell assets attributable to that protected cell.

(2)   Not extend to the protected cell assets of another protected cell or the assets of the SPFC's general account, and the person or counterparty, with respect to that obligation, is not entitled to have recourse to the protected cell assets of another protected cell or the assets of the SPFC's general account. The SPFC's capitalization held separate and apart from the capitalization of its protected cell or cells must be available at all times to pay expenses of or claims against the SPFC and may not be used to pay expenses or claims attributable to any protected cell.

(e)   Notwithstanding any other provision of law, an SPFC may allow for a security interest in accordance with applicable law to attach to protected cell assets or a protected cell account when in favor of a creditor of the protected cell or to facilitate an insurance securitization, including, without limitation, the issuance of the SPFC contract, to the extent those protected cell assets are not required at all times to support the risk, but without otherwise affecting the discharge of liabilities under the SPFC contract, or as otherwise approved by the Commissioner.

(f)   An SPFC shall establish administrative and accounting procedures necessary to properly identify the one or more protected cells of the SPFC and the protected cell assets and protected cell liabilities to each protected cell. An SPFC shall keep protected cell assets and protected cell liabilities:

(1)   Separate and separately identifiable from the assets and liabilities of the SPFC's general account.

(2) Attributable to one protected cell separate and separately identifiable from protected cell assets and protected cell liabilities attributable to other protected cells.

(g) All contracts or other documentation reflecting protected cell liabilities shall clearly indicate that only the protected cell assets are available for the satisfaction of those protected cell liabilities. In all SPFC insurance securitizations involving a protected cell, the contracts or other documentation effecting the transaction shall contain provisions identifying the protected cell to which the transaction is attributed. In addition, the contracts or other documentation shall clearly disclose that the assets of that protected cell, and only those assets, are available to pay the obligations of that protected cell. Notwithstanding this subsection, and subject to this Part and other applicable laws or regulations, the failure to include this language in the contracts or other documentation shall not be used as the sole basis by creditors, insureds or reinsureds, insurers or reinsurers, or other claimants to circumvent the provisions of this section.

(h) An SPFC with protected cells shall annually file with the Department accounting statements and financial reports required by this Part, which shall:

(1) Detail the financial experience of each protected cell and the SPFC separately.

(2) Provide the combined financial experience of the SPFC and all protected cells.

(i) An SPFC with protected cells shall notify the Commissioner in writing within 10 business days of a protected cell becoming insolvent. (2013-116, s. 1.)

§ 58-10-595. Issuing securities.

(a) An SPFC may issue securities, including surplus notes and other forms of financial instruments, subject to and in accordance with applicable law, its approved plan of operation, and its organizational documents.

(b) An SPFC, in connection with the issuance of securities, may enter into and perform all of its obligations under any required contracts to facilitate the issuance of these securities.

(c) Subject to the approval of the Commissioner, an SPFC may lawfully:

(1) Account for the proceeds of surplus notes as surplus and not as debt for purposes of statutory accounting.

(2) Submit for prior approval of the Commissioner periodic written requests for payments of interest on and repayments of principal of surplus notes. In lieu of approval of periodic written requests for authorization to make payments of interest on and repayments of principal of surplus notes and other debt obligations issued by the SPFC, the Commissioner may approve a formula or plan, which shall be included in the SPFC's plan of operation as amended from time to time, for payment of interest, principal, or both, with respect to such surplus notes and debt obligations.

(d) The Commissioner, without otherwise prejudicing the Commissioner's authority, may approve formulas for an ongoing plan of interest payments or principal repayments, or both, to provide guidance in connection with the Commissioner's ongoing reviews of requests to approve the payments on and principal repayments of the surplus notes.

(e) The obligation to repay principal or interest, or both, on the securities issued by the SPFC must reflect the risk associated with the obligations of the SPFC to the counterparty under the SPFC contract. (2013-116, s. 1.)

§ 58-10-600. Asset management agreements.

An SPFC may enter into swap agreements, or other forms of asset management agreements, including guaranteed investment contracts, or other transactions that have the objective of leveling timing differences in funding of up-front or ongoing transaction expenses, or managing asset, credit, or interest rate risk of the investments to ensure that the investments are sufficient to assure payment or repayment of the securities, and related interest or principal payments, issued pursuant to an SPFC insurance securitization transaction, or the obligations of the SPFC under the SPFC contract. (2013-116, s. 1.)

§ 58-10-605. Reinsurance.

(a) An SPFC may reinsure only the risks of a ceding insurer pursuant to a reinsurance contract. No SPFC shall issue a contract of insurance or a contract for assumption of risk or indemnification of loss other than such reinsurance contract.

(b) Unless otherwise approved in advance by the Commissioner, no SPFC shall assume or retain exposure to insurance or reinsurance losses for its own account that are not funded by:

(1) Proceeds from an insurance securitization, letters of credit, or other assets described in G.S. 58-10-340(22).

(2) Premium and other amounts payable by the ceding insurer to the SPFC pursuant to the reinsurance contract.

(3) Any return on investment of the items described in subdivisions (1) and (2) of this subsection.

(c) The reinsurance contract shall contain all provisions required or approved by the Commissioner, which requirements shall take into account the laws applicable to the ceding insurer regarding the ceding insurer taking credit for the reinsurance provided under such reinsurance contract.

(d) An SPFC may cede risks assumed through a reinsurance contract to one or more reinsurers through the purchase of reinsurance, subject to the prior approval of the Commissioner.

(e) An SPFC may enter into contracts and conduct other commercial activities related or incidental to and necessary to fulfill the purposes of the reinsurance contract, the insurance securitization, and this Part, provided such contracts and activities are included in the SPFC's plan of operation or are otherwise approved in advance by the Commissioner. Such contracts and activities may include the following:

(1) Entering into SPFC contracts.

(2) Issuing SPFC securities in accordance with applicable securities law.

(3) Complying with the terms of such contracts or securities.

(4) Entering into trust, guaranteed investment contract, letter of credit, swap, tax, administration, reimbursement, or fiscal agent transactions.

(5) Complying with trust indenture, reinsurance, or retrocession and other agreements necessary or incidental to effectuate an insurance securitization in compliance with this Part or the plan of operation approved by the Commissioner.

(f) Unless otherwise approved in advance by the Commissioner, a reinsurance contract shall not contain any provision for payment by the SPFC in discharge of its obligations under the reinsurance contract to any person other than the ceding insurer or any receiver of the ceding insurer.

(g) An SPFC shall notify the Commissioner immediately of any action by a ceding insurer or any other person to foreclose on or otherwise take possession of collateral provided by the SPFC to secure any obligation of the SPFC.

(h) In the SPFC insurance securitization, the contracts or other relating documentation shall contain provisions identifying the SPFC.

(i) Unless otherwise approved by the Commissioner, no SPFC shall enter into an SPFC contract with a person that is not licensed or otherwise authorized to transact the business of insurance or reinsurance in at least its state or country of domicile.

(j) No SPFC shall:

(1) Have any direct obligation to the policyholders or reinsureds of the counterparty.

(2) Perform any of the following activities with anyone convicted of a felony, anyone who is untrustworthy or of known bad character, or anyone convicted of a criminal offense involving the conversion or misappropriation of fiduciary funds or insurance accounts, theft, deceit, fraud, misrepresentation, or corruption:

a. Lend or otherwise invest assets.

b. Place any assets in custody, trust, or under management.

c. Borrow money or receive a loan or advance, other than by issuance of the securities pursuant to an insurance securitization. (2013-116, s. 1.)

§ 58-10-610. No securities considered to be insurance or reinsurance contracts.

No securities issued by an SPFC pursuant to an insurance securitization shall be considered to be insurance or reinsurance contracts. No investor in these securities or a holder of these securities, by sole means of this investment or holding, shall be considered to be transacting the business of insurance in this State. The underwriter's placement or selling agents and their partners, directors, officers, members, managers, employees, agents, representatives, and advisors involved in an insurance securitization pursuant to this Part shall not be considered to be insurance producers or brokers or conducting business as an insurance or reinsurance company or agency, brokerage, intermediary, advisory, or consulting business only by virtue of their activities in connection with an insurance securitization. (2013-116, s. 1.)

§ 58-10-615. Disposition of assets; investment limitations.

(a) The assets of an SPFC shall be preserved and administered by or on behalf of the SPFC to satisfy the liabilities and obligations of the SPFC incident to the reinsurance contract, the insurance securitization, and other related agreements.

(b) In the insurance securitization, the security offering memorandum or other document issued to prospective investors regarding the offer and sale of a surplus note or other security shall include a disclosure that all or part of the proceeds of such insurance securitization will be used to fund the SPFC's obligations to the ceding insurer.

(c) No SPFC shall be subject to any restriction on investments other than the following:

(1) The Commissioner may limit investments by an SPFC to those categories and amounts of authorized investments delineated in G.S. 58-7-167,

58-7-170, 58-7-172, 58-7-173, 58-7-178, 58-7-179, 58-7-180, 58-7-183, 58-7-185, 58-7-187, 58-7-188, 58-7-192, 58-7-193, 58-7-197, 58-7-200, and 58-7-205, as applicable and as amended from time to time.

(2) No SPFC shall make a loan to any person other than as permitted under its plan of operation or as otherwise approved in advance by the Commissioner.

(3) The Commissioner may prohibit or limit any investment that threatens the solvency or liquidity of the SPFC unless the investment is otherwise approved by the Commissioner in writing. (2013-116, s. 1.)

§ 58-10-620. Dividends.

(a) No SPFC shall declare or pay dividends in any form to its owners other than in accordance with the insurance securitization transaction agreements, and in no extent shall the dividends decrease the capital of the SPFC below two hundred fifty thousand dollars ($250,000). After giving effect to the dividends, the assets of the SPFC, including assets held in trust pursuant to the terms of the insurance securitization, shall be sufficient to satisfy the Commissioner that the SPFC can meet its obligations. Approval by the Commissioner of an ongoing plan for the payment of dividends or other distribution by an SPFC must be conditioned upon the retention at the time of each payment of capital or surplus equal to or in excess of amounts specified by or determined in accordance with formulas approved for the SPFC by the Commissioner.

(b) The dividends may be declared by the management of the SPFC if the dividends do not violate this Part or jeopardize the fulfillment of the obligations of the SPFC or the trustee pursuant to the SPFC insurance securitization agreements, the SPFC contract, or any related transaction and other provisions of this Part. (2013-116, s. 1.)

§ 58-10-625. Changes in plan of operation; filing of audit and statement of operation; examinations.

(a) Any material change of the SPFC's plan of operation, whether or not through an SPFC protected cell, shall require prior approval of the

Commissioner. The following transactions do not constitute material change for purposes of this section:

(1) If initially approved in the plan of operation, securities subsequently issued to continue the securitization activities of the SPFC either during or after expiration, redemption, or satisfaction of all of these, of part or all of the securities issued pursuant to initial insurance securitization transactions.

(2) A change and substitution in a counterparty to a swap transaction for an existing insurance securitization as allowed pursuant to this Part if the replacement swap counterparty carries a similar or higher rating to its predecessor with two or more nationally recognized rating agencies.

(b) No later than six months after the fiscal year-end of the SPFC, the SPFC shall file with the Commissioner an audit by a certified public accounting firm of the financial statements of the SPFC and the trust accounts.

(c) An SPFC shall report using statutory accounting principles, unless the Commissioner requires, approves, or accepts the use of generally accepted accounting principles or other comprehensive basis of accounting. In each case the Commissioner may require, approve, or accept any appropriate or necessary modifications or adaptations to the accounting basis, and may require the report to be supplemented by additional information.

(d) Each SPFC shall file by March 1 a statement of operations, using either generally accepted accounting principles or, if approved, accepted, or required by the Commissioner, statutory accounting principles with useful or necessary modifications or adaptations for the type of insurance and kinds of insurers to be reported upon, and as supplemented by additional information required by the Commissioner. The statement of operations shall include a statement of income, a balance sheet, and may include a detailed listing of invested assets, including identification of assets held in trust to secure the obligations of the SPFC under the SPFC contract. The SPFC also may include with the filing risk-based capital calculations and other adjusted capital calculations to assist the Commissioner with evaluating the levels of the surplus of the SPFC for the year ending on December 31 of the previous year. The statements shall be prepared on forms required by the Commissioner. In addition, the Commissioner may require the filing of performance assessments of the SPFC contract.

(e) An SPFC shall maintain the SPFC's records in this State unless otherwise approved by the Commissioner and shall make its records available for examination by the Commissioner at any time. The SPFC shall keep its books and records in such manner that its financial condition, affairs, and operations can be ascertained and so that the Commissioner may readily verify its financial statements and determine its compliance with this Part.

(f)   All original books, records, documents, accounts, and vouchers shall be preserved and kept available in this State for the purpose of examination and until authority to destroy or otherwise dispose of the records is secured from the Commissioner. The original records, however, may be kept and maintained outside this State if, according to a plan adopted by the management of the SPFC and approved by the Commissioner, the SPFC maintains suitable copies instead of the originals. The books or records may be photographed, reproduced on film, or stored and reproduced electronically. (2013-116, s. 1.)

§ 58-10-630. Cessation of business.

At the cessation of business of an SPFC following termination or cancellation of an SPFC contract and the redemption of any related securities issued in connection with the SPFC contract, the authority granted by the Commissioner expires or, in the case of retiring and surviving protected cells, is modified, the SPFC is no longer authorized to conduct activities unless and until a new or modified certificate of authority is issued pursuant to a new filing under this Part or as agreed by the Commissioner. (2013-116, s. 1.)

§ 58-10-635. Supervision, rehabilitation, or liquidation of SPFC.

(a)   Except as otherwise provided in this section, the terms and conditions set forth in Article 30 of this Chapter pertaining to supervision, rehabilitation, and liquidation of insurers apply in full to SPFCs or each of the SPFC's protected cells, independently, or both, without causing or otherwise effecting a supervision, rehabilitation, or liquidation of the SPFC or another protected cell.

(b)   Notwithstanding the provisions of Article 30 of this Chapter, and without causing or otherwise effecting a rehabilitation or liquidation of an otherwise solvent protected cell of an SPFC and subject to the provisions of subdivision (g)(5) of this section, the Commissioner may apply by petition to the court for an order authorizing the Commissioner to rehabilitate or liquidate an SPFC domiciled in this State on one or more of the following grounds:

(1) There has been embezzlement, wrongful sequestration, dissipation, or diversion of the assets of the SPFC intended to be used to pay amounts owed to the counterparty or the holders of SPFC securities.

(2) The SPFC is insolvent and the holders of a majority in outstanding principal amount of each class of SPFC securities request or consent to rehabilitation or liquidation pursuant to the provisions of this Part.

(c) Notwithstanding the provisions of Article 30 of this Chapter, the Commissioner may apply by petition to the Court for an order authorizing the Commissioner to rehabilitate or liquidate one or more of an SPFC's protected cells independently, without causing or otherwise effecting a rehabilitation or liquidation of the SPFC generally or another of its protected cells on one or more of the following grounds:

(1) There has been embezzlement, wrongful sequestration, dissipation, or diversion of the assets of the SPFC attributable to the affected protected cell or cells intended to be used to pay amounts owed to the counterparty or the holders of SPFC securities of the affected protected cell or cells.

(2) The affected protected cell is insolvent and the holders of a majority in outstanding principal amount of each class of SPFC securities attributable to that particular protected cell request or consent to rehabilitation or liquidation pursuant to the provisions of this Part.

(d) The Court may not grant relief provided by subdivision (b)(1) or (c)(1) of this section, unless after notice and a hearing, the Commissioner, who shall have the burden of proof, establishes by preponderance of the evidence that relief must be granted. The court's order may be made with respect to one or more protected cells by name, rather than the SPFC generally.

(e) Notwithstanding another provision in this Chapter, rules adopted under this Chapter, or another applicable law or regulation, upon any order of rehabilitation or liquidation of a SPFC, or one or more of the SPFC's protected cells, the receiver shall manage the assets and liabilities of the SPFC pursuant to the provisions of this Part. The receiver shall ensure that the assets linked to one protected cell are not applied to the liabilities linked to another protected cell or to the SPFC generally, unless an asset or liability is linked to more than one protected cell, in which case the receiver shall deal with the asset or liability in accordance with the terms of any relevant governing instrument or contract.

(f) With respect to amounts recoverable under an SPFC contract, the amount recoverable by the receiver must not be reduced or diminished as a result of the entry of an order of rehabilitation or liquidation with respect to the counterparty, notwithstanding another provision in the contracts or other documentation governing the SPFC insurance securitization.

(g) Notwithstanding the provisions of Article 30 of this Chapter or other laws of this State:

(1) An application or petition, or a temporary restraining order or injunction issued pursuant to the provisions of Article 30 of this Chapter, with respect to a counterparty does not prohibit the transaction of a business by an SPFC, including any payment by an SPFC made pursuant to an SPFC security, or any action or proceeding against an SPFC or its assets.

(2) The commencement of a summary proceeding or other interim proceeding commenced before a delinquency proceeding with respect to an SPFC, and any order issued by the court does not prohibit the payment by an SPFC made pursuant to an SPFC security, SPFC contract, or the SPFC from taking any action required to make the payment.

(3) A receiver of a counterparty may not void a nonfraudulent transfer by a counterparty to an SPFC of money or other property made pursuant to an SPFC contract.

(4) A receiver of an SPFC may not void a nonfraudulent transfer by the SPFC of money or other property made to a counterparty pursuant to an SPFC contract or made to or for the benefit of any holder of an SPFC security on account of the SPFC security.

(5) The Commissioner may not seek to have an SPFC with protected cells declared insolvent as long as at least one of the SPFC's protected cells remains solvent, and in the case of such an insolvency, the receiver shall handle the SPFC's assets in compliance with subsection (e) of this section and other laws of this State.

(h) Subsection (g) of this section does not prohibit the Commissioner from taking any action permitted under Article 30 of this Chapter with respect only to the rehabilitation of an SPFC with protected cell or cells, provided the Commissioner would have had sufficient grounds to seek to declare the SPFC insolvent, subject to and without otherwise affecting the provisions of subdivision (5) of subsection (g) of this section. In this case, with respect to the solvent protected cell or cells, the Commissioner may not prohibit payments made by the SPFC pursuant to the SPFC security, SPFC contract, or otherwise made under the insurance securitization transaction that are attributable to these protected cell or cells or prohibit the SPFC from taking any action required to make these payments.

(i) With the exception of the fulfillment of the obligations under an SPFC contract, and notwithstanding another provision of this Part or other laws of this State, the assets of an SPFC, including assets held in trust, must not be consolidated with or included in the estate of a counterparty in any delinquency proceeding against the counterparty, pursuant to the provisions of this Part for any purpose including, without limitation, distribution to creditors of the counterparty. (2013-116, s. 1.)

Subpart 5. Other Provisions.

§ 58-10-650. Other laws applicable to captive insurance companies.

In addition to the statutes and laws previously referred to in this Part, the following provisions of this Chapter are applicable to all captive insurance companies subject to this Part:

(1) G.S. 58-2-45. - Orders of Commissioner; when writing required.

(2) G.S. 58-2-160. - Reporting and investigation of insurance and reinsurance fraud and the financial condition of licensees; immunity from liability.

(3) G.S. 58-2-162. - Embezzlement by insurance agents, brokers, or administrators.

(4) G.S. 58-2-185. - Record of business kept by companies and agents; Commissioner may inspect.

(5) G.S. 58-2-190. - Commissioner may require special reports.

(6) G.S. 58-2-195. - Commissioner may require records, reports, etc., for agencies, agents, and others.

(7) G.S. 58-2-200. - Books and papers required to be exhibited.

(8) G.S. 58-5-1. - Deposits; use of master trust.

(9) G.S. 58-7-50. - Maintenance and removal of records and assets.

(10) G.S. 58-7-55. - Exceptions to requirements of G.S. 58-7-50. (2013-116, s. 1.)

Article 11.

Assessment Companies.

§ 58-11-1. Copies of charter and bylaws filed.

Every corporation, society, or organization of this or any other state or country, transacting business upon the cooperative or assessment plan, must file with the Commissioner, before beginning to do business in this State, a copy of its charter or articles of association, and the bylaws, rules, or regulations referred to in its policies or certificates and made a part of such contract. Bylaws or regulations not so filed with the Commissioner will not avoid or affect any policy or certificate issued by such company or association. (1899, c. 54, s. 86; Rev., s. 4790; C.S., s. 6356; 1991, c. 720, ss. 4, 66.)

§ 58-11-5. Contracts must accord with charter and bylaws.

Every policy or certificate or renewal receipt issued to a resident of this State by any corporation, association, or order transacting therein the business of insurance upon the assessment plan must be in accord with the provisions of the charter and bylaws of such corporation, association, or order, as filed with the Commissioner. It is unlawful for any such domestic or foreign insurance company or fraternal order to transact or offer to transact any business not authorized by the provisions of its charter and terms of its bylaws, or, through an agent or otherwise, to offer or issue any policy, renewal certificate, or other contract whose terms are not in clear accord with the powers, terms, and stipulations of its charter and bylaws. (1899, c. 54, s. 84; 1903, c. 438, s. 9; Rev., s. 4791; C.S., s. 6357; 1991, c. 720, s. 4.)

§ 58-11-10. "Assessment plan" printed on application and policy.

Every policy or certificate issued to a resident of the State by any corporation transacting in the State the business of life insurance upon the assessment plan, or admitted to do business in this State on the assessment plan, shall print in bold type near the top of the front page of the policy, upon every policy or certificate issued upon the life of any such resident of the State, the words "issued upon the assessment plan"; and the words "assessment plan" shall be printed conspicuously upon every application, circular, card, and any and all printed documents issued, circulated, or caused to be circulated by such corporation within the State. (1913, c. 159, s. 1; C.S., s. 6358; 1929, c. 93, s. 1; 1933, c. 34; 1945, c. 386.)

§ 58-11-15. Revocation for noncompliance.

If any corporation or association transacting insurance business in this State on the assessment plan or issuing any policy upon the life of a resident of North Carolina upon the assessment plan shall fail or refuse to comply with G.S. 58-11-10, the Commissioner shall forthwith suspend or revoke all authority of such corporation or association and of its agents to do business in this State. (1913, c. 159, s. 2; C.S., s. 6359; 1991, c. 720, ss. 4, 13.)

§ 58-11-20. Deposits and advance assessments required.

Every domestic insurance company, association, order, or fraternal benefit society doing business on the assessment plan shall collect and keep at all times in its treasury one regular loss assessment sufficient to pay one regular average loss; and no such company, association, order, or fraternal benefit society shall be licensed by the Commissioner unless it makes and maintains with him for the protection of its obligations at least five thousand dollars ($5,000) in United States or North Carolina bonds, in farm loan bonds issued by federal loan banks, or in the bonds of some city, county, or town of North Carolina to be approved by the Commissioner, or deposit with him a good and sufficient bond , secured by a deed of trust on real estate situated in North Carolina and approved by him, or by depositing with the Commissioner a bond in an amount of not less than five thousand dollars ($5,000), issued by any corporate surety company authorized to do business in this State. The Commissioner may increase the amount of deposit to the amount of reserve on the contracts of the association or society. The provisions of this section shall not apply to the farmers mutual fire insurance associations now doing business in the State and restricting their activities to not more than six adjacent counties. (Rev., s. 4792; 1913, c. 119, s. 1; 1917, c. 191, s. 2; C.S., s. 6360; 1933, c. 47; 1945, c. 386; 1991, c. 720, ss. 4, 87.)

§ 58-11-25. Deposits by foreign assessment companies or orders.

Each foreign insurance company, association, order, or fraternal benefit society doing business in this State on the assessment plan shall keep at all times deposited with the Commissioner or in its head office in this State, or in some responsible banking or trust company, one regular assessment sufficient to pay the average loss or losses occurring among its members in this State during the time allowed by it for the collection of assessments and payment of losses. It shall notify the Commissioner of the place of deposit and furnish him at all times such information as he requires in regard thereto; and no such company, association, order, or fraternal benefit society shall be licensed by the Commissioner unless it makes and maintains with him for the protection of its obligations at least five thousand dollars ($5,000) in United States or North Carolina bonds, in farm loan bonds issued by federal land banks, or in the bonds of some county, city, or town in North Carolina to be approved by the Commissioner, or a good and sufficient bond or note, secured by deed of trust on real estate situate in North Carolina, and approved by the Commissioner. (1899, c. 54, s. 84; 1903, c. 438, s. 9; Rev., s. 4713; 1913, c. 119, ss. 2, 3; 1917, c. 191, s. 2; C.S., s. 6361; 1945, c. 386; 1991, c. 720, s. 4.)

§ 58-11-30. Revocation of license.

If any such corporation, association, or order at any time fails to comply with the provisions of G.S. 58-11-20 and 58-11-25 or shall issue policies or certificates not in accord with its charter and bylaws, as provided in this Article, the Commissioner shall forthwith suspend or revoke all authority to it, and of all its agents or officers, to do business in this State, and shall publish such revocation in some newspaper published in this State. (1899, c. 54, s. 85; Rev., s. 4793; C.S., s. 6362; 1991, c. 720, s. 4.)

§ 58-11-35. Mutual life insurance companies; assessments prohibited.

No domestic mutual life insurance company shall, after March 6, 1945, be organized to issue any policy of life insurance or any annuity contract which provides for the payment of any assessment by any policyholder or member in addition to the regular premium charged for such insurance; nor shall any such company have power to levy or collect any such assessment. No foreign or alien life insurance company shall be permitted to do business in this State if it does business, in this State or elsewhere, on such or any other assessment plan. (1945, c. 386.)

Article 12.

Risk-Based Capital Requirements.

§ 58-12-1: Repealed by Session Laws 1993, c. 452, s. 65.

§ 58-12-2. Definitions.

As used in this Article, the following terms have the following meanings:

(1)	Adjusted risk-based capital report. - A risk-based capital report that has been adjusted by the Commissioner under G.S. 58-12-6.

(2) Corrective order. - An order issued by the Commissioner specifying corrective actions that the Commissioner has determined are required.

(3) Domestic insurer. - Any insurance company or health organization organized in this State under Article 7 of this Chapter as specified in subdivisions (4b) and (5a) of this section or under Article 15, 65, or 67 of this Chapter.

(4) Foreign insurer. - Any insurance company or health organization that is admitted to do business in this State under Article 16 or 67 of this Chapter but is not domiciled in this State.

(4a) Health organization. - Any insurer which is required by the Commissioner to use the NAIC Health Annual Statement Blank when filing the annual statement prescribed by G.S. 58-2-165 or any health maintenance organization, limited health service organization, dental or vision plan, hospital, medical, or dental indemnity or service corporation, or other organization licensed under Article 65 or 67 of this Chapter. "Health organization" does not include an insurer that is licensed as either a life or health insurer or a property or casualty insurer under this Chapter and that is otherwise subject to either the life or property and casualty risk-based capital requirements.

(4b) Life or health insurer. - Any insurance company licensed to write the kinds of insurance specified in G.S. 58-7-15(1), (2), or (3); or a licensed property and casualty insurer writing only the kinds of insurance specified in G.S. 58-7-15(3). "Life or health insurer" does not mean any insurer that is required by the Commissioner to use the NAIC Health Annual Statement Blank when it files the annual statement prescribed by G.S. 58-2-165.

(5) Negative trend. - A negative trend, with respect to a life or health insurer, over a period of time, as determined in accordance with the "trend test calculation" included in the risk-based capital instructions.

(5a) Property or casualty insurer. - Any insurance company licensed to write the kinds of insurance specified in G.S. 58-7-15(4) through (22); but not monoline mortgage guaranty insurers, financial guaranty insurers, or title insurers; nor any insurer that is required by the Commissioner to use the NAIC Health Annual Statement Blank when filing the annual statement prescribed by G.S. 58-2-165.

(6) Risk-based capital instructions. - The risk-based capital report including risk-based capital instructions adopted by the NAIC, as those risk-based capital instructions may be amended by the NAIC from time to time in accordance with the procedures adopted by the NAIC.

(7) Risk-based capital level. - An insurer's company action level risk-based capital, regulatory action level risk-based capital, authorized control level risk-based capital, or mandatory control level risk-based capital where:

a. "Company action level risk-based capital" means, with respect to any insurer, the product of 2.0 and its authorized control level risk-based capital.

b. "Regulatory action level risk-based capital" means the product of 1.5 and its authorized control level risk-based capital.

c. "Authorized control level risk-based capital" means the number determined under the risk-based capital formula in accordance with the risk-based capital instructions.

d. "Mandatory control level risk-based capital" means the product of .70 and the authorized control level risk-based capital.

(8) Risk-based capital plan. - A comprehensive financial plan containing the elements specified in G.S. 58-12-11(b). If the Commissioner rejects the risk-based capital plan, and it is revised by the insurer, with or without the Commissioner's recommendation, the plan shall be called the "revised risk-based capital plan".

(9) Risk-based capital report. - The report required in G.S. 58-12-6.

(10) Total adjusted capital. - The sum of:

a. An insurer's statutory capital and surplus, as determined in accordance with the statutory accounting applicable to the annual financial statements required under G.S. 58-2-165; and

b. Such other items, if any, as the risk-based capital instructions may provide. (1993 (Reg. Sess., 1994), c. 678, s. 1; 1995, c. 318, s. 2; 2001-223, ss. 12.1, 12.2, 12.3; 2011-196, s. 6.)

§ 58-12-4. Finding; endorsement of additional capital.

The General Assembly finds that an excess of capital over the amount produced by the risk-based capital requirements contained in this Article and in the formulas, schedules, and instructions referenced in this Article is desirable in the business of insurance. Accordingly, the General Assembly encourages insurers to seek to maintain capital above the risk-based capital levels required by this Article. Additional capital is used and useful in the insurance business and helps to secure an insurer against various risks inherent in or affecting the business of insurance but not accounted for or only partially measured by the risk-based capital requirements contained in this Article. (1995, c. 318, s. 3.)

§ 58-12-5. Repealed by Session Laws 1993, c. 452, s. 65.

§ 58-12-6. Risk-based capital reports.

(a)   Every domestic insurer shall, on or before each March 1 (the "filing date"), prepare and submit to the Commissioner a report of its risk-based capital levels as of the end of the calendar year just ended, in a form and containing such information as is required by the risk-based capital instructions. In addition, every domestic insurer shall file its risk-based capital report:

(1)   With the NAIC in accordance with the risk-based capital instructions; and

(2)   With the insurance regulator in any state in which the insurer is authorized to do business, if the Commissioner has notified the insurer of its request in writing, in which case the insurer shall file its risk-based capital report not later than the later of:

a.   Fifteen days after the receipt of notice to file its risk-based capital report with that state; or

b.   The filing date.

(b) A life or health insurer's risk-based capital shall be determined in accordance with the formula set forth in the risk-based capital instructions. The formula shall take into account (and may adjust for the covariance between):

(1) The risk with respect to the insurer's assets;

(2) The risk of adverse insurance experience with respect to the insurer's liabilities and obligations;

(3) The interest rate risk with respect to the insurer's business; and

(4) All other business risks and such other relevant risks as are set forth in the risk-based capital instructions.

These risks shall be determined in each case by applying the factors in the manner set forth in the risk-based capital instructions.

(c) If a domestic insurer files a risk-based capital report that in the judgment of the Commissioner is inaccurate, the Commissioner shall adjust the risk-based capital report to correct the inaccuracy and shall notify the insurer of the adjustment. The notice shall contain a statement of the reason for the adjustment. A risk-based capital report as adjusted is referred to as an "adjusted risk-based capital report".

(d) A property or casualty insurer's risk-based capital and a health organization's risk-based capital shall be determined in accordance with the formula set forth in the risk-based capital instructions. The formula shall take into account (and may adjust for the covariance between):

(1) Asset risk;

(2) Credit risk;

(3) Underwriting risk; and

(4) All business and other relevant risks set forth in the risk-based capital instructions, determined in each case by applying the factors in the manner set forth in the risk-based capital instructions. (1993 (Reg. Sess., 1994), c. 678, s. 1; 1995, c. 318, s. 4; 2001-223, s. 12.4.)

§ 58-12-10. Repealed by Session Laws 1993, c. 452, s. 65.

§ 58-12-11. Company action level event.

(a) "Company action level event" means any of the following events:

(1) The filing of a risk-based capital report by an insurer that indicates that:

a. The insurer's total adjusted capital is greater than or equal to its regulatory action level risk-based capital but less than its company action level risk-based capital; or

b. In the case of a life or health insurer, the insurer has total adjusted capital that is greater than or equal to its company action level risk-based capital but less than the product of its authorized control level risk-based capital and 2.5 and has a negative trend; or

c. In the case of a property or casualty insurer or a health organization, the insurer has total adjusted capital that is greater than or equal to its company action level risk-based capital but less than the product of its authorized control level risk-based capital and 3.0 and triggers the trend test determined in accordance with the trend test calculation included in the property and casualty or health organization risk-based capital instructions.

(2) The notification by the Commissioner to the insurer of an adjusted risk-based capital report that indicates the event in sub-subdivision (1)a., (1)b., or (1)c. of this subsection if the insurer does not challenge the adjusted risk-based capital report under G.S. 58-12-30.

(3) If the insurer challenges an adjusted risk-based capital report that indicates the event in sub-subdivision (1)a., (1)b., or (1)c. of this subsection under G.S. 58-12-30, the notification by the Commissioner to the insurer that the Commissioner has rejected the insurer's challenge.

(b) In the event of a company action level event, the insurer shall prepare and submit to the Commissioner a comprehensive financial plan that:

(1) Identifies the conditions in the insurer that contribute to the company action level event.

(2) Contains proposals of corrective actions that the insurer intends to take and would be expected to result in the elimination of the company action level event.

(3) Provides forecasts of the insurer's financial results in the current year and at least the four succeeding years (except for health organizations, which must provide forecasts in the current year and at least the two succeeding years), both in the absence of proposed corrective actions and giving effect to the proposed corrective actions, including forecasts of statutory balance sheets, operating income, net income, capital and surplus, and risk-based capital levels (the forecasts for both new and renewal business should include separate forecasts for each major line of business and separately identify each significant income, expense, and benefit component).

(4) Identifies the key assumptions affecting the insurer's forecasts and the sensitivity of the forecasts to the assumptions.

(5) Identifies the quality of, and problems associated with, the insurer's business, including its assets, anticipated business growth and associated surplus strain, extraordinary exposure to risk, mix of business, and use of reinsurance in each case, if any.

(c) The risk-based capital plan shall be submitted:

(1) Within 45 days after the company action level event; or

(2) If the insurer challenges an adjusted risk-based capital report pursuant to G.S. 58-12-30, within 45 days after notification to the insurer that the Commissioner has rejected the insurer's challenge.

(d) Within 60 days after the submittal by an insurer of a risk-based capital plan to the Commissioner, the Commissioner shall notify the insurer whether the risk-based capital plan shall be implemented or is, in the judgment of the Commissioner, unsatisfactory. If the Commissioner determines the risk-based capital plan is unsatisfactory, the notification to the insurer shall set forth the reasons for the determination, and may set forth proposed revisions that will render the risk-based capital plan satisfactory, in the judgment of the Commissioner. Upon notification from the Commissioner, the insurer shall prepare a revised risk-based capital plan, which may incorporate by reference any revisions proposed by the Commissioner, and shall submit the revised risk-based capital plan to the Commissioner:

(1) Within 45 days after notification from the Commissioner; or

(2) If the insurer challenges the notification from the Commissioner under G.S. 58-12-30, within 45 days after a notification to the insurer that the Commissioner has rejected the insurer's challenge.

(e) In the event of a notification by the Commissioner to an insurer that the insurer's risk-based capital plan or revised risk-based capital plan is unsatisfactory, the Commissioner may, subject to the insurer's right to a hearing under G.S. 58-12-30, specify in the notification that the notification constitutes a regulatory action level event.

(f) Every domestic insurer that files a risk-based capital plan or revised risk-based capital plan with the Commissioner shall file a copy of the risk-based capital plan or revised risk-based capital plan with the insurance regulator in any state in which the insurer is authorized to do business if:

(1) That state has a risk-based capital provision substantially similar to G.S. 58-12-21(a); and

(2) The insurance regulator of that state has notified the insurer of its request for the filing in writing, in which case the insurer shall file a copy of the risk-based capital plan or revised risk-based capital plan in that state no later than the later of:

a. Fifteen days after the receipt of notice to file a copy of its risk-based capital plan or revised risk-based capital plan with the state; or

b. The date on which the risk-based capital plan or revised risk-based capital plan is filed under subsection (c) or (d) of this section. (1993 (Reg. Sess., 1994), c. 678, s. 1; 1995, c. 193, s. 21; c. 318, s. 5; 2001-223, ss. 12.5, 12.6; 2011-196, s. 7; 2013-199, s. 4.)

§ 58-12-15. Repealed by Session Laws 1993, c. 452, s. 65.

§ 58-12-16. Regulatory action level event.

(a) "Regulatory action level event" means, with respect to any insurer, any of the following events:

(1) The filing of a risk-based capital plan report by the insurer that indicates that the insurer's total adjusted capital is greater than or equal to its authorized control level risk-based capital but less than its regulatory action level risk-based capital.

(2) The notification by the Commissioner to an insurer of an adjusted risk-based capital report that indicates the event in subdivision (1) of this subsection, if the insurer does not challenge the adjusted risk-based capital report under G.S. 58-12-30.

(3) If the insurer challenges an adjusted risk-based capital report that indicates the event in subdivision (1) of this subsection under G.S. 58-12-30, the notification by the Commissioner to the insurer that the Commissioner has rejected the insurer's challenge.

(4) The failure of the insurer to file a risk-based capital report by the filing date, unless the insurer has provided an explanation for the failure that is satisfactory to the Commissioner and has cured the failure within 10 days after the filing date.

(5) The failure of the insurer to submit a risk-based capital plan to the Commissioner within the time period set forth in G.S. 58-12-11(c).

(6) Notification by the Commissioner to the insurer that:

a. The risk-based capital plan or revised risk-based capital plan submitted by the insurer is, in the judgment of the Commissioner, unsatisfactory; and

b. The notification constitutes a regulatory action level event with respect to the insurer, provided the insurer has not challenged the determination under G.S. 58-12-30.

(7) If the insurer challenges a determination by the Commissioner under subdivision (6) of this subsection pursuant to G.S. 58-12-30, the notification by

the Commissioner to the insurer that the Commissioner has rejected the challenge.

(8) Notification by the Commissioner to the insurer that the insurer has failed to adhere to its risk-based capital plan or revised risk-based capital plan; but only if the failure has a substantial adverse effect on the ability of the insurer to eliminate the company action level event in accordance with its risk-based capital plan or revised risk-based capital plan and the Commissioner has so stated in the notification, provided the insurer has not challenged the determination under G.S. 58-12-30.

(9) If the insurer challenges a determination by the Commissioner under subdivision (8) of this subsection pursuant to G.S. 58-12-30, the notification by the Commissioner to the insurer that the Commissioner has rejected the challenge (unless the failure of the insurer to adhere to its risk-based capital plan or revised risk-based capital plan has no substantial adverse effect on the ability of the insurer to eliminate the regulatory action level event with respect to the insurer).

(b) In the event of a regulatory action level event the Commissioner shall:

(1) Require the insurer to prepare and submit a risk-based capital plan or, if applicable, a revised risk-based capital plan.

(2) Perform such examination or analysis, as the Commissioner deems necessary, of the assets, liabilities, and operations of the insurer, including a review of its risk-based capital plan or revised risk-based capital plan.

(3) After the examination or analysis, issue an order specifying such corrective actions as the Commissioner shall determine are required (a "Corrective Order").

(c) In determining corrective actions, the Commissioner may take into account such factors as are deemed relevant with respect to the insurer based upon the Commissioner's examination or analysis of the assets, liabilities, and operations of the insurer, including, but not limited to, the results of any sensitivity tests undertaken pursuant to risk-based capital instructions. The risk-based capital plan or revised risk-based capital plan shall be submitted:

(1) Within 45 days after the occurrence of the regulatory action level event;

(2) If the insurer challenges an adjusted risk-based capital report pursuant to G.S. 58-12-30 and the challenge is not in the judgment of the Commissioner frivolous, within 45 days after the notification to the insurer that the Commissioner has, after a hearing, rejected the insurer's challenge; or

(3) If the insurer challenges a revised risk-based capital plan under G.S. 58-12-30, within 45 days after notification to the insurer that the Commissioner has rejected the challenge.

(d) The Commissioner may retain actuaries and investment experts and other consultants as may be necessary in the judgment of the Commissioner to review the insurer's risk-based capital plan or revised risk-based capital plan, examine or analyze the assets, liabilities, and operations of the insurer and formulate the Corrective Order with respect to the insurer. The fees, costs, and expenses relating to consultants shall be borne by the affected insurer or such other party as directed by the Commissioner. (1993 (Reg. Sess., 1994), c. 678, s. 1.)

§ 58-12-20. Repealed by Session Laws 1993, c. 452, s. 65.

§ 58-12-21. Authorized control level event.

(a) "Authorized control level event" means any of the following events:

(1) The filing of a risk-based capital report by the insurer that indicates that the insurer's total adjusted capital is greater than or equal to its mandatory control level risk-based capital but less than its authorized control level risk-based capital.

(2) The notification by the Commissioner to the insurer of an adjusted risk-based capital report that indicates the event in subdivision (1) of this subsection if the insurer does not challenge the adjusted risk-based capital report under G.S. 58-12-30.

(3) If the insurer challenges an adjusted risk-based capital report that indicates the event in subdivision (1) of this subsection under G.S. 58-12-30,

notification by the Commissioner to the insurer that the Commissioner has rejected the challenge.

(4)   The failure of the insurer to respond, in a manner satisfactory to the Commissioner, to a Corrective Order if the insurer has not challenged the Corrective Order under G.S. 58-12-30.

(5)   If the insurer has challenged a Corrective Order under G.S. 58-12-30 and the Commissioner has rejected the challenge or modified the Corrective Order, the failure of the insurer to respond, in a manner satisfactory to the Commissioner, to the Corrective Order after the rejection or modification by the Commissioner.

(b)   In the event of an authorized control level event with respect to an insurer, the Commissioner shall:

(1)   Take such actions as are required under G.S. 58-12-30 regarding an insurer with respect to which a regulatory action level event has occurred; or

(2)   If the Commissioner deems it to be in the best interests of the policyholders and creditors of the insurer and of the public, take such actions as are necessary to cause the insurer to be placed under regulatory control under Article 30 of this Chapter. If the Commissioner takes such actions, the authorized control level event shall be deemed sufficient grounds for the Commissioner to take action under Article 30 of this Chapter, and the Commissioner shall have the rights, powers, and duties with respect to the insurer as are set forth in Article 30 of this Chapter. If the Commissioner takes actions under this subdivision pursuant to an adjusted risk-based capital report, the insurer shall be entitled to such protections as are afforded to insurers under the provisions of Article 30 of this Chapter pertaining to summary proceedings. (1993 (Reg. Sess., 1994), c. 678, s. 1.)

§ 58-12-25. Mandatory control level event.

(a)   "Mandatory control level event" means any of the following events:

(1)   The filing of a risk-based capital report that indicates that the insurer's total adjusted capital is less than its mandatory control level risk-based capital.

(2) Notification by the Commissioner to the insurer of an adjusted risk-based capital report that indicates the event in subdivision (1) of this subsection if the insurer does not challenge the adjusted risk-based capital report under G.S. 58-12-30.

(3) If the insurer challenges an adjusted risk-based capital report that indicates the event in subdivision (1) of this subsection under G.S. 58-12-30, notification by the Commissioner to the insurer that the Commissioner has rejected the challenge.

(b) In the event of a mandatory control level event with respect to a life insurer or a health organization, the Commissioner shall take actions as are necessary to cause the insurer to be placed under regulatory control under Article 30 of this Chapter. The mandatory control level event is sufficient grounds for the Commissioner to take action under Article 30 of this Chapter, and the Commissioner shall have the rights, powers, and duties with respect to the insurer as are set forth in Article 30 of this Chapter. If the Commissioner takes actions pursuant to an adjusted risk-based capital report, the insurer shall be entitled to such protections as are afforded to insurers under the provisions of Article 30 of this Chapter pertaining to summary proceedings.
Notwithstanding any of the foregoing, the Commissioner may forego action for up to 90 days after the mandatory control level event if the Commissioner finds there is a reasonable expectation that the mandatory control level event may be eliminated within the 90-day period.

(c) In the event of a mandatory control level event with respect to a property and casualty insurer, the Commissioner shall take actions as are necessary to cause the insurer to be placed under regulatory control under Article 30 of this Chapter, or, in the case of an insurer which is writing no business and which is running off its existing business, may allow the insurer to continue its runoff under the supervision of the Commissioner. In either event, the mandatory control level event is sufficient grounds for the Commissioner to take action under Article 30 of this Chapter, and the Commissioner shall have the rights, powers, and duties with respect to the insurer as are set forth in Article 30 of this Chapter. If the Commissioner takes actions under an adjusted risk-based capital report, the insurer shall be entitled to such protections as are afforded to insurers under the provisions of Article 30 of this Chapter pertaining to summary proceedings. Notwithstanding any of the foregoing, the Commissioner may forego action for up to 90 days after the mandatory control level event if the Commissioner finds there is a reasonable expectation that the mandatory control level event may be eliminated within the 90-day period. (1993 (Reg. Sess., 1994), c. 678, s. 1; 2001-223, ss. 12.7, 12.8.)

§ 58-12-30. Hearings.

Upon (i) notification to an insurer by the Commissioner of an adjusted risk-based capital report; or (ii) notification to an insurer by the Commissioner that the insurer's risk-based capital plan or revised risk-based capital plan is unsatisfactory, and the notification constitutes a regulatory action level event with respect to the insurer; or (iii) notification to any insurer by the Commissioner that the insurer has failed to adhere to its risk-based capital plan or revised risk-based capital plan and that the failure has a substantial adverse effect on the ability of the insurer to eliminate the company action level event with respect to the insurer in accordance with its risk-based capital plan or revised risk-based capital plan; or (iv) notification to an insurer by the Commissioner of a corrective order with respect to the insurer, the insurer has a right to a confidential hearing, at which the insurer may challenge any determination or action by the Commissioner. The insurer shall notify the Commissioner of its request for a hearing within five days after the notification by the Commissioner under this section. Upon receipt of the insurer's request for a hearing, the Commissioner shall set a date for the hearing; the date shall be no less than 10 days nor more than 30 days after the date of the insurer's request. (1993 (Reg. Sess., 1994), c. 678, s. 1; 1995, c. 517, s. 5.)

§ 58-12-35. Confidentiality and prohibition on announcements.

(a) All risk-based capital reports, to the extent the information therein is not required to be set forth in a publicly available annual statement schedule, and the risk-based capital plans, including the results or report of any examination or analysis of an insurer performed pursuant hereto and any corrective order issued by the Commissioner pursuant to examination or analysis, with respect to any domestic insurer or foreign insurer that are filed with the Commissioner constitute information that shall be kept confidential by the Commissioner. This information shall not be made public and shall not be subject to subpoena, discovery, or admissible in evidence in any private civil action, other than by the Commissioner, and then only for the purpose of enforcement actions taken by the Commissioner under this Article or any other provision of this Chapter. In order to assist in the performance of the Commissioner's duties, the Commissioner may share and receive confidential and privileged risk-based capital information in a manner consistent with that information shared and received pursuant to G.S. 58-2-132(g) and (h). Neither the Commissioner nor any person who received documents, materials, or other information while acting under the authority of the Commissioner shall be permitted or required to testify in any private civil action concerning any confidential documents, materials, or information subject to this subsection.

(b) The General Assembly finds that the comparison of an insurer's total adjusted capital to any of its risk-based capital levels is a regulatory tool that may indicate the need for possible corrective action with respect to the insurer, and is not intended as a means to rank insurers generally. Therefore, except as otherwise required under this Article, the making, publishing, disseminating, circulating, or placing before the public, or causing, directly or indirectly, to be made, published, disseminated, circulated, or placed before the public, in a newspaper, magazine, or other publication, or in the form of a notice, circular, pamphlet, letter, or poster, or over any radio or television station, or in any other way, an advertisement, announcement, or statement containing an assertion, representation, or statement with regard to the risk-based capital levels of any insurer, or of any component derived in the calculation by any insurer, agent, broker, or other person engaged in any manner in the insurance business is prohibited; provided, however, that if any materially false statement with respect to the comparison regarding an insurer's total adjusted capital to its risk-based capital levels (or any of them) or an inappropriate comparison of any other amount to the insurers' risk-based capital levels is published in any written publication and the insurer is able to demonstrate to the Commissioner, with substantial proof, the falsity of the statement, or the inappropriateness, as the case may be, then the insurer may publish an announcement in a written publication if the sole purpose of the announcement is to rebut the materially false statement. (1993 (Reg. Sess., 1994), c. 678, s. 1; 1995, c. 193, s. 22; 2013-199, s. 5.)

§ 58-12-40. Supplemental provisions; rules; exemptions.

(a) The provisions of this Article are supplemental to any other provisions of the laws of this State, and do not preclude or limit any other powers or duties of the Commissioner under those laws, including Article 30 of this Chapter.

(b) Risk-based capital instructions, risk-based capital reports, adjusted risk-based capital reports, risk-based capital plans, and revised risk-based capital plans are solely for use by the Commissioner in monitoring the solvency of insurers and the need for possible corrective action with respect to insurers. The Commissioner shall not use any of these reports or plans for rate making nor consider or introduce them as evidence in any rate proceeding. The Commissioner shall not use these reports or plans to calculate or derive any elements of an appropriate premium level or rate of return for any kind of insurance that an insurer or any affiliate is authorized to write.

(c) The Commissioner may exempt from the application of this Article any domestic property or casualty insurer that:

(1) Writes direct business only in this State.

(2) Writes direct annual premiums of two million dollars ($2,000,000) or less.

(3) Assumes no reinsurance in excess of five percent (5%) of direct written premiums.

(d) The Commissioner may, in the Commissioner's discretion, exempt from the application of this Article:

(1) Any domestic town or county mutual insurance company organized under G.S. 58-7-75(5)d.

(2) Any domestic life or health insurer that:

a. Has no direct or assumed annual premiums; and

b. Has no direct or assumed policyholder obligations.

(3) Any domestic health maintenance organization that:

a. Writes only direct business in this State;

b. Assumes no reinsurance in excess of five percent (5%) of direct written premiums; and

c. Writes direct annual premiums for a comprehensive medical business of two million dollars ($2,000,000) or less, or is a single service health maintenance organization that covers less than 2,000 lives. (1993 (Reg. Sess., 1994), c. 678, s. 1; 1995, c. 318, s. 6; 2005-215, s. 22.)

§ 58-12-45. Foreign insurers.

(a) Any foreign insurer shall, upon written request of the Commissioner, submit to the Commissioner a risk-based capital report as of the end of the calendar year just ended the later of:

(1) The date a risk-based capital report would be required to be filed by a domestic insurer under this Article; or

(2) Fifteen days after the request is received by the foreign insurer.

Any foreign insurer shall, at the written request of the Commissioner, promptly submit to the Commissioner a copy of any risk-based capital plan that is filed with the insurance regulator of any other state.

(b) In the event of a company action level event, regulatory action level event, or authorized control level event with respect to any foreign insurer as determined under the risk-based capital statute or rule applicable in the state of domicile of the insurer, or if no risk-based capital statute or rule is in force in that state under the provisions of this Article, if the insurance regulator of the state of domicile of the foreign insurer fails to require the foreign insurer to file a risk-based capital plan in the manner specified under the risk-based capital statute or, if no risk-based capital provision is in force in that state, under G.S. 58-12-11, the Commissioner may require the foreign insurer to file a risk-based capital plan with the Commissioner. In that event the failure of the foreign insurer to file a risk-based capital plan with the Commissioner is grounds to order the insurer to cease and desist from writing new insurance business in this State.

(c) In the event of a mandatory control level event with respect to any foreign insurer, if no domiciliary receiver has been appointed with respect to the foreign insurer under the rehabilitation or liquidation statutes of the state of domicile of the foreign insurer, the Commissioner may make application to the Superior Court of Wake County as permitted under Article 30 of this Chapter with respect to the liquidation of property of foreign insurers found in this State;

and the occurrence of the mandatory control level event is an adequate ground for the application. (1993 (Reg. Sess., 1994), c. 678, s. 1; 1995, c. 193, s. 23.)

§ 58-12-50. Notices.

All notices by the Commissioner to an insurer that may result in regulatory action under this Article are effective upon dispatch if transmitted by registered or certified mail; or in the case of any other transmission are effective upon the insurer's receipt of the notice. (1993 (Reg. Sess., 1994), c. 678, s. 1.)

§ 58-12-55. Phase-in provision.

For risk-based capital reports required to be filed with respect to 1994, the following requirements apply in lieu of the provisions of G.S. 58-12-11:

(1) In the event of a company action level event with respect to a domestic insurer, the Commissioner shall take no regulatory action hereunder.

(2) In the event of a regulatory action level event under G.S. 58-12-16(a)(1), (2), or (3) the Commissioner shall take the actions required under G.S. 58-12-11.

(3) In the event of a regulatory action level event under G.S. 58-12-16(a)(4), (5), (6), (7), (8), or (9) or an authorized control level event, the Commissioner shall take the actions required under G.S. 58-12-16 with respect to the insurer.

(4) In the event of a mandatory control level event with respect to an insurer, the Commissioner shall take the actions required under G.S. 58-12-21 with respect to the insurer. (1993 (Reg. Sess., 1994), c. 678, s. 1.)

§ 58-12-60. Property or casualty phase-in provision.

For risk-based capital reports required to be filed by property or casualty insurers with respect to 1995, the following requirements apply in lieu of the provisions of G.S. 58-12-11, 58-12-16, 58-12-21, and 58-12-25:

(1) In the event of a company action level event with respect to a domestic insurer, the Commissioner shall take no regulatory action under this Article.

(2) In the event of a regulatory action level event under G.S. 58-12-16(a)(1), (2), or (3), the Commissioner shall take the actions required under G.S. 58-12-11.

(3) In the event of a regulatory action level event under G.S. 58-12-16(a)(4), (5), (6), (7), (8), or (9), or an authorized control level event, the Commissioner shall take the actions required under G.S. 58-12-16 with respect to the insurer.

(4) In the event of a mandatory control level event with respect to an insurer, the Commissioner shall take the actions required under G.S. 58-12-21 with respect to the insurer. (1995, c. 318, s. 7.)

§ 58-12-65. Health organization phase-in provision.

For risk-based capital reports required to be filed by health organizations with respect to calendar year 2001, the following requirements apply in lieu of the provisions of G.S. 58-12-11, 58-12-16, 58-12-21, and 58-12-25:

(1) In the event of a company action level event with respect to a domestic insurer, the Commissioner shall take no regulatory action under this Article.

(2) In the event of a regulatory action level event under G.S. 58-12-16(a)(1), (2), or (3), the Commissioner shall take the actions required under G.S. 58-12-11.

(3) In the event of a regulatory action level event under G.S. 58-12-16(a)(4), (5), (6), (7), (8) or (9), or an authorized control level event, the Commissioner shall take the actions required under G.S. 58-12-16 with respect to the insurer.

(4) In the event of a mandatory control level event with respect to an insurer, the Commissioner shall take the actions required under G.S. 58-12-21 with respect to the insurer. (2001-223, s. 12.9.)

§ 58-12-70. HMO net worth requirements.

The Commissioner may require an HMO to have and maintain a larger amount of net worth than prescribed in G.S. 58-67-110, based upon the principles of risk-based capital as determined by the NAIC or the Commissioner. (2001-223, s. 12.10.)

Article 13.

Asset Protection Act.

§ 58-13-1. Title.

This Article shall be known and may be cited as the "Asset Protection Act." (1985, c. 327, s. 1.)

§ 58-13-5. Purposes.

The purposes of this Article are to require insurers to maintain unencumbered assets in amounts equal to policyholder-related liabilities and minimum required capital and minimum required surplus; to provide preferential claims against insurers' assets in favor of owners, beneficiaries, assignees, and holders of insurance policies and certificates; and to prevent the pledging, hypothecation, or encumbrance of assets without a prior written order of the Commissioner. (1985, c. 327, s. 1; 1991, c. 681, s. 30.1; 1993, c. 504, s. 7.)

§ 58-13-10. Scope.

This Article applies to all domestic insurers and to all kinds of insurance written by those insurers under Articles 1 through 68 of this Chapter. Foreign insurers shall comply in substance with the requirements and limitations of this Article. This Article does not apply to the following:

(1) Variable contracts or guaranteed investment contracts for which separate accounts are required to be maintained.

(2) Statutory deposits that are required by insurance regulatory agencies to be maintained as a requirement for doing business in such jurisdictions.

(3) Real estate, authorized under G.S. 58-7-187, encumbered by a mortgage loan with a first lien. (1985, c. 327, s. 1; 1991, c. 681, s. 30.2; 1993, c. 452, s. 25; 1993 (Reg. Sess., 1994), c. 678, s. 13; 1999-244, s. 4; 2001-223, s. 13.1; 2002-187, s. 2.8.)

§ 58-13-15. Definitions.

As used in this Article:

(1) "Assets" means all property, real or personal, tangible or intangible, legal or equitable, owned by an insurer.

(2) "Claimants" means any owners, beneficiaries, assignees, certificate holders, or third-party beneficiaries of any insurance benefit or right arising out of and within the coverage of an insurance policy covered by this Article.

(3) "Reserve assets" means those assets of an insurer that are authorized investments for policy reserves in accordance with this Chapter.

(4) "Policyholder-related liabilities" means those liabilities that are required to be established by an insurer for all of its outstanding insurance policies in accordance with this Chapter. (1985, c. 327, s. 1; 1993, c. 504, s. 8; 2001-223, ss. 13.2, 13.3.)

§ 58-13-20. Exception.

(a) This Article does not apply to those reserve assets of an insurer that are held, deposited, pledged, hypothecated, or otherwise encumbered as provided in this section to secure, offset, protect, or meet those policyholder-related liabilities of the insurer that are established, incurred, or required under the provisions of a reinsurance agreement whereby the insurer has reinsured the insurance policy liabilities of a ceding insurer, provided:

(1) The ceding insurer and the reinsurer are both licensed to transact business in this State;

(2) Pursuant to a written agreement between the ceding insurer and the reinsurer, reserve assets substantially equal to the policyholder-related liabilities required to be established by the reinsurer on the reinsured business are either (i) deposited by or are withheld from the reinsurer and are in the custody of the ceding insurer as security for the payment of the reinsurer's obligations under the reinsurance agreement, and such assets are held subject to withdrawal by and under the separate or joint control of the ceding insurer, or (ii) deposited and held in trust account for that purpose and under those conditions with a qualified United States financial institution.

(b) The Commissioner has the right to examine any of such assets, reinsurance agreements, or deposit arrangements at any time in accordance with his authority to make examinations of insurers as conferred by other provisions of this Chapter.

(c) For purposes of subdivision (a)(2) of this section, "qualified United States financial institution" means an institution that:

(1) Is organized or, in the case of a United States office of a foreign banking organization, licensed under the laws of the United States or any of its states;

(2) Is regulated, supervised, and examined by United States federal or state authorities having regulatory authority over banks and trust companies; and

(3) Has been determined by either the Commissioner or the Securities Valuation Office of the NAIC to meet the standards of financial condition and standing considered necessary and appropriate to regulate the quality of financial institutions who serve as trustees. (1985, c. 327, s. 1; 1993, c. 504, s. 9; 2001-223, s. 13.4; 2005-215, s. 25.)

§ 58-13-25. Prohibition of hypothecation.

(a) Every insurer subject to this Article shall at all times have and maintain free and unencumbered reserve assets equal to an amount that is the total of its policyholder-related liabilities and its required minimum capital and minimum surplus and shall not pledge, hypothecate, or otherwise encumber those reserve assets. The Commissioner, upon application made to the Commissioner, may issue a written order approving the pledging, hypothecation, or encumbrance of any of the assets of an insurer not otherwise prohibited upon a finding that the pledging, hypothecation, or encumbrance will not adversely affect the insurer's solvency.

(b) Every insurer shall file, along with any statement filed under G.S. 58-2-165, a statement sworn to by the chief executive officer of the insurer that: (i) Title to assets in an amount equal to the policyholder-related liabilities and minimum required capital and minimum required surplus of the insurer that are not pledged, hypothecated, or otherwise encumbered is vested in the insurer; (ii) the only assets of the insurer that are pledged, hypothecated, or otherwise encumbered are as identified and reported in the sworn statement and no other assets of the insurer are pledged, hypothecated, or otherwise encumbered; and (iii) the terms and provisions of the transaction of the pledge, hypothecation, or encumbrance are as reported in the sworn statement.

(c) Any person that accepts a pledge, hypothecation, or encumbrance of any asset of an insurer, as security for a debt or other obligation of the insurer, not in accordance with this Article, is deemed to have accepted the asset subject to a superior, preferential, and automatically perfected lien in favor of claimants: Provided, that said lien does not apply to the assets of an insurer in a delinquency proceeding under Article 30 of this Chapter if the Commissioner or the court, whichever is appropriate, approves the pledge, hypothecation, or encumbrance of the assets.

(d) In the event of the liquidation of any insurer subject to this Article, claimants of the insurer shall have a prior and preferential claim against all assets of the insurer except those that have been pledged, hypothecated, or encumbered in accordance with this Article. Subject to Article 30 of this Chapter, all claimants have equal status; and their prior and preferential claims are superior to any claim or cause of action against the insurer by any other person. (1985, c. 327, s. 1; 1989, c. 452, s. 4; 1991, c. 681, s. 30.3; 1993, c. 504, s. 10; 2002-187, s. 2.9.)

Article 14.

Unauthorized Insurance by Domestic Companies.

§ 58-14-1. Purpose of Article.

It is the purpose of this Article to effectively control and regulate the activities of domestic insurance companies so as to prevent them from engaging in and transacting insurance business in states and jurisdictions in which they are not authorized to do a business of insurance. The General Assembly recognizes that insofar as domestic companies of this State engage in transacting insurance business in states and jurisdictions in which they are not authorized to do business that such activity subjects the domestic companies of this State to the penalties for such unlawful activities in other states and jurisdictions, and that such activities tend to substantially impair the effectiveness of the domestic companies in this State. The General Assembly also recognizes that the practices of unauthorized insurers could be largely corrected if each state would effectively regulate the activities of its domestic companies. The provisions of this Article are in addition to all other statutory provisions designed to control the activities of domestic companies and nothing herein shall be construed to amend, modify or repeal the provisions of existing laws. (1967, c. 935, s. 1.)

§ 58-14-5. Domestic insurers prohibited from transacting business in foreign states without authorization; exceptions.

Except as hereinafter provided, no domestic insurer organized under the laws of this State shall transact or attempt to transact or solicit business in any manner or accept risks in any jurisdiction in which such insurer is not licensed in accordance with the laws of such jurisdiction. There is excepted from the terms of this section the following acts and transactions:

(1)   Contracts entered into by a domestic company insuring a risk within a foreign state or jurisdiction, where the law of the foreign state or jurisdiction permits an unauthorized insurer to so contract;

(2) Contracts entered into where the prospective insured is personally present in the state in which the insurer is authorized to transact business when he signs the application;

(3) Contracts of reinsurance between a licensed insurer of the foreign state or jurisdiction and a domestic company;

(4) The issuance of certificates under a lawfully transacted group life or group disability policy, where the master policy was entered into in a state in which the insurer was then authorized to transact business;

(5) The renewal or continuance in force, with or without modification, of contracts otherwise lawful and which were not originally executed in violation of this section. (1967, c. 935, s. 1.)

§ 58-14-10. Domestic insurers; advertising; exceptions.

No domestic insurer shall knowingly solicit or advertise its insurance business in a state or jurisdiction in which it is not licensed as an authorized insurer. Provided, however, that this section shall not prohibit a domestic insurer from advertising through publications, radio or television if such advertising is not expressly directed toward the residents or subjects of insurance in a foreign state or other jurisdiction. Nor shall this section apply to trade journals or directories. (1967, c. 935, s. 1.)

§ 58-14-15. Penalties provided for unauthorized acts.

When any domestic insurer knowingly engages in the practice of soliciting, advertising or making contracts for insurance in states or jurisdictions in which it is not licensed, the Commissioner may issue an order requiring the company to cease and desist from engaging in such activities and, for the purposes of this section, the acts prohibited by G.S. 58-14-10 and the foregoing sections, are declared to be an unfair trade practice within the meaning of G.S. 58-63-15 and G.S. 58-63-40. When the Commissioner has reason to believe that any domestic company has been engaged or is engaging in the practice of knowingly soliciting, advertising or writing contracts of insurance on risks within a state or jurisdiction in which it is not licensed, the Commissioner shall serve the company with notice of hearing and the hearing shall conform with the hearing procedure set forth in G.S. 58-63-25. Any action taken by the Commissioner after the hearing shall comply with G.S. 58-63-32, and any company aggrieved by an order of the Commissioner is entitled to the judicial review provided in G.S. 58-63-35. (1967, c. 935, s. 1; 1991, c. 720, ss. 4, 54; 1995, c. 193, s. 24; 1995 (Reg. Sess., 1996), c. 742, s. 23.)

Article 15.

Reciprocal Insurance.

Part 1. General Provisions.

§ 58-15-1. Scope.

This Article applies to all reciprocals and reciprocal insurance. (1989, c. 425, s. 1.)

§ 58-15-5. Definitions.

As used in this Article:

(1)   "Attorney" means the person designated and authorized by subscribers as the attorney-in-fact having authority to obligate them on reciprocal and other insurance contracts.

(2)   "License" means a license to transact the business of insurance in this State, issued by the Commissioner.

(3)   In addition to the meaning of the term as defined in G.S. 12-3(6) and G.S. 58-1-5(9), "person" means any county, city, school board, hospital authority, or any other local governmental authority or local agency or public service corporation owned, operated or controlled by a local government or local government authority, that has the power to enter into contractual undertakings within or without the State.

(4) "Reciprocal" means an aggregation of subscribers under a common name.

(5) "Reciprocal insurance" means insurance resulting from the mutual exchange of insurance contracts among persons in an unincorporated association under a common name through an attorney-in-fact having authority to obligate each person both as insured and insurer.

(6) "Subscriber" means a person obligated under a reciprocal insurance agreement. (1989, c. 425, s. 1; 1991, c. 720, s. 15; 1999-132, s. 9.1.)

§ 58-15-10. Kinds of insurance.

A reciprocal licensed in this State may write the kinds of insurance enumerated in G.S. 58-7-15, except life insurance, annuities, and title insurance. (1989, c. 425, s. 1.)

§ 58-15-15. Risk limitations.

(a) Except for Article 11 of this Chapter and as otherwise specifically provided, all the provisions of Articles 1 through 64 of this Chapter relating to insurers generally, and those relating to insurers writing the same kinds of insurance that reciprocals are permitted to write, are applicable to reciprocals.

(b) A reciprocal shall be deemed to comply with G.S. 58-3-105 if:

(1) It issues policies containing a contingent assessment liability, provided for in G.S. 58-15-60; and

(2) It maintains reinsurance in an amount that the Commissioner considers adequate to reasonably limit the reciprocal's aggregate losses to the lesser of:

a. Ten percent (10%) of the surplus to policyholders of the reciprocal multiplied by the number of subscribers;

b. The surplus to policyholders of the reciprocal multiplied by three; or

c. Five million dollars ($5,000,000). (1989, c. 425, s. 1.)

§ 58-15-20. Eligible contracting persons.

(a) Persons of this State may enter into reciprocal insurance contracts with each other and with persons of other states and countries.

(b) For any corporation now existing or subsequently organized under the laws of this State, the authority to enter into reciprocal insurance contracts is in addition to the authority conferred upon it in its charter and is incidental to the purposes for which the corporation is organized. (1989, c. 425, s. 1.)

§ 58-15-25. Business name.

Every reciprocal shall have and use an appropriate business name that includes the word or words "reciprocal," "interinsurer," "interinsurance," or "exchange". (1989, c. 425, s. 1.)

§ 58-15-30. License, surplus, and deposit requirements.

(a) No reciprocal shall engage in any insurance transaction in this State until it has obtained a license to do so in accordance with the applicable provisions of Articles 1 through 64 of this Chapter. The license shall continue in full force and effect, subject to timely payment of an annual license continuation fee in accordance with G.S. 58-6-7 and subject to any other applicable provision of the insurance laws of this State.

(b) No domestic or foreign reciprocal shall be licensed in this State unless it has a surplus to policyholders of at least eight hundred thousand dollars ($800,000); and no alien reciprocal shall be licensed unless it has a trusteed surplus of at least eight hundred thousand dollars ($800,000).

(c) Each domestic, foreign, or alien reciprocal licensed in this State shall deposit and maintain deposits with the Commissioner of at least four hundred thousand dollars ($400,000) in cash or in value of securities of the kind specified in G.S. 58-5-15, which shall be subject to Article 5 of this Chapter. (1989, c. 425, s. 1; 2003-212, s. 26(e); 2004-203, s. 74(a); 2005-215, s. 24.)

§ 58-15-35. Continuation of business under prior requirements.

(a) Notwithstanding other provisions of Articles 1 through 64 of this Chapter regarding minimum required surplus, any reciprocal that was licensed to write and was writing any kind of insurance in this State on January 1, 1990 may continue to write that kind of insurance under the appropriate license from the Commissioner. Such reciprocal shall maintain at all times the minimum surplus, and the minimum trusteed surplus if an alien reciprocal, that was required before January 1, 1990.

(b) Before any reciprocal obtains a license to write in this State any kind of insurance that it was not licensed to write and writing in this State on January 1, 1990, it shall comply with all the requirements of this Part regarding surplus. (1989, c. 425, s. 1.)

§ 58-15-40. Certification of foreign and alien reciprocals.

No foreign reciprocal shall be licensed in this State until it files with the Commissioner a certificate of the insurance regulator of the state in which it is organized. The certificate shall show that the foreign reciprocal is licensed to write and is writing actively in that state the kind of insurance it proposes to write in this State. No alien reciprocal shall be licensed in this State until it files with the Commissioner a certificate of the insurance regulator of (i) the state through which it entered the United States or (ii) the alien reciprocal's domiciliary country. The certificate shall show that the alien reciprocal is licensed to write and is writing actively in that state or country the kind of insurance it proposes to write in this State. Foreign and alien reciprocals must also satisfy the appropriate provisions of Article 16 of this Chapter pertaining to admission requirements. (1989, c. 425, s. 1.)

§ 58-15-45. Attorney's domicile.

Nothing in Articles 1 through 64 of this Chapter regarding the admission and licensing of foreign and alien insurers requires that the attorney of a foreign or alien reciprocal be resident or domiciled in this State, or that the principal office of the attorney be maintained in this State. The office or offices of the attorney shall be determined by the subscribers through the power of attorney. (1989, c. 425, s. 1.)

§ 58-15-50. Contracts and property.

A reciprocal may enter into contracts and acquire, hold title to, and convey property in its business name. All contracts of a reciprocal, including its insurance contracts, shall be executed on behalf of the reciprocal by the attorney of the reciprocal. (1989, c. 425, s. 1.)

§ 58-15-55. Agent's license.

No person shall act in this State as an agent of a reciprocal in the solicitation or procurement of applications for insurance, subscriber's agreements, or powers of attorney, or in the collection of premiums in connection with the reciprocal, without first procuring an agent's license from the Commissioner pursuant to Article 33 of this Chapter. An agent shall be appointed by each reciprocal the agent represents. (1989, c. 425, s. 1.)

§ 58-15-60. Subscribers' contingent liability.

(a) Each subscriber insured under an assessable policy has a contingent assessment liability for payment of actual losses and expenses incurred by the reciprocal while his policy was in force. This liability is in the amount provided for in the power of attorney or subscriber's agreement.

(b) The contingent assessment liability on any one policy in any one calendar year equals the premiums earned, as defined in G.S. 58-15-135, on the policy for that year multiplied by not more than ten.

(c) The contingent assessment liability is several and not joint.

(d) Each assessable policy issued by the reciprocal shall plainly set forth a statement of the contingent assessment liability on the front of the policy in capital letters, in contrasting color, and in no less than ten-point type. (1989, c. 425, s. 1.)

§ 58-15-65. Nonassessable policies.

(a) The Commissioner may issue a certificate authorizing the reciprocal to reduce or extinguish the contingent assessment liability of subscribers under its policies then in force in this State and to omit provisions imposing contingent assessment liability in all policies delivered or issued for delivery in this State for as long as all such surplus to policyholders remains unimpaired. The certificate may be issued if (i) a reciprocal has surplus to policyholders of at least two million dollars ($2,000,000), and (ii) an application of the attorney has been approved by the subscribers' advisory committee.

(b) The Commissioner shall issue this certificate if the conditions of subsection (a) of this section are met and if he determines that the reciprocal's surplus to policyholders is reasonable in relation to the reciprocal's outstanding liabilities and is adequate to meet its financial needs. In making that determination the following factors, among others, shall be considered:

(1) The size of the reciprocal as measured by its assets, capital and surplus, reserves, premium writings, insurance in force, and other appropriate criteria;

(2) The extent to which the reciprocal's business is diversified among different kinds of insurance;

(3) The number and size of risks insured in each kind of insurance;

(4) The extent of the geographic dispersion of the reciprocal's insured risks;

(5) The nature and extent of the reciprocal's reinsurance program;

(6) The quality, diversification, and liquidity of the reciprocal's investment portfolio;

(7) The recent past and trend in the size of the reciprocal's surplus to policyholders;

(8) The surplus to policyholders maintained by other comparable insurers; and

(9) The adequacy of the reciprocal's reserves.

(c) Upon impairment of the surplus to policyholders as described in subsection (a) of this section, the Commissioner shall revoke the certificate. After revocation, the reciprocal shall not issue or renew any policy without providing for the contingent assessment liability of subscribers.

(d) The Commissioner shall not authorize a domestic reciprocal to extinguish the contingent assessment liability of any of its subscribers or in any of its policies to be issued, unless it has the required surplus to policyholders and extinguishes the contingent assessment liability of all of its subscribers and in all policies to be issued for all kinds of insurance it writes. However, if required by the laws of another state in which the domestic reciprocal is transacting the business of insurance as a licensed insurer, it may issue policies providing for the contingent assessment liability of its subscribers that acquire policies in that state and need not extinguish the contingent assessment liability applicable to policies already in force in that state. (1989, c. 425, s. 1.)

§ 58-15-70. Distribution to subscribers.

A reciprocal may return to its subscribers any savings or credits accruing to their accounts. Any such distribution shall not unfairly discriminate between classes of risks or policies or between subscribers. However, the distribution may vary for classes of subscribers based upon the experience of those classes. (1989, c. 425, s. 1.)

§ 58-15-75. Reserves.

Each reciprocal shall maintain the same unearned premium and loss or claim reserves required for stock and mutual companies writing the same kinds of insurance. (1989, c. 425, s. 1.)

§ 58-15-80: Reserved for future codification purposes.

§ 58-15-85. Service of process.

(a) Each attorney of a domestic reciprocal who files the declaration required by G.S. 58-15-100, and each attorney of a foreign or alien reciprocal that applies for a license, shall file with the Commissioner a written power of attorney executed in duplicate by the attorney that appoints the Commissioner as agent of the reciprocal. Upon the appointment, the Commissioner may be served all legal process against such reciprocal pursuant to G.S. 58-16-30. A copy of the power of attorney, duly certified by the Commissioner, is admissible as evidence in the courts of this State.

(b) Whenever any such process is served upon the Commissioner, G.S. 58-16-45 is applicable, except that the process shall be directed to the attorney at the address shown on the power of attorney. Nothing in this section limits the right to serve any process upon any reciprocal in any other manner permitted by law. (1989, c. 425, s. 1.)

§ 58-15-90. Legal proceedings.

(a) Any reciprocal doing business in this State may sue or be sued in its business name.

(b) Any action or suit against a reciprocal may be brought in any county (i) where its principal office is located, or (ii) where the cause of action or any part of the cause of action arose. If the action or suit is to recover a loss under a policy of property insurance, it may also be brought in the county where the property insured was situated at the date of the policy. Any action or suit against a foreign or alien reciprocal may also be brought in any county of this State in which it has any debts owed to it.

(c) In an action against a reciprocal, process against the reciprocal may be served upon the Commissioner. If the defendant in the action is a domestic reciprocal, process against that domestic reciprocal shall be served upon the attorney for that domestic reciprocal unless service upon that attorney is not feasible. (1989, c. 425, s. 1.)

§ 58-15-95. Liability on judgments.

Any judgment against a reciprocal based upon legal process duly served as provided in this Article is binding upon the reciprocal and upon each of the reciprocal's subscribers as their respective interests may appear, in an amount not exceeding their respective contingent assessment liabilities. There is no derivative liability on the part of the attorney, officers, employees, agents, or subscribers' advisory committee of the reciprocal arising merely by reason of the status of such persons. (1989, c. 425, s. 1.)

Part 2. Domestic Reciprocals.

§ 58-15-100. Declaration for license.

(a) One hundred or more persons domiciled in this State and designated as subscribers may organize a domestic reciprocal and apply to the Commissioner for a license to transact the business of insurance. The Commissioner may authorize such a reciprocal to form with a lesser number of subscribers upon being satisfied that the risks are adequately spread and financial projections indicate that such a reciprocal will have a reasonable potential to succeed in its business with such a lesser number of subscribers. The original subscribers and the proposed attorney shall execute and file with the Commissioner a declaration setting forth:

(1) The name of the attorney and the business name of the reciprocal;

(2) The location of the reciprocal's principal office, which shall be the same as that of the attorney and shall be in this State;

(3) The kinds of insurance proposed to be written;

(4) The names and addresses of the original subscribers;

(5) The designation and appointment of the attorney, and a copy of the power of attorney and subscriber's agreement;

(6) The names and addresses of the officers and directors of the attorney, if a corporation, or of its members if not a corporation;

(7) The powers of the subscribers' advisory committee, and the names and terms of office of its members;

(8) A statement that each of the original subscribers has in good faith applied for insurance of the kind proposed to be written and that the reciprocal has received from each original subscriber the anticipated premium or premium deposit for a term of not less than six months for the policy for which application is made;

(9) A statement of the financial condition of the reciprocal, including a schedule of its assets;

(10) A statement that the reciprocal has the surplus to policyholders required by G.S. 58-15-30;

(11) A copy of each policy, endorsement, and application form it proposes to issue or use; and

(12) Financial projections of the anticipated operational results of the reciprocal for a five-year period based upon the initial surplus of the proposed reciprocal and its plan of operation.

(b) The declaration shall be acknowledged by each original subscriber and by the attorney. (1989, c. 425, s. 1.)

§ 58-15-105. Attorney's bond.

(a) Concurrent with the filing of the declaration provided for in G.S. 58-15-100, the attorney of a domestic reciprocal shall file with the Commissioner a fidelity bond payable to this State. The bond shall be executed by the attorney and by a licensed insurer and is subject to the approval of the Commissioner.

(b) The bond shall be in an amount established in the discretion of the Commissioner, which amount shall be at least fifty thousand dollars ($50,000). The bond shall be on the condition that the attorney faithfully accounts for all moneys and other property of the reciprocal coming into the attorney's control and that the attorney does not withdraw or appropriate for his own use from the funds of the reciprocal any moneys or property to which he is not entitled under the power of attorney.

(c) The bond is not subject to cancellation unless 30-days' written notice of intent to cancel is given to the attorney and the Commissioner. (1989, c. 425, s. 1.)

§ 58-15-110. Deposit in lieu of bond.

Instead of filing the bond required by G.S. 58-15-105, the attorney may maintain on deposit with the Commissioner an equal amount in cash or in value of securities of the kind specified in G.S. 58-5-20 and subject to the same conditions as the bond. (1989, c. 425, s. 1.)

§ 58-15-115. Advisory committee.

The advisory committee exercising the subscribers' rights in a domestic reciprocal shall be selected under rules adopted by the subscribers. At least three-fourths of the committee shall comprise subscribers or their representatives other than the attorney or any person employed by, representing, or having a financial interest in the attorney. The committee shall supervise the finances of the reciprocal and the reciprocal's operations to the extent required to assure their conformity with the subscriber's agreement and power of attorney and shall exercise any other powers conferred on it by the subscriber's agreement. (1989, c. 425, s. 1.)

§ 58-15-120. Subscriber's agreement and power of attorney.

(a) Every subscriber of a domestic reciprocal shall execute a subscriber's agreement and power of attorney setting forth the rights, privileges, and obligations of the subscriber as an underwriter and as a policyholder, and the powers and duties of the attorney. The subscriber's agreement and power of attorney shall contain in substance the following provisions:

(1) A designation and appointment of the attorney to act for and bind the subscriber in all transactions relating to or arising out of the operations of the reciprocal;

(2) A provision empowering the attorney (i) to accept service of legal process on behalf of the reciprocal and (ii) to appoint the Commissioner agent of the reciprocal upon whom may be served all legal process against the reciprocal;

(3) Except for nonassessable policies, a provision for a contingent assessment liability of each subscriber in a specified amount in accordance with G.S. 58-15-60; and

(4) The maximum amount to be deducted from advance premiums or deposits to be paid the attorney, and the items of expense, in addition to losses, to be paid by the reciprocal.

(b) The subscriber's agreement may:

(1) Provide for the right of substitution of the attorney and revocation of the power of attorney;

(2) Impose any restrictions upon the exercise of the power agreed upon by the subscribers;

(3) Provide for the exercise of any right reserved to the subscribers directly or through an advisory committee;

(4) Provide for indemnification of the attorney, officers, employees, agents, and subscribers' advisory committee of the reciprocal against liability and litigation expenses to the extent permitted in the case of domestic business corporations; or

(5) Contain other lawful provisions considered advisable. (1989, c. 425, s. 1.)

§ 58-15-125. Modification of subscriber's agreement and power of attorney.

Modification of the terms of the subscriber's agreement and the power of attorney of a domestic reciprocal shall be made jointly by the attorney and the subscriber's advisory committee. No modification is retroactive nor does it affect any insurance contract issued prior to the modification. (1989, c. 425, s. 1.)

§ 58-15-130. Advance of funds.

The attorney or other interested persons may advance to a domestic reciprocal any funds required for its operations. The funds advanced shall not be treated as a liability of the reciprocal and shall not be withdrawn or repaid except out of the reciprocal's earned surplus in excess of its minimum required surplus. This section does not apply to loans made by commercial lenders in the ordinary course of their businesses. (1989, c. 425, s. 1.)

§ 58-15-135. Assessments.

(a) Assessments may be levied upon the subscribers of a domestic reciprocal by the attorney in accordance with G.S. 58-15-60. The assessments shall be approved in advance by the subscribers' advisory committee.

(b) Each domestic reciprocal subscriber's share of an assessment shall be computed by multiplying the premiums earned on the subscriber's policies during the period to be covered by the assessment by the ratio of the total assessment to the total premiums earned during the period upon all policies subject to the assessment. However, no assessment shall exceed the aggregate contingent assessment liability computed in accordance with G.S. 58-15-60. For the purposes of this section, the premiums earned on the subscriber's policies are the gross premiums charged by the reciprocal for the policies minus any charges not recurring upon the renewal or extension of the policies. No subscriber shall have an offset against any assessment for which he is liable on account of any claim for unearned premium or losses payable. (1989, c. 425, s. 1.)

§ 58-15-140. Duration of liability for assessment.

Every subscriber of a domestic reciprocal having contingent assessment liability shall be liable for and shall pay his share of any assessment computed in accordance with this Part, if, while the policy is in force or for such period after its termination as the Commissioner may establish by rule, the subscriber is notified (i) by the attorney of his intention to levy the assessment or (ii) that delinquency proceedings have been commenced against the reciprocal under the provisions of Article 30 of this Chapter, and the Commissioner or receiver intends to levy an assessment. In adopting such rules the Commissioner may take into account factors including the kinds of insurance issued by such reciprocals. (1989, c. 425, s. 1, c. 770, s. 70; 1989 (Reg. Sess., 1990), c. 1021, s. 1.)

§ 58-15-145. Distribution of assets after liquidation.

Upon the liquidation of a domestic reciprocal, the assets remaining after (i) discharge of its indebtedness and policy obligations, (ii) the return of any contributions of the attorney or other person made as provided in G.S. 58-15-130, and (iii) the return of any unused deposits, savings, or credits, shall be distributed. The distribution shall be according to a formula approved by the Commissioner or the Court to the persons who were its subscribers within the 12 months prior to the final termination of its license. (1989, c. 425, s. 1.)

§ 58-15-150. Financial impairment; assessment; liquidation.

(a) If (i) the assets of a domestic reciprocal are at any time insufficient to settle the sum of its liabilities, except those on account of funds contributed by the attorney or other parties, and its required surplus to policyholders, and (ii) the deficiency is not cured from other sources, its attorney shall levy an assessment upon subscribers made subject to assessment by the terms of their policies for the amount needed to make up the deficiency. However, the assessment shall be subject to G.S. 58-15-60.

(b) If the attorney fails to make the assessment within 30 days after the Commissioner orders him to do so, or if the deficiency is not fully made up within 60 days after the date the assessment is made, delinquency proceedings may be instituted and conducted against the insurer as provided in Article 30 of this Chapter.

(c) If liquidation of the reciprocal is ordered, an assessment shall be levied upon the subscribers for the amount the Commissioner or the Court, as the case may be, determines to be necessary to discharge all liabilities of the reciprocal. This assessment shall exclude any funds contributed by the attorney or other persons, but shall include the reasonable cost of the liquidation. However, the assessment is subject to G.S. 58-15-60. (1989, c. 425, s. 1; c. 770, s. 71.)

Article 16.

Foreign or Alien Insurance Companies.

§ 58-16-1. Admitted to do business.

Foreign or alien insurance companies, upon complying with the conditions of Articles 1 through 64 of this Chapter applicable to them, may be admitted to transact in this State any class of insurance authorized by the laws in force relative to the duties, obligations, prohibitions, and penalties of insurance companies, and subject to all laws applicable to the transaction of such business by foreign or alien insurance companies and their agents. (1899, c. 54, s. 61; Rev., s. 4746; C.S., s. 6410; 1945, c. 384; 1987, c. 629, s. 17.)

§ 58-16-5. Conditions of licensure.

A foreign or alien insurance company may be licensed to do business when it:

(1) Deposits with the Commissioner a certified copy of its charter or certificate of organization and a statement of its financial condition and business, in the form and detail that the Commissioner requires, signed and sworn to by its president and secretary or other proper officer, and pays for the filing of this statement the sum required by law.

(2) Satisfies the Commissioner that it is fully and legally organized under the laws of its state or government to do the business it proposes to transact as direct insurance or assumed reinsurance; that it has, if a stock company, a free surplus and a fully paid-up and unimpaired capital, exclusive of stockholders' obligations of any description of an amount not less than that required for the organization of a domestic company writing the same kinds of business; and if a mutual company that its free surplus is not less than that required for the organization of a domestic company writing the same kind of business, and that the capital, surplus, and other funds are invested substantially in accordance with the requirements of this Chapter.

(3) Repealed by Session Laws 1995, c. 517, s. 6.

(4) Repealed by Session Laws 1987, c. 629, s. 20.

(5) Files with the Commissioner a certificate that it has complied with the laws of the state or government under which it was organized and is authorized to make contracts of insurance.

(6) Satisfies the Commissioner that it is in substantial compliance with G.S. 58-7-21, 58-7-26, 58-7-30, and 58-7-31 and Article 13 of this Chapter.

(7) Satisfies the Commissioner that it is in compliance with the company name requirements of G.S. 58-7-35.

(8) Satisfies the Commissioner that the operation of the company in this State would not be hazardous to prospective policyholders, creditors, or the general public.

(9) Satisfies the Commissioner that it is in substantial compliance with the requirements of G.S. 58-7-37 pertaining to the background of its officers and directors.

(10) Files with the Commissioner an instrument appointing the Commissioner as the company's agent on whom any legal process under G.S. 58-16-30 may

be served. This appointment is irrevocable as long as any liability of the company remains outstanding in this State. A copy of this instrument, certified by the Commissioner, is sufficient evidence of this appointment; and service upon the Commissioner is sufficient service upon the company. (1899, c. 54, s. 62; 1901, c. 391, s. 5; 1903, c. 438, s. 6; Rev., s. 4747; C.S., s. 6411; 1945, c. 384; 1951, c. 781, s. 3; 1985 (Reg. Sess., 1986), c. 1027, s. 32; 1987, c. 629, s. 20; 1987 (Reg. Sess., 1988), c. 975, s. 16; 1991, c. 681, s. 24; 1995, c. 193, s. 25; c. 517, s. 6; 1999-294, s. 7; 2001-223, s. 14.1; 2009-172, s. 8.)

§ 58-16-6. Conditions of continued licensure.

In order for a foreign insurance company to continue to be licensed, it shall report any changes in the documents filed under G.S. 58-16-5(1) or G.S. 58-16-5(5); maintain the amounts of capital and surplus specified in G.S. 58-16-5(2); and remain in compliance with G.S. 58-16-5(6), (7), and (8) and with G.S. 58-7-46. (1995, c. 517, s. 7; 2001-223, s. 14.2; 2005-215, s. 13.)

§ 58-16-10. Limitation as to kinds of insurance.

Any foreign or alien company admitted to do business in this State shall be limited with respect to doing kinds of insurance in this State in the same manner and to the same extent as are domestic companies, provided that any foreign insurance company which has been licensed to do the business of life insurance in this State continuously during a period of 20 years next preceding March 6, 1945, may continue to be licensed, in the discretion of the Commissioner, to do the kind or kinds of insurance business which it was authorized to do immediately prior to March 6, 1945. (1899, c. 44, s. 65; 1901, c. 391, s. 5; 1903, c. 438, s. 6; Rev., s. 4748; 1911, c. 111, s. 2; C.S., s. 6412; 1945, c. 384; 1985 (Reg. Sess., 1986), c. 1027, s. 53; 1987 (Reg. Sess., 1988), c. 975, s. 17.)

§ 58-16-15. Foreign companies; requirements for admission.

A company organized under the laws of any other of these United States for the transaction of life insurance may be admitted to do business in this State if it complies with the other provisions of Articles 1 through 64 of this Chapter regulating the terms and conditions upon which foreign life insurance companies may be admitted and authorized to do business in this State, and, in the opinion of the Commissioner, is in sound financial condition and has policies in force upon not less than 500 lives for an aggregate amount of not less than five hundred thousand dollars ($500,000). Any life company organized under the laws of any other country than the United States, in addition to the above requirements, must make and maintain the deposit required of such companies by Article 5 of this Chapter. (1899, c. 54, s. 56; Rev., s. 4774; C.S., s. 6456; 1945, c. 379; 1991, c. 720, ss. 4, 16.)

§ 58-16-20. Company owned or controlled by foreign government prohibited from doing business.

(a) Any insurance company or other insurance entity that is owned or controlled by any foreign government outside the continental limits of the United States or the territories of the United States is prohibited from doing any kind of insurance business in the State of North Carolina. For the purposes of this section, "foreign government" means any foreign government or any state, province, municipality, or political subdivision of any foreign government, and shall not be construed to apply to any insurance company organized under the laws of a foreign nation that is owned or controlled by the private citizens or private business interest of that foreign nation.

(b) The Commissioner shall not license any insurance company or other insurance entity that is owned or controlled by any foreign government outside the continental limits of the United States or the territories of the United States, nor shall the Commissioner authorize any such company or entity to transact any kind of insurance business in the State of North Carolina.

(c) Any insurance company or other insurance entity that is owned or controlled by any foreign government outside the continental limits of the United States or the territories of the United States, or any representative or agent of any such company or entity that violates the provisions of this section, is guilty of a Class 3 misdemeanor.

(d) This section does not apply to the operating subsidiary of any insurance company or other insurance entity, where the company or entity is owned or controlled by any foreign government outside the continental limits of the United States or the territories of the United States, as long as the operating subsidiary is domesticated in and licensed by another state of the United States as an insurer or reinsurer and as a separate subsidiary. (1955, c. 449; 1991, c. 720, s. 4; 1993, c. 539, s. 449; 1994, Ex. Sess., c. 24, s. 14(c); 1997-179, s. 1.)

§ 58-16-25. Retaliatory laws.

When, by the laws of any other state or nation, any fines, penalties, licenses, fees, deposits of money or of securities, or other obligations or prohibitions are imposed upon insurance companies of this State doing business in such other state or nation or upon their agents therein greater than those imposed by this State upon insurance companies of such other state, then, so long as such laws continue in force, the same fines, penalties, licenses, fees, deposits, obligations and prohibitions, of whatever kind, may in the discretion of the Commissioner be imposed upon all such insurance companies of such other state or nation doing business within this State and upon their agents here. Nothing herein repeals or reduces the license, fees, taxes, and other obligations now imposed by the laws of this State or to go into effect with the companies of any other state or nation unless some company of this State is actually doing or seeking to do business in such state or nation. When an insurance company organized under the laws of any state or country is prohibited by the laws of such state or country or by its charter from investing its assets other than capital stock in the bonds of this State, then and in such case the Commissioner is authorized and directed to refuse to grant a license to transact business in this State to such insurance company. (1899, c. 54, s. 71; 1903, c. 536, s. 11; Rev., s. 4749; C.S., s. 6413; 1927, c. 32; 1945, c. 384; 1987, c. 814, s. 3; 1991, c. 720, s. 4.)

§ 58-16-30. Service of legal process upon Commissioner.

As an alternative to service of legal process under G.S. 1A-1, Rule 4, the service of such process upon any insurance company or any foreign or alien entity licensed or admitted and authorized to do business in this State under the provisions of this Chapter may be made by the sheriff or any other person delivering and leaving a copy of the process in the office of the Commissioner with a deputy or any other person duly appointed by the Commissioner for that purpose; or acceptance of service of the process may be made by the Commissioner or a duly appointed deputy or person. Service may also be made by mailing a copy of the summons and of the complaint, registered or certified mail, return receipt requested, addressed to the Commissioner. As a condition precedent to a valid service of process under this section, the party obtaining such service shall pay to the Commissioner at the time of service or acceptance of service the sum of ten dollars ($10.00), which the party shall recover as part of the taxable costs if the party prevails in the action. (1899, c. 54, ss. 16, 62; 1903, c. 438, s. 6; Rev., s. 4750; C.S., s. 6414; 1927, c. 167, s. 1; 1931, c. 287; 1951, c. 781, s. 9; 1971, c. 421, s. 1; 1985, c. 666, s. 5; 1989, c. 645, s. 2; 1991, c. 720, s. 4; 1995, c. 517, s. 8.)

§ 58-16-35. Unauthorized Insurers Process Act.

(a) Purpose of Section. - The purpose of this section is to subject certain insurers to the jurisdiction of courts of this State in suits by or on behalf of insureds or beneficiaries under insurance contracts. The General Assembly declares that it is a subject of concern that many residents of this State hold policies of insurance issued by insurers not authorized to do business in this State, thus presenting to such residents the often insuperable obstacle of resorting to distant forums for the purpose of asserting legal rights under such policies. In furtherance of such State interest, the General Assembly herein provides a method of substituted service of process upon such insurers and declares that in so doing it exercises its power to protect its residents and to define, for the purpose of this statute, what constitutes doing business in this State, and also exercises powers and privileges available to the State by virtue of Public Law 15, 79th Congress of the United States, Chapter 20, 1st Session, s. 340, as amended, which declares that the business of insurance and every person engaged therein shall be subject to the laws of the several states.

(b) Service of Process upon Unauthorized Insurer. -

(1) Any of the following acts in this State, effected by mail or otherwise, by an unauthorized foreign or alien insurer:

a. The issuance or delivery of contracts of insurance to residents of this State or to corporations authorized to do business therein,

b. The solicitation of applications for such contracts,

c. The collection of premiums, membership fees, assessments or other considerations for such contracts, or

d.   Any other transaction of business,

is equivalent to and shall constitute an appointment by such insurer of the Commissioner and his successor or successors in office, to be its true and lawful attorney, upon whom may be served all lawful process in any action, suit, or proceeding instituted by or on behalf of an insured or beneficiary arising out of any such contract of insurance, and any such act shall be signification of its agreement that such service of process is of the same legal force and validity as personal service of process in this State upon such insurer.

(2)   Such service of process shall be made by delivering to and leaving with the Commissioner or some person in apparent charge of his office two copies thereof and the payment to him of ten dollars ($10.00). The Commissioner shall within four business days mail by certified or registered mail one of the copies of such process to the defendant at its last known principal place of business, and shall keep a record of all process so served upon him. Such service of process is sufficient, provided notice of such service and a copy of the process are sent within 10 days thereafter by certified or registered mail by plaintiff or plaintiff's attorney to the defendant at its last known principal place of business, and the defendant's receipt, or receipt issued by the transmitting post office, showing the name of the sender of the letter and the name and address of the person to whom the letter is addressed, and the affidavit of the plaintiff or plaintiff's attorney showing a compliance herewith are filed with the clerk of the court in which such action is pending on or before the date the defendant is required to appear, or within such further time as the court may allow.

(3)   Service of process in any such action, suit or proceeding shall in addition to the manner provided in subdivision (2) of this subsection be valid if:

a.   It is served on a person within this State who is in the State on behalf of the insurer to solicit insurance, make, issue, or deliver a contract of insurance, or collect or receive a premium, membership fee, assessment, or other consideration for insurance;

b.   A copy of the process is sent within 10 days after service by certified or registered mail by the plaintiff or plaintiff's attorney to the defendant at the defendant's last known principal place of business; and

c.   The defendant's receipt, or the receipt issued by the transmitting post office, showing the name of the sender of the letter and the name and address of the person to whom the letter is addressed, and the affidavit of the plaintiff or plaintiff's attorney showing a compliance herewith are filed with the clerk of the court in which such action is pending on or before the date the defendant is required to appear, or within such further time as the court may allow.

(4)   No plaintiff or complainant shall be entitled to a judgment by default under this section until the expiration of 30 days from the date of the filing of the affidavit of compliance.

(5)   Nothing in this section contained shall limit or abridge the right to serve any process, notice or demand upon any insurer in any other manner now or hereafter permitted by law.

(c)   Defense of Action by Unauthorized Insurer. -

(1)   Before any unauthorized foreign or alien insurer shall file or cause to be filed any pleading in any action, suit or proceeding instituted against it, such unauthorized insurer shall either

a.   Deposit with the clerk of the court in which such action, suit or proceeding is pending cash or securities or file with such clerk a bond with good and sufficient sureties, to be approved by the court, in an amount to be fixed by the court sufficient to secure the payment of any final judgment which may be rendered in such action; or

b.   Procure a license to transact the business of insurance in this State.

(2)   The court in any action, suit, or proceeding, in which service is made in the manner provided in subdivisions (2) or (3) of subsection (b) may, in its discretion, order such postponement as may be necessary to afford the defendant reasonable opportunity to comply with the provisions of subdivision (1) of this subsection and to defend such action.

(3)   Nothing in subdivision (1) of this subsection is to be construed to prevent an unauthorized foreign or alien insurer from filing a motion to quash a writ or to set aside service thereof made in the manner provided in subdivisions (2) or (3) of subsection (b) on the ground either

a.   That such unauthorized insurer has not done any of the acts enumerated in subdivision (1) of subsection (b), or

b. That the person on whom service was made pursuant to subdivision (3) of subsection (b) was not doing any of the acts therein enumerated.

(d) Attorney Fees. - In any action against an unauthorized foreign or alien insurer upon a contract of insurance issued or delivered in this State to a resident thereof or to a corporation authorized to do business therein, if the insurer has failed for 30 days after demand prior to the commencement of the action to make payment in accordance with the terms of the contract, and it appears to the court that such refusal was vexatious and without reasonable cause, the court may allow to the plaintiff a reasonable attorney fee and include such fee in any judgment that may be rendered in such action; providing, however, that the fee or portion of fee included in the judgment shall be not less than twenty-five dollars ($25.00) nor more than twelve and one-half percent (12 1/2%) of the amount which the court or jury finds the plaintiff is entitled to recover against the insurer. Failure of an insurer to defend any such action shall be deemed prima facie evidence that its failure to make payment was vexatious and without reasonable cause.

(e) Short Title. - This section may be cited as the Unauthorized Insurers Process Act. (1955, c. 1040; 1985, c. 666, ss. 5, 8; 1987, c. 752, s. 11; 1989, c. 645, s. 3; 1991, c. 720, s. 4; 1999-132, s. 9.1.)

§ 58-16-40. Alternative service of process on insurers.

In addition to the procedures set out in Articles 1 through 64 of this Chapter, insurers may be served with process and subjected to the jurisdiction of the courts of this State pursuant to applicable provisions of Chapter 1 and Chapter 1A of the General Statutes. (1967, c. 954, s. 3.)

§ 58-16-45. Commissioner to notify company of service or acceptance of service of process.

When service of legal process is made in the manner provided in G.S. 58-16-30, the Commissioner or his duly appointed deputy shall within four business days thereafter notify the company served of such service or acceptance of service by registered or certified mail directed to its secretary, or its resident manager in the case of a foreign company having no secretary in the United States. Such notification shall be accompanied by a copy of the process served or accepted and any pleading or order accompanying the process. The Commissioner shall keep a record which shall show the day and hour of such service or acceptance of service of process and whether any pleading or order accompanied the process. When service is made under the provisions of G.S. 58-16-30, the time within which to file a responsive pleading, as provided by Chapter 1A of the General Statutes, shall be deemed extended by 12 days. (1899, c. 54, s. 16; Rev., s. 4751; C.S., s. 6415; 1927, c. 167, s. 2; 1971, c. 421, s. 2; 1985, c. 666, s. 7; 1987, c. 752, s. 11; 1991, c. 720, s. 4.)

§ 58-16-50. Action to enforce compliance with this Chapter.

Compliance with the provisions of Articles 1 through 64 of this Chapter as to deposits, obligations, and prohibitions, and the payment of taxes, fines, fees, and penalties by foreign or alien insurance companies, may be enforced in the ordinary course of legal procedure by action brought in the Superior Court of Wake County by the Attorney General in the name of the State upon the relation of the Commissioner of Insurance. (1899, c. 54, s. 102; 1903, c. 438, s. 10; Rev., s. 4752; C.S., s. 6416; 1945, c. 384.)

§ 58-16-55. Amendments to documents.

Any change in or amendment to any document required to be filed under G.S. 58-16-5 shall be promptly filed with the Commissioner. (1989, c. 485, s. 49.)

Article 17.

"Lloyds" Insurance Associations.

§ 58-17-1. "Lloyds" insurance associations may transact business of insurance other than life, on certain conditions.

Associations of individuals, whether organized within the State or elsewhere, formed upon the plan known as "Lloyds" - whereby each associate underwriter becomes liable for a proportionate part of the whole amount insured by policy - may be authorized to transact business of insurance, other than life, in this State, in like manner and upon the same terms and conditions as are required of and imposed upon insurance companies regularly organized; but all such "Lloyds" whether organized within the State or elsewhere, shall make the same deposit, and upon the same terms and conditions as required by Articles 5 and 16 of this Chapter for foreign or alien insurance companies incorporated under the laws of any government or state other than the United States or one of the several states of the Union. Provided, such associations shall be subject to all of the laws and regulations of the State of North Carolina relating to the transaction of insurance business within this State. (1967, c. 844.)

Article 18.

Promoting and Holding Companies.

§§ 58-18-1 through 58-18-25: Repealed by Session Laws 2001-223, s. 15, effective June 15, 2001.

Article 19.

Insurance Holding Company System Regulatory Act.

§ 58-19-1. Findings; purpose; legislative intent.

(a) The General Assembly finds that the public interest and the interests of policyholders are or may be adversely affected when any of the following occur:

(1) Control of an insurer is sought by persons who would utilize such control adversely to the interests of policyholders.

(2) Acquisition of control of an insurer would substantially lessen competition or create a monopoly in the insurance business in this State.

(3) An insurer that is part of a holding company system is caused to enter into transactions or relationships with affiliated companies on terms that are not fair and reasonable.

(4) An insurer pays dividends to shareholders that jeopardize the financial condition of such insurer.

(b) The General Assembly declares that the policies and purposes of this Article are to promote the public interest by doing all of the following:

(1) Requiring disclosure of pertinent information relating to changes in control of an insurer.

(2) Requiring disclosure by an insurer of material transactions and relationships between the insurer and its affiliates, including certain dividends to shareholders paid by the insurer.

(3) Providing standards governing material transactions between an insurer and its affiliates. (1989, c. 722, s. 1.)

§ 58-19-2. Compliance with federal law.

(a) As used in this section, "depository institution" has the same meaning as in section 3 of the Federal Deposit Insurance Act, 12 U.S.C. § 1813, and includes any foreign bank that maintains a branch, an agency, or a commercial lending company in the United States.

(b) With respect to affiliations between a depository institution or any affiliate of a depository institution and any insurer, the provisions of section 104(c) of the Gramm-Leach-Bliley Act, P.L. 106-102, shall apply to this Article. (2001-215, s. 2.)

§ 58-19-5. Definitions.

As used in this Article, unless the context requires otherwise, the following terms have the following meanings:

(1) An "affiliate" of or person "affiliated" with a specific person is a person that indirectly through one or more intermediaries or directly controls, is controlled by, or is under common control with the person specified.

(2) "Control", including the terms "controlling", "controlled by", and "under common control with", means the direct or indirect possession of the power to direct or cause the direction of the management and policies of a person, whether through the ownership of voting securities, by contract other than a commercial contract for goods or nonmanagement services, or otherwise. Control is presumed to exist if any person directly or indirectly owns, controls, holds with the power to vote, or holds proxies representing, ten percent (10%) or more of the voting securities of any other person. This presumption may be rebutted by a showing made in the manner provided by G.S. 58-19-25(j) that control does not exist in fact. The Commissioner may determine, after furnishing all persons in interest notice and opportunity to be heard and making specific findings of fact to support such determination, that control exists in fact, notwithstanding the absence of a presumption to that effect.

(3) "Insurance holding company system" means an entity comprising two or more affiliated persons, one or more of which is an insurer.

(4) "Insurer" includes a person subject to Articles 65 and 66 or 67 of this Chapter. "Insurer" does not include (1) an agency, authority, or instrumentality of the United States; any of its possessions and territories; the Commonwealth of Puerto Rico; the District of Columbia; nor a state or political subdivision of a state; nor (2) fraternal benefit societies or fraternal orders.

(5) "Person" means an individual, corporation, partnership, limited liability company, association, joint stock company, trust, unincorporated organization, or any similar entity or any combination of the foregoing acting in concert.

(6) A "security holder" of a specified person is one who owns any security of such person, including common stock, preferred stock, debt obligations, or any other security convertible into or evidencing the right to acquire any of the foregoing.

(7) A "subsidiary" of a specified person is an affiliate controlled by such person indirectly through one or more intermediaries or directly.

(8) "Voting security" includes any security convertible into or evidencing a right to acquire a voting security. (1989, c. 722, s. 1; 1995, c. 517, ss. 9, 10; 2001-223, s. 16.1.)

§ 58-19-10. Subsidiaries of insurers.

(a) Any domestic insurer, either by itself or in cooperation with one or more persons, may organize or acquire one or more subsidiaries engaged in the following kinds of business:

(1) Any kind of insurance business authorized by the jurisdiction in which it is incorporated.

(2) Acting as an insurance broker or as an insurance agent for its parent or for any of its parent's insurer subsidiaries.

(3) Investing, reinvesting, or trading in securities for its own account, that of its parent, any subsidiary of its parent, or any affiliate or subsidiary.

(4) Management of any investment company subject to or registered pursuant to the federal Investment Company Act of 1940, as amended, including related sales and services.

(5) Acting as a broker-dealer subject to or registered pursuant to the federal Securities Exchange Act of 1934, as amended.

(6) Rendering investment advice to governments, government agencies, corporations, or other organizations or groups.

(7) Rendering other services related to the operations of an insurance business, including actuarial, loss prevention, safety engineering, data processing, accounting, claims, appraisal, and collection services.

(8) Ownership and management of assets that the parent corporation could itself own or manage.

(9) Acting as an administrative agent for a governmental instrumentality that is performing an insurance function.

(10) Financing of insurance premiums, agents, and other forms of consumer financing.

(11) Any other business activity that is reasonably ancillary to an insurance business.

(12) Owning a corporation or corporations engaged or organized to engage exclusively in one or more of the businesses specified in this section.

(b) In addition to investments in common stock, preferred stock, debt obligations, and other securities permitted under this Chapter, a domestic insurer may also:

(1) Invest, in common stock, preferred stock, debt obligations, and other securities of one or more subsidiaries, amounts that do not exceed the lesser of ten percent (10%) of the insurer's admitted assets or fifty percent (50%) of the insurer's policyholders' surplus, provided that after those investments, the insurer's policyholders' surplus will be reasonable in relation to the insurer's outstanding liabilities and adequate to its financial needs. In calculating the amount of the investments, investments in domestic or foreign insurance subsidiaries and health maintenance organizations shall be excluded, and there shall be included: (i) total net monies or other consideration expended and obligations assumed in the acquisition or formation of a subsidiary, including all organizational expenses and contributions to capital and surplus of the subsidiary whether or not represented by the purchase of capital stock or issuance of other securities; and (ii) all amounts expended in acquiring additional common stock, preferred stock, debt obligations, and other securities, and all contributions to the capital or surplus, of a subsidiary subsequent to its acquisition or formation;

(2) Invest any amount in common stock, preferred stock, debt obligations and other securities of one or more subsidiaries engaged or organized to engage exclusively in the ownership and management of assets authorized as investments for the insurer; provided that such subsidiary agrees to limit its investments in any asset so that such investments will not cause the amount of the total investment of the insurer to exceed any of the investment limitations specified in subdivision (b)(1) of this section or in Article 7 of this Chapter applicable to the insurer. For the purposes of this section, "the total investment of the insurer" includes: (i) any direct investment by the insurer in an asset; and (ii) the insurer's proportionate share of any investment in an asset by any

subsidiary of the insurer, which shall be calculated by multiplying the amount of the subsidiary's investment by the percentage of the ownership of such subsidiary.

(3) With the approval of the Commissioner, invest any greater amount in common stock, preferred stock, debt obligations, or other securities of one or more subsidiaries; provided that after such investment the insurer's policyholders' surplus will be reasonable in relation to the insurer's outstanding liabilities and adequate to its financial needs.

(c) Investments in common stock, preferred stock, debt obligations, or other securities of subsidiaries made pursuant to subsection (b) of this section are not subject to any of the otherwise applicable restrictions or prohibitions contained in this Chapter applicable to such investments of insurers.

(d) Whether any investment pursuant to subsection (b) of this section meets the applicable requirements of that subsection is to be determined, before such investment is made, by calculating the applicable investment limitations as though the investment had already been made, taking into account the then outstanding principal balance on all previous investments in debt obligations, and the value of all previous investments in equity securities as of the day they were made, net of any return of capital invested, not including dividends.

(e) If an insurer ceases to control a subsidiary, it shall dispose of any investment therein made pursuant to this section within three years from the time of the cessation of control or within such further time as the Commissioner may prescribe, (i) unless after cessation of control such investment meets the requirements for investment under any other provision of Articles 1 through 64 of this Chapter, or (ii) unless the Commissioner authorizes the insurer to continue the investment. (1989, c. 722, s. 1; 1993, c. 504, s. 11; 2001-223, ss. 16.2, 16.3, 16.4.)

§ 58-19-15. Acquisition of control of or merger with domestic insurer.

(a) No person other than the issuer shall make a tender offer for or a request or invitation for tenders of, or enter into any agreement to exchange securities, or seek to acquire, or acquire, in the open market or otherwise, any voting security of a domestic insurer, if, after the consummation thereof, the person would, directly or indirectly (or by conversion or by exercise of any right to acquire), be in control of the insurer, and no person shall enter into an agreement to merge with or otherwise to acquire control of a domestic insurer or any person controlling a domestic insurer unless the offer, request, invitation, agreement, or acquisition is conditioned upon the approval of the Commissioner under this section. No such merger or other acquisition of control is effective until a statement containing the information required by this section has been filed with the Commissioner and all other provisions of this section have been complied with and the merger or acquisition of control has been approved by the Commissioner under this section. The statement containing the information required by this section shall also be filed with the domestic insurer when it is filed with the Commissioner.

(a1)   For the purposes of this section a "domestic insurer" includes any person controlling a domestic insurer. Further, for the purposes of this section, "person" does not include any securities broker holding, in the usual and customary broker's function, less than twenty percent (20%) of the voting securities of an insurance company or of any person that controls an insurance company.

(a2)   Any acquisition of control of a domestic insurer must be completed not later than 90 days after the date of the Commissioner's order approving the acquisition under this section, unless the Commissioner grants an extension in writing on a showing of good cause for the delay. Any increase in a company's capital and surplus required under this Article as a result of the change of control of a domestic insurer must be completed not later than 90 days after the date of the Commissioner's order approving the change of control and before the company writes any new insurance business.

(a3)   If the deadlines for completion in subsection (a2) of this section are not met, the person seeking to acquire control of the domestic insurer must resubmit the statement required by subsection (b) of this section, and the Commissioner may reconsider approval of acquisition of control under this section.

(b)   The statement to be filed with the Commissioner under subsection (a) of this section shall be made under oath or affirmation and shall contain the following information:

(1)   The name and address of each person by whom or on whose behalf the merger or other acquisition of control referred to in subsection (a) of this section is to be effected (hereinafter called "acquiring party"), and: (i) if such person is

an individual, his principal occupation and all offices and positions held during the past five years, and any conviction of crimes other than minor traffic violations during the past 10 years; (ii) if such person is not an individual, a report of the nature of its business operations during the past five years or for such lesser period as such person and any predecessors thereof shall have been in existence; an informative description of the business intended to be done by such person and such person's subsidiaries; and a list of all individuals who are or who have been selected to become directors or executive officers of such person, or who perform or will perform functions appropriate to such positions. Such list shall include for each such individual the information required by sub-subdivision (1)(i) of this subsection.

(2) The source, nature, and amount of the consideration used or to be used in effecting the merger or other acquisition of control; a description of any transaction wherein funds were or are to be obtained for any such purpose, including any pledge of the insurer's stock, or the stock of any of its subsidiaries or controlling affiliates; and the identity of persons furnishing such consideration; provided, however, that where a source of such consideration is a loan made in the lender's ordinary course of business, the identity of the lender shall remain confidential, if the person filing such statement so requests.

(3) Fully audited financial information as to the earnings and financial condition of each acquiring party for the preceding five fiscal years of each such acquiring party, or for such lesser period as such acquiring party and any predecessors thereof have been in existence; and similar unaudited information as of a date not earlier than 90 days prior to the filing of the statement.

(4) Any plans or proposals that each acquiring party may have to liquidate such insurer, to sell its assets or merge or consolidate it with any person, or to make any other material change in its business or corporate structure or management.

(5) The number of shares of any security referred to in subsection (a) of this section that each acquiring party proposes to acquire; the terms of the offer, request, invitation, agreement, or acquisition referred to in subsection (a) of this section; and a statement as to the method by which the fairness of the proposal was arrived at.

(6) The amount of each class of any security referred to in subsection (a) of this section that is beneficially owned or concerning which there is a right to acquire beneficial ownership by each acquiring party.

(7) A full description of any contracts, arrangements, or understandings with respect to any security referred to in subsection (a) of this section in which any acquiring party is involved, including transfer of any of the securities, joint ventures, loan or option arrangements, puts or calls, guarantees of loans, guarantees against loss or guarantees of profits, division of losses or profits, or the giving or withholding of proxies. Such description shall identify the persons with whom such contracts, arrangements, or understandings have been entered into.

(8) A description of the purchase of any security referred to in subsection (a) of this section during the 12 calendar months preceding the filing of the statement, by any acquiring party, including the dates of purchase, names of the purchasers, and consideration paid or agreed to be paid therefor.

(9) A description of any recommendations to purchase any security referred to in subsection (a) of this section made during the 12 calendar months preceding the filing of the statement, by any acquiring party, or by anyone based upon interviews or at the suggestion of such acquiring party.

(10) Copies of all tender offers for, requests, or invitations for tenders of, exchange offers for, and agreements to acquire or exchange any securities referred to in subsection (a) of this section, and any related additional soliciting material that has been distributed.

(11) The term of any agreement, contract, or understanding made with or proposed to be made with any third party in connection with any acquisition of control of or merger with a domestic insurer, and the amount of any fees, commissions, or other compensation to be paid to the third party with regard thereto.

(12) Such additional information as the Commissioner may by rule prescribe as necessary or appropriate for the protection of policyholders of the insurer or in the public interest.

If the person required to file the statement referred to in subsection (a) of this section is a partnership, limited partnership, syndicate, or other group, the Commissioner shall require that the information called for by subdivisions (1) through (12) of this subsection be given with respect to each partner of such partnership or limited partnership, each member of such syndicate or group, and each person who controls such partner or member. If any such partner, member, or person is a corporation or the person required to file the statement referred to in subsection (a) of this section is a corporation, the Commissioner shall require that the information called for by subdivisions (1) through (12) of this subsection be given with respect to such corporation, each officer and director of such corporation, and each person who is, directly or indirectly, the beneficial owner of more than ten percent (10%) of the outstanding voting securities of such corporation.

If any material change occurs in the facts set forth in the statement filed with the Commissioner and sent to such insurer pursuant to this section, an amendment setting forth such change, together with copies of all documents and other material relevant to such change, shall be filed with the Commissioner and sent to such insurer by the filer within two business days after the person learns of such change.

(c)   If any offer, request, invitation, agreement, or acquisition referred to in subsection (a) of this section is proposed to be made by means of a registration statement under the Federal Securities Act of 1933, in circumstances requiring the disclosure of similar information under the Federal Securities Exchange Act of 1934, or under any State law requiring similar registration or disclosure, the person required to file the statement referred to in subsection (a) may utilize such documents in furnishing the information called for by that statement.

(d)   The Commissioner shall approve any merger or other acquisition of control referred to in subsection (a) of this section unless, after a public hearing thereon, he finds any of the following:

(1)   After the change of control, the domestic insurer referred to in subsection (a) of this section would not be able to satisfy the requirements for the issuance of a license to write the kind or kinds of insurance for which it is presently licensed.

(2)   The effect of the merger or other acquisition of control would be substantially to lessen competition in insurance or tend to create a monopoly in this State.

(3)   The financial condition of any acquiring party might jeopardize the financial stability of the insurer or prejudice the interest of its policyholders.

(4)   Any plans or proposals that the acquiring party has to liquidate the insurer, sell its assets or consolidate or merge it with any person, or to make

any other material change in its business or corporate structure or management, are unfair and unreasonable to policyholders of the insurer and not in the public interest.

(5)   The competence, experience, and integrity of those persons who would control the operation of the insurer are such that it would not be in the interests of policyholders of the insurer and of the public to permit the merger or other acquisition of control.

(6)   The acquisition is likely to be hazardous or prejudicial to the insurance-buying public.

(e)   The public hearing referred to in subsection (d) of this section shall be held within 120 days after the statement required by subsection (a) of this section is filed, and the Commissioner shall give at least 30 days notice of the hearing to the person filing the statement, to the insurer, and to such other persons as may be designated by the Commissioner. The Commissioner shall make a determination as expeditiously as is reasonably practicable after the conclusion of the hearing. At the hearing, the person filing the statement, the insurer, any person to whom notice of hearing was sent, and any other person whose interest may be affected by the hearing shall have the right to present evidence, examine and cross-examine witnesses, and offer oral or written arguments; and in connection therewith shall be entitled to conduct discovery proceedings at any time after the statement is filed with the Commissioner under this section and in the same manner as is presently allowed in the superior courts of this State. In connection with discovery proceedings authorized by this section, the Commissioner may issue such protective orders and other orders governing the timing and scheduling of discovery proceedings as might otherwise have been issued by a superior court of this State in connection with a civil proceeding. If any party fails to make reasonable and adequate response to discovery on a timely basis or fails to comply with any order of the Commissioner with respect to discovery, the Commissioner on the Commissioner's own motion or on motion of any other party or person may order that the hearing be postponed, recessed, convened, or reconvened, as the case may be, following proper completion of discovery and reasonable notice to the person filing the statement, to the insurer, and to such other persons as may be designated by the Commissioner.

(f)   The Commissioner may retain, at the acquiring person's expense, any attorneys, actuaries, economists, accountants, or other experts not otherwise a part of the Commissioner's staff as may be reasonably necessary to assist the Commissioner in reviewing the proposed acquisition of control.

(g) The expenses of mailing any notices and other materials required by this section shall be borne by the person making the filing. As security for the payment of such expenses, such person shall file with the Commissioner an acceptable bond or other deposit in an amount to be determined by the Commissioner.

(h) The provisions of this section do not apply to any offer, request, invitation, agreement, or acquisition that the Commissioner by order exempts therefrom as (i) not having been made or entered into for the purpose and not having the effect of changing or influencing the control of a domestic insurer, or (ii) as otherwise not comprehended within the purposes of this section. Any acquisition of stock of a former domestic mutual insurer by a parent company that occurs in connection with the conversion of a mutual insurer to a stock insurer under G.S. 58-10-10 is not subject to this section, provided that no person acquires control of the parent company.

(i) The following are violations of this section:

(1) The failure to file any statement, amendment, or other material required to be filed pursuant to subsection (a) or (b) of this section; or

(2) The effectuation or any attempt to effectuate an acquisition of control of or merger with a domestic insurer, unless the Commissioner has given his approval thereto.

(j) The courts of this State are vested with jurisdiction over every person not resident, domiciled, or authorized to do business in this State who files a statement with the Commissioner under this section; and each such person is deemed to have performed acts equivalent to and constituting an appointment by such person of the Commissioner to be his true and lawful attorney upon whom may be served all legal process in any action, suit, or proceeding arising out of violations of this section. Copies of all such process shall be handled in accordance with the provisions of G.S. 58-16-30, 58-16-35, and 58-16-45. (1989, c. 722, s. 1; 1991, c. 681, ss. 31, 32; c. 720, s. 17; 1993, c. 452, ss. 26-29; c. 504, s. 12; c. 553, s. 16; 1995, c. 517, ss. 11, 12; 2001-223, s. 16.5.)

§ 58-19-17. Foreign or alien insurer's report of change of control.

(a) As used in this section, "controlling capital stock" means enough of an insurer's shares of the issued and outstanding stock, as defined in G.S. 58-19-5(2), to give its owner the power to exercise a controlling influence over the management or policies of the insurer.

(b) If there is a change in the controlling capital stock or a change of twenty-five percent (25%) or more of the assets of a foreign or alien insurer, the insurer shall report the change in writing to the Commissioner within 30 days after the effective date of the change. The report shall be in a form prescribed by the Commissioner and shall contain the name and address of the new owners of the controlling stock or assets, the nature and value of the new assets, and other relevant information that the Commissioner requires. (1991, c. 681, s. 38.)

§ 58-19-20: Repealed by Session Laws 1993, c. 452, s. 65.

§ 58-19-25. Registration of insurers.

(a) Every insurer that is licensed to do business in this State and that is a member of an insurance holding company system shall register with the Commissioner, except a foreign insurer subject to the registration requirements and standards adopted by statute or regulation in the jurisdiction of its domicile that are substantially similar to those contained in:

(1) This section.

(2) G.S. 58-19-30(a), G.S. 58-19-30(c), and G.S. 58-19-30(d).

(3) G.S. 58-19-30(b) or a statutory or regulatory provision such as the following: Each registered insurer shall keep current the information required to be disclosed in its registration statement by reporting all material changes or additions within 15 days after the end of the month in which it learns of each change or addition. The insurer shall also file a copy of its registration statement and any amendments to the statement in each state in which that insurer is authorized to do business, if requested by the insurance regulator of that state.

Any insurer that is subject to registration under this section shall register within 30 days after it becomes subject to registration, and an amendment to the registration statement shall be filed by April 1 of each year for the previous calendar year; unless the Commissioner for good cause shown extends the time for registration or filing, and then within the extended time. All registration statements shall contain a summary, on a form prescribed by the Commissioner, outlining all items in the current registration statement representing changes from the prior registration statement. The Commissioner may require any insurer that is a member of a holding company system that is not subject to registration under this section to furnish a copy of the registration statement or other information filed by the insurance company with the insurance regulator of its domiciliary jurisdiction.

(b)   Every insurer subject to registration shall file the registration statement on a form prescribed by the Commissioner, which shall contain the following current information:

(1)   The bylaws, capital structure, general financial condition, ownership, and management of the insurer and any person controlling the insurer.

(2)   The identity and relationship of every member of the insurance holding company system.

(3)   The following agreements in force, and transactions currently outstanding or that have occurred during the last calendar year between such insurer and its affiliates:

a.   Loans, other investments, or purchases, sales or exchanges of securities of the affiliates by the insurer or of the insurer by its affiliates.

b.   Purchases, sales, or exchange of assets.

c.   Transactions not in the ordinary course of business.

d.   Guarantees or undertakings for the benefit of an affiliate that result in an actual contingent exposure of the insurer's assets to liability, other than insurance contracts entered into in the ordinary course of the insurer's business.

e.   All management agreements, service contracts, and cost-sharing arrangements.

f. Reinsurance agreements.

g. Dividends and other distributions to shareholders.

h. Consolidated tax allocation agreements.

(4) Any pledge of the insurer's stock, including stock of any subsidiary or controlling affiliate, for a loan made to any member of the insurance holding company system.

(5) Other matters concerning transactions between registered insurers and any affiliates as may be included from time to time in any registration forms adopted or approved by the Commissioner.

(c) No information need be disclosed on the registration statement filed pursuant to subsection (b) of this section if such information is not material for the purposes of this section. Unless the Commissioner by rule or order provides otherwise, all sales, purchases, exchanges, loans or extensions of credit, investments, or guarantees involving one-half of one percent (1/2%) or less of an insurer's admitted assets as of the preceding December 31 are not material for the purposes of this section.

(d) Subject to G.S. 58-7-130(b) and G.S. 58-19-30(c), each domestic insurer shall report to the Commissioner all dividends and other distributions to shareholders within five business days following the declaration thereof and at least 30 days before the payment thereof. The Commissioner may adopt rules to further the requirements of this section.

(e) Any person within an insurance holding company system subject to registration shall provide complete and accurate information to an insurer, where such information is reasonably necessary to enable the insurer to comply with the provisions of this Article.

(f) The Commissioner shall terminate the registration of any insurer that demonstrates that it no longer is a member of an insurance holding company system.

(g) The Commissioner may require or allow two or more affiliated insurers subject to registration under this section to file a consolidated registration statement.

(h)   The Commissioner may allow an insurer that is authorized to do business in this State and that is part of an insurance holding company system to register on behalf of any affiliated insurer that is required to register under subsection (a) of this section and to file all information and material required to be filed under this section.

(i)   The provisions of this section do not apply to any insurer, information, or transaction if and to the extent that the Commissioner by rule or order exempts the same from the provisions of this section.

(j)   Any person may file with the Commissioner a disclaimer of affiliation with any authorized insurer, or such a disclaimer may be filed by such insurer or any member of an insurance holding company system. The disclaimer shall fully disclose all material relationships and bases for affiliation between such person and such insurer as well as the basis for disclaiming such affiliation. After a disclaimer has been filed, the insurer shall be relieved of any duty to register or report under this section that may arise out of the insurer's relationship with such person unless the Commissioner disallows such a disclaimer. The Commissioner shall disallow such a disclaimer only after furnishing all parties in interest with notice and opportunity to be heard and after making specific findings of fact to support such disallowance.

(k)   The failure to file a registration statement or any summary of the registration statement thereto required by this section within the time specified for such filing is a violation of this section. (1989, c. 722, s. 1; 1991, c. 681, ss. 33, 34; 1993, c. 452, ss. 30-32; c. 504, s. 13; 1993 (Reg. Sess., 1994), c. 678, s. 14; 1995, c. 193, s. 26; 2001-223, s. 16.6; 2006-105, s. 3.2.)

§ 58-19-30. Standards and management of an insurer within a holding company system.

(a)   Transactions within a holding company system to which an insurer subject to registration is a party are subject to all of the following standards:

(1)   The terms shall be fair and reasonable.

(2)   Charges or fees for services performed shall be reasonable.

(3) Expenses incurred and payment received shall be allocated to the insurer in conformity with customary insurance accounting practices consistently applied.

(4) The books, accounts, and records of each party to all such transactions shall be so maintained as to clearly and accurately disclose the nature and details of the transactions, including such accounting information as is necessary to support the reasonableness of the charges or fees to the respective parties.

(5) The insurer's surplus as regards policyholders following any dividends or distributions to shareholder affiliates shall be reasonable in relation to the insurer's outstanding liabilities and adequate to its financial needs.

(b) The following transactions involving a domestic insurer and any person in its holding company system may not be entered into unless the insurer has notified the Commissioner in writing of its intention to enter into the transaction at least 30 days before the transaction, or such shorter period as the Commissioner permits, and the Commissioner has not disapproved it within that period:

(1) Sales, purchases, exchanges, loans or extensions of credit, or investments, provided the transactions equal or exceed: (i) with respect to nonlife insurers, the lesser of three percent (3%) of the insurer's admitted assets or twenty-five percent (25%) of surplus as regards policyholders; (ii) with respect to life insurers, three percent (3%) of the insurer's admitted assets; each as of the preceding December 31.

(2) Loans or extensions of credit to any person who is not affiliated, where the insurer makes the loans or extensions of credit with the agreement or understanding that the proceeds of the transactions, in whole or in substantial part, are to be used to make loans or extensions of credit to, to purchase assets of, or to make investments in, any affiliate of the insurer making the loans or extensions of credit provided the transactions equal or exceed: (i) with respect to nonlife insurers, the lesser of three percent (3%) of the insurer's admitted assets or twenty-five percent (25%) of surplus as regards policyholders; (ii) with respect to life insurers, three percent (3%) of the insurer's admitted assets; each as of the preceding December 31.

(3) Reinsurance agreements or modifications to the agreements in which the reinsurance premium or a change in the insurer's liabilities equals or

exceeds five percent (5%) of the insurer's surplus as regards policyholders, as of the preceding December 31, including those agreements that may require as consideration the transfer of assets from an insurer to a nonaffiliate, if an agreement or understanding exists between the insurer and nonaffiliate that any portion of the assets will be transferred to one or more affiliates of the insurer.

(4)   All management agreements, service contracts, guarantees, or cost-sharing arrangements.

(5)   Any material transactions, specified by rule, that the Commissioner determines may adversely affect the interests of the insurer's policyholders.

Nothing in this section authorizes or permits any transactions that, in the case of an insurer, not a member of the same holding company system, would be otherwise contrary to law. A domestic insurer may not enter into transactions that are part of a plan or series of like transactions with persons within the holding company system if the purpose of those separate transactions is to avoid the statutory threshold amount and thus avoid the review that would otherwise occur. If the Commissioner determines that such separate transactions were entered into over any 12-month period for that purpose, the Commissioner may exercise the Commissioner's authority under G.S. 58-19-50. The Commissioner, in reviewing transactions pursuant to this subsection, shall consider whether the transactions comply with the standards set forth in subsection (a) of this section and whether they may adversely affect the interests of policyholders. The Commissioner shall be notified within 30 days after any investment of a domestic insurer in any one corporation if, as a result of the investment, the total investment in the corporation by the insurance holding company system exceeds ten percent (10%) of the corporation's voting securities.

(c)   No domestic insurer shall pay any extraordinary dividend or make any other extraordinary distribution to its shareholders until (i) 30 days after the Commissioner has received notice of the declaration thereof and has not within that period disapproved the payment or (ii) the Commissioner has approved the payment within the 30-day period.

For the purposes of this section, an "extraordinary dividend" or "extraordinary distribution" includes any dividend or distribution of cash or other property, whose fair market value together with that of other dividends or distributions made within the preceding 12 months exceeds the greater of (i) ten percent (10%) of the insurer's surplus as regards policyholders as of the preceding

December 31, or (ii) the net gain from operations of the insurer, if the insurer is a life insurer, or the net income, if the insurer is not a life insurer, not including realized capital gains, for the 12-month period ending the preceding December 31; but does not include pro rata distributions of any class of the insurer's own securities.

Notwithstanding any other provision of law, an insurer may declare an extraordinary dividend or distribution that is conditional upon the Commissioner's approval, and the declaration shall confer no rights upon shareholders until (i) the Commissioner has approved the payment of the dividend or distribution or (ii) the Commissioner has not disapproved the payment within the 30-day period referred to above.

(d)   For the purposes of this Article, in determining whether an insurer's surplus as regards policyholders is reasonable in relation to the insurer's outstanding liabilities and adequate to its financial needs, all of the following factors, among others, shall be considered:

(1)   The size of the insurer as measured by its assets, capital and surplus, reserves, premium writings, insurance in force, and other appropriate criteria.

(2)   The extent to which the insurer's business is diversified among the several kinds of insurance.

(3)   The number and size of risks insured in each kind of insurance.

(4)   The extent of the geographic dispersion of the insurer's insured risks.

(5)   The nature and extent of the insurer's reinsurance program.

(6)   The quality, diversification, and liquidity of the insurer's investment portfolio.

(7)   The recent past and projected future trend in the size of the insurer's surplus as regards policyholders.

(8)   The surplus as regards policyholders maintained by other comparable insurers.

(9)   The adequacy of the insurer's reserves.

(10) The quality and liquidity of investments in affiliates. The Commissioner may treat any such investment as a disallowed asset for purposes of determining the adequacy of surplus as regards policyholders whenever in his judgment such investment so warrants.

(11) The quality of the insurer's earnings and the extent to which the reported earnings of the insurer include extraordinary items. (1989, c. 722, s. 1; 1991, c. 681, ss. 35, 36; c. 720, s. 18; 1993, c. 452, s. 33; 2001-223, s. 16.7; 2005-215, s. 14; 2006-105, ss. 3.3, 3.4.)

§ 58-19-35. Examination.

(a) Subject to the limitation contained in this section and in addition to the powers that the Commissioner has under other provisions of Articles 1 through 64 of this Chapter relating to the examination of insurers, the Commissioner also has the power to order any insurer registered under G.S. 58-19-25 or any acquiring party to produce such records, books, or other information in the possession of the insurer or its affiliates or the acquiring party as are reasonably necessary to ascertain the financial condition of such insurer or acquiring party or to determine compliance with Articles 1 through 64 of this Chapter. In the event such insurer or acquiring party fails to comply with such order, the Commissioner shall have the power to examine such insurer or its affiliates or such acquiring party to obtain such information.

(b) The Commissioner may retain, at the expense of the registered insurer or acquiring party that is being examined, such attorneys, actuaries, economists, accountants, and other experts not otherwise a part of the Commissioner's staff as are reasonably necessary to assist in the conduct of the examination under subsection (a) of this section. Any persons so retained shall be under the direction and control of the Commissioner and shall act in a purely advisory capacity.

(c) Repealed by Session Laws 1995, c. 360, s. 2(h).

(d) The Commissioner shall exercise his power under subsection (a) of this section only if the examination of the insurer or acquiring party under other provisions of Articles 1 through 64 of this Chapter is inadequate or the interests of the policyholders of such insurer may be adversely affected. (1989, c. 722, s. 1; 1995, c. 193, s. 27; c. 360, s. 2(h).)

§ 58-19-40. Confidential treatment.

All information, documents, and copies thereof obtained by or disclosed to the Commissioner or any other person in the course of an examination or investigation made pursuant to G.S. 58-19-35, and all information reported pursuant to G.S. 58-19-25 and G.S. 58-19-30, shall be given confidential treatment; shall not be subject to subpoena; and shall not be made public by the Commissioner, the NAIC, or any other person, except to insurance regulators of other states, without the prior written consent of the insurer or acquiring party to which it pertains unless the Commissioner, after giving the insurer and its affiliates or the acquiring party that would be affected thereby notice and opportunity to be heard, determines that the interest of the insurer's policyholders or the public will be served by the publication thereof, in which event he may publish all or any part thereof in such manner as he considers appropriate. (1989, c. 722, s. 1.)

§ 58-19-45. Injunctions; prohibitions against the voting of securities; sequestration of voting securities.

(a)   Whenever it appears to the Commissioner that any person has committed or is about to commit a violation of this Article or of any rule or order of the Commissioner under this Article, the Commissioner may apply to the Superior Court of Wake County for an order enjoining such person from violating or continuing to violate this Article or any such rule or order; and for such other equitable relief as the nature of the case and the interest of the domestic insurer's policyholders or the public may require.

(b)   No security that is the subject of any agreement or arrangement regarding acquisition, or that is acquired or to be acquired, in contravention of the provisions of this Article or of any rule or order of the Commissioner under this Article, may be voted at any shareholder's meeting nor may be counted for quorum purposes; and any action of shareholders requiring the affirmative vote of a percentage of shares may be taken as though such securities were not issued and outstanding. No action taken at any such meeting shall be invalidated by the voting of such securities, unless the action would materially affect control of the insurer or unless the courts of this State have so ordered. If an insurer or the Commissioner has reason to believe that any security of the insurer has been or is about to be acquired in contravention of the provisions of this Article or of any rule or order issued by the Commissioner under this Article, the insurer or the Commissioner may apply to the Superior Court of Wake County to enjoin any offer, request, invitation, agreement, or acquisition made in contravention of G.S. 58-19-15 or any rule or order of the Commissioner under that section to enjoin the voting of any security so acquired, to void any vote of such security already cast at any meeting of shareholders, and for such other equitable relief as the nature of the case and the interest of the insurer's policyholders or the public may require.

(c) In any case where a person has acquired or is proposing to acquire any voting securities in violation of this Article or any rule or order of the Commissioner under this Article, the Superior Court of Wake County may, on such notice as the court considers appropriate and upon the application of the insurer or the Commissioner, seize or sequester any voting securities of the insurer owned directly or indirectly by the person, and issue an order with respect thereto as may be appropriate to effectuate the provisions of this Article. Notwithstanding any other provision of law, for the purposes of this Article the sites of the ownership of the securities of domestic insurers are in this State. (1989, c. 722, s. 1; 1991, c. 681, s. 37; 1993, c. 452, s. 34.)

§ 58-19-50. Sanctions.

(a) Any person failing, without just cause, to file any registration statement as required in this Article shall pay, after notice and hearing, a civil penalty of one hundred dollars ($100.00) for each day's delay, not to exceed a total penalty of one thousand dollars ($1,000), to the Commissioner. The clear proceeds of civil penalties provided for in this section shall be remitted to the Civil Penalty and Forfeiture Fund in accordance with G.S. 115C-457.2.

(b) Every director or officer of an insurance holding company system who knowingly and willfully violates, participates in, or assents to, or who knowingly and willfully permits any of the officers or agents of the insurer to engage in transactions or make investments that have not been properly reported or submitted pursuant to G.S. 58-19-25(a), 58-19-30(b), or 58-19-30(c), or that violate this Article, shall pay, in his individual capacity, after notice and hearing, a civil penalty of one hundred dollars ($100.00) per violation, not to exceed a total penalty of one thousand dollars ($1,000), to the Commissioner, who shall forward the clear proceeds to the General Fund of this State.

(c) Whenever it appears to the Commissioner that any insurer subject to this Article or any director, officer, employee, or agent thereof has engaged in any transaction or entered into a contract that is subject to G.S. 58-19-30 and that would not have been approved had such approval been requested, the Commissioner may order the insurer to immediately cease and desist from any further activity under that transaction or contract. After notice and hearing the Commissioner may also order the insurer to void any such contracts and restore the status quo if such action is in the best interest of the policyholders, creditors, or the public.

(d) Whenever it appears to the Commissioner that any insurer or any director, officer, employee, or agent thereof has knowingly and willfully committed a violation of this Article, the Commissioner may cause criminal proceedings to be instituted by the Superior Court of Wake County against such insurer or the responsible director, officer, employee, or agent thereof. Any insurer that knowingly and willfully violates this Article may be fined not more than one thousand dollars ($1,000). Any individual who knowingly and willfully violates this Article is guilty of a Class I felony.

(e) Any officer, director, or employee of an insurance holding company system who knowingly and willfully subscribes to or makes or causes to be made any false statements or false reports or false filings with the intent to deceive the Commissioner in the performance of his duties under this Article, is guilty of a Class I felony. Any fines imposed shall be paid by the officer, director, or employee in his individual capacity. (1989, c. 722, s. 1; 1993, c. 504, s. 14; c. 539, ss. 1271, 1272; 1994, Ex. Sess., c. 24, s. 14(c); 1998-215, s. 84.)

§ 58-19-55. Receivership.

Whenever it appears to the Commissioner that any person has committed a violation of this Article that so impairs the financial condition of a domestic insurer as to threaten insolvency or make the further transaction of business by it hazardous to its policyholders, creditors, shareholders, or the public, then the Commissioner may proceed as provided in Article 30 of this Chapter. (1989, c. 722, s. 1.)

§ 58-19-60. Recovery.

(a)   If an order for liquidation or rehabilitation of a domestic insurer has been entered, the receiver appointed under such order has a right to recover on behalf of the insurer, (i) from any parent corporation or holding company or person or affiliate who otherwise controlled the insurer, the amount of distributions (other than distributions of shares of the same class of stock) paid by the insurer on its capital stock, or (ii) any payment in the form of a bonus, termination settlement, or extraordinary lump sum salary adjustment made by the insurer or its subsidiary or subsidiaries to a director, officer, or employee, where the distribution or payment pursuant to (i) or (ii) above is made at any time during the one year preceding the petition for liquidation or rehabilitation, as the case may be, subject to the limitations of subsections (b), (c), and (d) of this section.

(b)   No such distribution is recoverable if the parent or affiliate shows that when paid such distribution was lawful and reasonable, and that the insurer did not know and could not reasonably have known that such distribution might adversely affect the ability of the insurer to fulfill its contractual obligations.

(c)   Any person that was a parent corporation or holding company or a person that otherwise controlled the insurer or affiliate at the time such distributions were paid is liable up to the amount of distributions or payments under subsection (a) of this section such person received. Any person who otherwise controlled the insurer at the time such distributions were declared is liable up to the amount of distributions he would have received if they had been paid immediately. If two or more persons are liable with respect to the same distributions, they are jointly and severally liable.

(d)   The maximum amount recoverable under this section is the amount needed in excess of all other available assets of the insurer to pay its contractual obligations and to reimburse any guaranty funds.

(e)   To the extent that any person liable under subsection (c) of this section is insolvent or otherwise fails to pay claims due from it pursuant to that subsection, its parent corporation, holding company, or person who otherwise controlled it at the time that the distribution was paid, are jointly and severally liable for any resulting deficiency in the amount recovered from such parent corporation or holding company or person who otherwise controlled it. (1989, c. 722, s. 1.)

§ 58-19-65. Revocation or suspension of insurer's license.

Whenever it appears to the Commissioner that any person has committed a violation of this Article that makes the continued operation of an insurer contrary to the interests of policyholders or the public, the Commissioner may, after giving notice and an opportunity to be heard, suspend or revoke such insurer's license to do business in this State for such period as he finds is required for the protection of policyholders or the public. Any such determination shall be accompanied by specific findings of fact and conclusions of law. (1989, c. 722, s. 1; 2003-212, s. 26(f).)

§ 58-19-70. Judicial review; mandatory injunction or writ of mandamus.

(a) Any person aggrieved by any order made by the Commissioner pursuant to this Article may appeal in accordance with G.S. 58-2-75.

(b) Any person aggrieved by any failure of the Commissioner to act or make a determination required by this Article may petition the Superior Court of Wake County for a mandatory injunction or a writ of mandamus directing the Commissioner to act or make such determination forthwith. (1989, c. 722, s. 1.)

Article 20.

Hull Insurance, and Protection and Indemnity Clubs.

§ 58-20-1. Short title.

This Article may be cited as the "Commercial Fishermen's Hull Insurance, and Protection and Indemnity Club Act". (1987, c. 330.)

§ 58-20-5. Definitions.

For purposes of this Article:

(1)   "Association" means a trade or professional association that has been in existence for at least five years, and has adopted a written constitution, and a written set of bylaws, and was created for purposes other than for participating in a club.

(2)   "Club" means a commercial fishermen's hull insurance and protection and indemnity club created under this Article.

(3)   "Commercial fisherman" means any individual, corporation, or other business entity whose earned income is at least fifty percent (50%) derived from taking and selling food resources living in any ocean, bay, river, gulf, estuary, tidal wetlands, spoil area, estuation exit or entrance, or any other body of water or tidal wetlands from which a commercial harvest of fish may be taken.

(4)   "Hull Insurance and Protection and Indemnity" means:

a.   Insurance against loss or damage to a vessel's hull, lifeboats, rafts, and other operating equipment of the vessel other than its electrical machinery; and

b.   Insurance against loss of life, personal injury, or illness to the master, the crew, and other third parties, and against damage to any other vessel or property, such as cargo, for which the insured is legally liable. (1987, c. 330.)

§ 58-20-10. Commercial Fishermen Hull Insurance, and Protection and Indemnity Clubs authorized.

In addition to other authority granted under Articles 1 through 64 of this Chapter, ten or more commercial fishermen who are members of an association may enter into contracts or agreements under this Article for the joint protection and retention of their risk for Hull Insurance, and Protection and Indemnity, and for the payment of losses or claims made against any member. Any group of commercial fishermen intending to organize and operate a Club under this

Article shall give the Commissioner 30 days' advance written notification of its intention in a form prescribed by the Commissioner. (1987, c. 330.)

§ 58-20-15. Board of trustees.

(a)   A Club shall be operated by a board of trustees. Each trustee shall also be a member of an association. The trustees shall be selected by the Club members under the rules of organization of the Club. The board of trustees shall:

(1)   Establish the terms and conditions of hull insurance and protection and indemnity coverage within the Club, including underwriting and exclusions of coverage;

(2)   Ensure that all valid claims are paid promptly;

(3)   Take all necessary precautions to safeguard the assets of the Club;

(4)   Maintain minutes of its meeting and make those minutes available to the Commissioner;

(5)   Designate an administrator to carry out the policies established by the trustees; and

(6)   Establish guidelines for membership in the Club.

(b)   The board of trustees shall not:

(1)   Extend credit to an individual member for payment of a premium, except under a payment plan approved by the Commissioner; or

(2)   Borrow money from the Club, or in the name of the Club, except in the ordinary course of business.

§ 58-20-20. Mutual agreement for indemnification.

(a)   An agreement made under this Article shall contain provisions for:

(1)   A system or program of loss control;

(2) The termination of membership;

(3) The payment by the Club of all claims for which a member incurred liability during the period of his membership;

(4) The non-payment of claims where a member has individually retained the risk, or where the risk is not specifically covered, or where the amount of the claim exceeds the coverage provided by the Club;

(5) The assessment of members;

(6) The payment of contributions from members to satisfy deficiencies;

(7) The maintenance of claim reserves equal to known incurred losses and loss adjustment expenses and to an estimate of incurred but not reported losses; and

(8) Final accounting and settlement of the obligations or refunds to a terminating member when all incurred claims are settled.

(b) The agreement required by this section may also include provisions authorizing the Club to:

(1) To establish offices where necessary in this State, and employ necessary staff to carry out its purposes;

(2) Retain legal counsel, actuaries, claims adjusters, auditors, engineers, private consultants, and advisors, and other persons as the board of trustees or the administrator deem to be necessary;

(3) Amend or repeal its bylaws;

(4) Purchase, lease, or rent real and personal property as it deems necessary; and

(5) Enter into agreements with financial institutions that permit it to issue checks or other negotiable instruments in its own name. (1987, c. 330.)

§ 58-20-25. Termination of Club membership; notice.

If a member fails to pay his contributions calls, or assessment, or other property required by the board of trustees as authorized by this Article, he shall not be entitled to any hull insurance and protection and indemnity coverage under this Article, and the Club may terminate his membership upon giving the member at least 10 days' notice. The Club may terminate a membership for any other reason upon giving the member at least 90 days' written notice of the termination. A member may terminate his membership with the Club upon giving at least 90 days' written notice of the termination. (1987, c. 330.)

§ 58-20-30. Financial monitoring and evaluation of clubs.

Each club shall be audited annually, at the Club's expense, by a certified public accounting firm. A copy of the audit report shall be furnished to each member, and to the Commissioner. The trustees shall obtain an appropriate actuarial evaluation of the loss and loss adjustment expenses reserves of the Club, including estimate of losses and loss adjustment expenses incurred but not reported. The provisions of G.S. 58-2-131 through G.S. 58-2-134, G.S. 58-2-150, 58-2-160, 58-2-165, 58-2-180, 58-2-185, 58-2-190, 58-2-200, and G.S. 58-6-5 apply to each Club and to persons that administer the Clubs. (1987, c. 330, s. 1; 1991, c. 681, s. 5; 1999-132, s. 11.2.)

§ 58-20-35. Insolvency or impairment of Club.

(a) If an annual audit or an examination by the Commissioner reveals that the assets of a Club are insufficient to discharge its legal liabilities and other obligations, the Commissioner shall notify the administrator and board of trustees of the Club's deficiency; and he shall recommend the measures to be taken in order to abate the deficiency. He may recommend that the Club refrain from adding new members until the deficiency is abated. If the Club fails to comply with the recommendations within 30 days after the date of the notice, the Commissioner may apply to the Superior Court of Wake County for an order requiring the Club to abate the deficiency and authorizing the Commissioner to appoint one or more special deputy commissioners, counsel, clerks, or assistants to oversee the implementation of the Court's order. The compensation and expenses of such persons shall be fixed by the

Commissioner, subject to the approval of the Court, and shall be paid out of the funds or assets of the Club.

(b) If a Club is determined to be insolvent, financially impaired, or is otherwise unable to discharge its legal liabilities and other obligations, each member shall be assessed on a pro rata basis as provided under G.S. 58-20-15. (1987, c. 330.)

§ 58-20-40. Immunity of administrators and boards of trustees.

There is no liability on the part of and no cause of action arises against any board of trustees established under this Article, or against any administrator appointed as their representative, or any Club, its members or its employees, agents, contractors, or subcontractors for any good faith action taken by them in the performance of their powers and duties in creating or administering any Club under this Article. (1987, c. 330.)

Article 21.

Surplus Lines Act.

§ 58-21-1. Short title.

This Article shall be known and may be cited as the "Surplus Lines Act". (1985, c. 688, s. 1.)

§ 58-21-2. Relationship to other insurance laws.

Unless surplus lines insurance, surplus lines licensees, or nonadmitted insurers are specifically referenced in a particular section of this Chapter, no sections contained in Articles of this Chapter other than this Article apply to surplus lines insurance, surplus lines licensees, or nonadmitted insurers. (1999-219, s. 6.2.)

§ 58-21-4. Nonadmitted and Reinsurance Reform Act duties.

(a) For the purposes of carrying out the provisions of the Nonadmitted and Reinsurance Reform Act of 2010, the Commissioner is authorized to utilize the national insurance producer database of the NAIC, or any other equivalent uniform national database, for the licensure of an individual or an entity as a surplus lines producer and for renewal of such license.

(b) In order to assist in the performance of the Commissioner's duties, under the Nonadmitted and Reinsurance Reform Act of 2010, the Commissioner may contract with nongovernmental entities, including the NAIC or any affiliates or subsidiaries that the NAIC oversees, to perform any ministerial functions that the Commissioner and the nongovernmental entity may deem to be appropriate, including (i) the collection of fees related to producer licensing and (ii) the collection of the premium tax under G.S. 58-21-85. The NAIC or other entity with whom the Commissioner contracts may charge a reasonable fee to the insurer, insured, or other appropriate person for the functions performed. (2011-120, s. 1.1.)

§ 58-21-5. Purposes; necessity for regulation.

This Article shall be liberally construed and applied to promote its underlying purposes, which include:

(1) Protecting persons in this State seeking insurance;

(2) Permitting surplus lines insurance to be placed with reputable and financially sound nonadmitted insurers and exported from this State pursuant to this Article;

(3) Establishing a system of regulation that will permit orderly access to surplus lines insurance in this State and encourage admitted insurers to provide new and innovative types of insurance available to consumers in this State; and

(4) Protecting revenues of this State. (1985, c. 688, s. 1.)

§ 58-21-10. Definitions.

As used in this Article:

(1) "Admitted insurer" means an insurer licensed to engage in the business of insurance in this State.

(1a) "Affiliate" means, with respect to an insured, any entity that controls, is controlled by, or is under common control with the insured.

(1b) "Affiliated group" means any group of entities that are all affiliated.

(2) "Capital", as used in the financial requirements of G.S. 58-21-20, means funds paid in for stock or other evidence of ownership.

(2a) "Control" means an entity that has "control" over another entity if either of the following occurs:

a. The entity directly or indirectly or acting through one or more other persons owns, controls, or has the power to vote twenty-five percent (25%) or more of any class of voting securities of the other entity.

b. The entity controls in any manner the election of a majority of the directors or trustees of the other entity.

(3) "Eligible surplus lines insurer" means a nonadmitted insurer with which a surplus lines licensee may place surplus lines insurance under G.S. 58-21-20.

(4) "Export" means to place surplus lines insurance with a nonadmitted insurer.

(5) "Nonadmitted insurer" means an insurer not licensed to do an insurance business in this State. "Nonadmitted insurer" includes insurance exchanges authorized under the laws of various states. "Nonadmitted insurer" does not include a risk retention group, as defined in G.S. 58-22-10(10).

(6) "Producing broker" means an agent or broker licensed under Article 33 of this Chapter who deals directly with the party seeking insurance and who may also be a surplus lines licensee.

(6a) "Salary protection insurance" means insurance against financial loss caused by the cessation of earned income because of disability from sickness, ailment, or bodily injury.

(7) "Surplus", as used in the financial requirements of G.S. 58-21-20, means funds over and above liabilities and capital of the company for the protection of policyholders.

(8) "Surplus lines insurance" means any insurance in this State of risks resident, located, or to be performed in this State, permitted to be placed through a surplus lines licensee with a nonadmitted insurer eligible to accept such insurance, including salary protection insurance. The term does not include reinsurance, commercial aircraft insurance, wet marine and transportation insurance, insurance independently procured pursuant to G.S. 58-28-5, life and accident or health insurance, and annuities.

(9) "Surplus lines licensee" means a person licensed under G.S. 58-21-65 to place insurance on risks resident, located, or to be performed in this State with nonadmitted insurers eligible to accept such insurance.

(10) "Wet marine and transportation insurance" means:

a. Insurance upon vessels, crafts, hulls and of interests therein or with relation thereto;

b. Insurance of marine builder's risks, marine war risks and contracts of marine protection and indemnity insurance;

c. Insurance of freights and disbursements pertaining to a subject of insurance coming within this subsection; and

d. Insurance of personal property and interests therein, in the course of exportation from or importation into any country, or in the course of transportation coastwise or on inland waters including transportation by land, water, or air from point of origin to final destination, in connection with any and all risks or perils of navigation, transit or transportation, and while being prepared for and while awaiting shipment, and during any delays, transshipment, or reshipment incident thereto. (1985, c. 688, s. 1; 1985 (Reg. Sess., 1986), c. 1027, s. 45; 1987, c. 629, s. 19; c. 727, s. 6; c. 864, s. 73; 1998-211, s. 3; 1999-219, s. 5.3; 2011-120, s. 2; 2011-370, s. 1.)

§ 58-21-11. Home state.

(a)   The provisions of this Article shall apply to those transactions in which North Carolina is the home state of the insured.

(b)   Except as provided in subsection (c) of this section, the term "home state" means, with respect to an insured, either of the following:

(1)   The state in which an insured maintains its principal place of business or, in the case of an individual, the individual's principal residence.

(2)   If one hundred percent (100%) of the insured risk is located out of the state referred to in subdivision (1) of this subsection, the state to which the greatest percentage of the insured's taxable premium for that insurance contract is allocated.

(c)   Affiliated Groups. - If two or more insureds from an affiliated group are named insureds on a single nonadmitted insurance contract, the term "home state" means the home state, as determined pursuant to subsection (b) of this section, of the member of the affiliated group that has the largest percentage of premium attributed to it under that insurance contract. (2011-120, s. 3.)

§ 58-21-15. Placement of surplus lines insurance.

Surplus lines may be placed by a surplus lines licensee if all of the following apply:

(1)   Each insurer is an eligible surplus lines insurer.

(1a)   Each insurer is authorized to write the kind of insurance in its domiciliary jurisdiction.

(2)   The full amount or kind of insurance cannot be obtained from insurers who are admitted to do business in this State. Such full amount or kind of insurance may be procured from eligible surplus lines insurers, provided that a diligent search is made among the insurers who are admitted to transact and are actually writing the particular kind and class of insurance in this State.

(3) All other requirements of this Article are met. (1985, c. 688, s. 1; 1985 (Reg. Sess., 1986), c. 1013, s. 5; 2011-120, s. 4.)

§ 58-21-16. Streamlined application for commercial purchasers.

(a) A surplus lines licensee seeking to procure or place nonadmitted insurance in this State for an exempt commercial purchaser shall not be required to satisfy any requirement under G.S. 58-21-15 to make a due diligence search to determine whether the full amount or type of insurance sought by such exempt commercial purchaser can be obtained from admitted insurers if all of the following apply:

(1) The licensee procuring or placing the surplus lines insurance has disclosed to the exempt commercial purchaser that such insurance may or may not be available from the admitted market that may provide greater protection with more regulatory oversight.

(2) The exempt commercial purchaser has subsequently requested in writing the licensee to procure or place such insurance from a nonadmitted insurer.

(b) As used in this section, the following definitions apply:

(1) "Exempt commercial purchaser" means any person purchasing commercial insurance that, at the time of placement, meets all of the following requirements:

a. The person employs or retains a qualified risk manager to negotiate insurance coverage.

b. The person has paid aggregate nationwide commercial property and casualty insurance premiums in excess of one hundred thousand dollars ($100,000) in the immediately preceding 12 months.

c. The person meets at least one of the following criteria:

1. The person possesses a net worth in excess of twenty million dollars ($20,000,000), as such amount is adjusted pursuant to subsection (c) of this section.

2. The person generates annual revenues in excess of fifty million dollars ($50,000,000), as such amount is adjusted pursuant to subsection (c) of this section.

3. The person employs more than 500 full-time or full-time equivalent employees per individual insured or is a member of an affiliated group employing more than 1,000 employees in the aggregate.

4. The person is a not-for-profit organization or public entity generating annual budgeted expenditures of at least thirty million dollars ($30,000,000), as such amount is adjusted pursuant to subsection (c) of this section.

5. The person is a municipality with a population in excess of 50,000 persons.

(2) "Qualified risk manager" means, with respect to a policyholder of commercial insurance, a person who meets all of the following requirements:

a. Is an employee of, or third-party consultant retained by, the commercial policyholder.

b. Provides skilled services in loss prevention, loss reduction, or risk and insurance coverage analysis, and purchase of insurance.

c. Has one of the following:

1. A bachelor's degree or higher from an accredited college or university in risk management, business administration, finance, economics, or any other field determined by the Commissioner to demonstrate minimum competence in risk management and one of the following:

I. Three years of experience in risk financing, claims, administration, loss prevention, risk and insurance analysis, or purchasing commercial lines of insurance.

II. One of the following designations:

A. Chartered Property and Casualty Underwriter (CPCU) issued by the American Institute for CPCU/Insurance Institute of America.

B. Associate in Risk Management (ARM) issued by the American Institute for CPCU/Insurance Institute of America.

C. Certified Risk Manager (CRM) issued by the National Alliance for Insurance Education & Research.

D. RIMS Fellow (RF) issued by the Global Risk Management Institute.

E. A designation, certification, or license determined by the Commissioner to demonstrate minimum competency in risk management.

2. Seven years of experience in risk financing, claims administration, loss prevention, risk and insurance coverage analysis, or purchasing commercial lines of insurance; and has any one of the designations specified in sub-sub-sub-sub-subdivisions A. through E. of sub-sub-sub-subdivision II. of this sub-subdivision.

3. Ten years of experience in risk financing, claims administration, loss prevention, risk and insurance coverage analysis, or purchasing commercial lines of insurance.

4. A graduate degree from an accredited college or university in risk management, business administration, finance, economics, or any other field determined by the Commissioner to demonstrate minimum competence in risk management.

(c) Effective on the fifth January 1 occurring after the date of the enactment of this section [July 21, 2011] and each fifth January 1 occurring thereafter, the dollar amounts in sub-sub-subdivisions (b)(1)c.1., 2., 3., and 4. of this section shall be adjusted to reflect the percentage change for such five-year period in the Consumer Price Index for All Urban Consumers published by the Bureau of Labor Statistics of the U.S. Department of Labor. (2011-120, s. 5.)

§ 58-21-17. Placement with alien insurers.

Nothing in this Article prohibits a surplus lines licensee from placing surplus lines insurance with, or procuring surplus lines insurance from, a nonadmitted insurer domiciled outside the United States that is listed on the Quarterly Listing of Alien Insurers maintained by the International Insurers Department of the NAIC. (2011-120, s. 5.)

§ 58-21-20. Eligible surplus lines insurers required.

(a) A surplus lines licensee shall not place coverage with a nonadmitted insurer unless, at the time of placement, the surplus lines licensee has determined that the nonadmitted insurer satisfies the following:

(1) Repealed by Session Laws 2011-120, s. 6, effective July 21, 2011.

(2) Qualifies under one of the following subdivisions:

a. Has capital and surplus or its equivalent under the laws of its domiciliary jurisdiction, which equals the greater of either:

1. This State's minimum capital and surplus requirements under G.S. 58-7-75.

2. Fifteen million dollars ($15,000,000).

The requirements of this sub-subdivision may be satisfied by an insurer's possessing less than the minimum capital and surplus upon an affirmative finding of acceptability by the Commissioner. The finding shall be based upon such factors as quality of management, capital and surplus of any parent company, company underwriting profit and investment income trends, market availability, and company record and reputation within the industry. In no event shall the Commissioner make an affirmative finding of acceptability when the nonadmitted insurer's capital and surplus is less than four million five hundred thousand dollars ($4,500,000).

b. In the case of any Lloyd's plans or other similar group of insurers, which consists of unincorporated individual insurers, or a combination of both unincorporated and incorporated insurers, maintains a trust fund in an amount of not less than one hundred million dollars ($100,000,000) as security to the full amount thereof for all policyholders and creditors in the United States of each member of the group, and the trust shall likewise comply with the terms and conditions established in subdivision (2)a. of this section for alien insurers.

  c. In the case of an "insurance exchange" created by the laws of individual states, maintain capital and surplus, or the substantial equivalent thereof, of not less than seventy-five million dollars ($75,000,000) in the aggregate. For insurance exchanges which maintain funds in an amount of not less than fifteen million dollars ($15,000,000) for the protection of all insurance exchange policyholders, each individual syndicate shall maintain minimum capital and surplus, or the substantial equivalent thereof, of not less than five million dollars ($5,000,000). If the insurance exchange does not maintain funds in an amount of not less than fifteen million dollars ($15,000,000) for the protection of all insurance exchange policyholders, each individual syndicate shall meet the minimum capital and surplus requirements of subdivision (2)a. of this section.

  d. In the case of a group of incorporated insurers under common administration, which has continuously transacted an insurance business outside the United States for at least three years immediately before this time, and which submits to this State's authority to examine its books and records and bears the expense of the examination, and maintains an aggregate policyholders' surplus of not less than ten billion dollars ($10,000,000,000), and maintains in trust a surplus of not less than one hundred million dollars ($100,000,000) for the benefit of United States surplus lines policyholders of any member of the group, and each insurer maintains capital and surplus of not less than twenty-five million dollars ($25,000,000) per company.

(3) Has caused to be provided to the Commissioner a copy of its current annual statement certified by such insurer; such statement to be provided no more than two months, and for alien insurers six months, after the close of the period reported upon and that is either:

  a. Filed with and approved by the regulatory authority in the domicile of the nonadmitted insurer; or

  b. Certified by an accounting or auditing firm licensed in the jurisdiction of the insurer's domicile; or

  c. In the case of an insurance exchange, the statement may be an aggregate combined statement of all underwriting syndicates operating during the period reported.

(b) In addition to meeting the requirements in subdivisions (a)(1) through (a)(3) of this section, an insurer shall be an eligible surplus lines insurer if it appears on the most recent list of eligible surplus lines insurers published by the Commissioner. Nothing in this subsection shall require the Commissioner to place or maintain the name of any nonadmitted insurer on the list of eligible surplus lines insurers. There shall be no liability on the part of, and no cause of action of any nature shall arise against, the Commissioner or his employees or representatives for any action taken or not taken by them in the performance of their powers and duties under this subsection.

(c) Every surplus lines insurer that applies for eligibility under this section shall pay a nonrefundable fee of five hundred dollars ($500.00). In order to renew eligibility, such insurer shall pay a nonrefundable renewal fee of one thousand dollars ($1,000) on or before January 1 of each year thereafter. Such fees shall not be prorated. (1985, c. 688, s. 1; c. 793; 1985 (Reg. Sess., 1986), c. 1027, s. 46; 1989 (Reg. Sess., 1990), c. 1069, s. 13; 1991, c. 681, s. 39; 1993 (Reg. Sess., 1994), c. 678, s. 15; 1995, c. 507, s. 11A(c); 2001-223, s. 17.1; 2009-451, s. 21.14(a); 2011-120, s. 6.)

§ 58-21-22. Limitation on amount of salary protection insurance.

When salary protection insurance benefits are payable to an individual or an individual's beneficiary, the amount of salary protection insurance plus the amount of any in-force disability income insurance, if the individual can obtain disability insurance from an admitted insurer, shall not exceed seventy-five percent (75%) of the individual's annual earned income. As used in this section, "disability income insurance" has the same meaning as "accident and health insurance" in G.S. 58-7-15(3). (2011-370, s. 2.)

§ 58-21-25. Other nonadmitted insurers.

Only that portion of any risk eligible for export for which the full amount of coverage is not procurable from eligible surplus lines insurers may be placed with any other nonadmitted insurer that does not appear on the list of eligible surplus lines insurers published by the Commissioner pursuant to G.S. 58-21-20(b), but nonetheless meets the requirements set forth in G.S. 58-21-20(a)(1) through (a)(3) and any regulations of the Commissioner. The surplus lines licensee seeking to provide coverage through an unlisted nonadmitted insurer shall make a filing specifying the amount and percentage of each risk to be placed, and naming the nonadmitted insurer with which placement is intended. Within 30 days after the coverage has been placed, the producing broker or surplus lines licensee shall send written notice to the insured that the insurance, or a portion thereof, has been placed with such nonadmitted insurer. (1985, c. 688, s. 1.)

§ 58-21-30. Withdrawal of eligibility from a surplus lines insurer.

If at any time the Commissioner has reason to believe that an eligible surplus lines insurer:

(1)   Is in unsound financial condition or has acted in an untrustworthy manner,

(2)   Is no longer eligible under G.S. 58-21-20,

(3)   Has willfully violated the laws of this State, or

(4)   Does not make reasonably prompt payment of just losses and claims in this State or elsewhere, the Commissioner may declare it ineligible. The Commissioner shall promptly mail notice of all such declarations to each surplus lines licensee. (1985, c. 688, s. 1; 2001-223, s. 17.2.)

§ 58-21-35. Duty to file and retain reports.

(a)   Within 30 days after the placing of any surplus lines insurance, the surplus lines licensee shall file with the Commissioner a report in a format prescribed by the Commissioner regarding the insurance and including the following information:

(1)   The name of the insured.

(2)   The identity of the insurer or insurers.

(3)   A description of the subject and location of the risk.

(4)   The amount of premium charged for the insurance.

(5)   The amount of premium tax for the insurance.

(6)   The policy period.

(7)   The policy number.

(7a)   An acknowledged statement that the surplus lines licensee has complied with G.S. 58-21-15 or G.S. 58-21-16, whichever is applicable.

(8)   The name, address, telephone number, facsimile telephone number, and electronic mail address of the licensee, as applicable.

(9)   Any other relevant information the Commissioner may reasonably require.

(b)   The licensee shall complete and retain a copy of the report in paper or electronic form as required by the Commissioner. The report required by this section and the quarterly report required by G.S. 58-21-80 shall be completed on a standardized form or forms prescribed by the Commissioner and are not public records under G.S. 132-1 or G.S. 58-2-100. (1985, c. 688, s. 1; 1987, c. 864, s. 35; 1993 (Reg. Sess., 1994), c. 678, s. 16; 1999-219, s. 6.1; 2006-105, s. 2.6; 2011-120, s. 7.)

§ 58-21-40. Surplus lines regulatory support organization.

(a)   A surplus lines regulatory support organization of surplus lines licensees shall be formed to:

(1)   Facilitate and encourage compliance by resident and nonresident surplus lines licensees with the laws of this State and the rules and regulations of the Commissioner relative to surplus lines insurance;

(2)   Communicate with organizations of admitted insurers with respect to the proper use of the surplus lines market;

(3) Receive and disseminate to surplus lines licensees information about surplus lines insurance, including, without limitation, new electronic filing procedures approved by the Commissioner, changes in the list of eligible surplus lines insurers, and modifications in coverages, procedures, and requirements as may be requested by the Commissioner; and

(4) Countersign nonresident produced surplus lines coverages and remit premium taxes for those coverages under G.S. 58-21-70 by means satisfactory to the Commissioner; and charge the nonresident surplus lines licensee a fee for the certification and countersignature as approved by the Commissioner.

(b) The regulatory support organization shall file with the Commissioner:

(1) A copy of its constitution, articles of agreement or association, or certificate of incorporation;

(2) A copy of its bylaws and rules governing its activities;

(3) An annually updated list of resident and nonresident licensees;

(4) The name and address of a resident of this State upon whom notices or orders of the Commissioner or processes issued at his direction may be served; and

(5) An agreement that the Commissioner may examine the regulatory support organization in accordance with subsection (c) of this section.

(c) The Commissioner may, at times deemed appropriate, make or cause to be made an examination of each regulatory support organization; in which case the provisions of G.S. 58-2-131, 58-2-132, 58-2-133, 58-2-134, 58-2-150, 58-2-155, 58-2-180, 58-2-185, 58-2-190, 58-2-195, and 58-2-200 shall apply. If the Commissioner finds the regulatory support organization or any surplus lines licensee, whether resident or nonresident, to be in violation of this Article, the Commissioner may issue an order requiring the discontinuance of the violation.

(d) Each resident surplus lines licensee shall maintain active membership in a regulatory support organization as a condition of continued licensure under this Article. (1985, c. 688, s. 1; 1987 (Reg. Sess., 1988), c. 975, s. 13; 1995, c. 193, s. 28; 1999-132, s. 11.3; 2001-203, s. 28; 2001-451, ss. 2.1, 2.2; 2001-487, s. 63.)

§ 58-21-45. Evidence of the insurance; changes; penalty.

(a)   As soon as surplus lines insurance has been placed, the producing broker or surplus lines licensee shall promptly deliver the policy to the insured. If the policy is not then available, the broker or licensee shall promptly deliver to the insured a certificate described in subsection (d) of this section, cover note, binder, or other evidence of insurance. The certificate described in subsection (d), cover note, binder, or other evidence of insurance shall be executed by the surplus lines licensee and shall show the description and location of the subject of the insurance, coverages including any material limitations other than those in standard forms, a general description of the coverages of the insurance, the premium and rate charged and taxes to be collected from the insured, and the name and address of the insured and surplus lines insurer or insurers and proportion of the entire risk assumed by each, and the name of the surplus lines licensee and the licensee's license number.

(b)   No producing broker or surplus lines licensee shall issue or deliver any evidence of insurance or purport to insure or represent that insurance will be or has been written by any eligible surplus lines insurer, or a nonadmitted insurer pursuant to G.S. 58-21-25, unless he has authority from the insurer to cause the risk to be insured, or has received information from the insurer in the regular course of business that such insurance has been granted.

(c)   If, after delivery of any such evidence of insurance there is any change in the identity of the insurers, or the proportion of the risk assumed by any insurer, or any other material change in coverage as stated in the producing broker's or surplus lines licensee's original evidence of insurance, or in any other material as to the insurance coverage so evidenced, the producing broker or surplus lines licensee shall promptly issue and deliver to the insured an appropriate substitute for or endorsement of the original document, accurately showing the current status of the coverage and the insurers responsible thereunder.

(d)   As soon as reasonably possible after the placement of any such insurance the producing broker or surplus lines licensee shall deliver a copy of the policy or, if not available, a certificate of insurance to the insured to replace any evidence of insurance previously issued. Each certificate or policy of insurance shall contain or have attached thereto a complete record of all policy insuring agreements, conditions, exclusions, clauses, endorsements, or any other material facts that would regularly be included in the policy.

(e) Any surplus lines licensee or producing broker who fails to comply with the requirements of this section shall be subject to the penalties provided in G.S. 58-21-105.

(f) Every evidence of insurance negotiated, placed, or procured under the provisions of this Article issued by the surplus lines licensee shall bear the name of the licensee and the following legend in 12 point type and in contrasting color or in 12 point type and underlined and in bold print: "The insurance company with which this coverage has been placed is not licensed by the State of North Carolina and is not subject to its supervision. In the event of the insolvency of the insurance company, losses under this policy will not be paid by any State insurance guaranty or solvency fund." (1985, c. 688, s. 1; 2006-105, s. 2.7.)

§ 58-21-50. Duty to notify insured.

No contract of insurance placed by a surplus lines licensee under this Article shall be binding upon the insured and no premium charged therefor shall be due and payable until the producing broker or surplus lines licensee notifies the insured in writing, a copy of which shall be maintained by the broker or licensee with the records of the contract and available for possible examination, that:

(1) The insurer with which the coverage has been placed is not licensed by this State and is not subject to its supervision; and

(2) In the event of the insolvency of the surplus lines insurer, losses will not be paid by any State insurance guaranty or solvency fund.

Nothing in this section shall nullify any agreement by any insurer to provide insurance. (1985, c. 688, s. 1.)

§ 58-21-55. Valid surplus lines insurance.

Insurance contracts procured under this Article shall be valid and enforceable as to all parties. (1985, c. 688, s. 1.)

§ 58-21-60. Effect of payment to surplus lines licensee.

A payment of premium to a surplus lines licensee acting for a person other than himself in negotiating, continuing, or reviewing any policy of insurance under this Article shall be deemed to be payment to the insurer, notwithstanding any conditions or stipulations inserted in the policy or contract. (1985, c. 688, s. 1.)

§ 58-21-65. Licensing of surplus lines licensee.

(a)   For insureds whose home state is this State, no agent or broker licensed by the Commissioner shall procure any contract of surplus lines insurance with any nonadmitted insurer, unless he possesses a current surplus lines insurance license issued by the Commissioner.

(b)   The Commissioner shall issue a surplus lines license to any qualified holder of a current property broker's or agent's license, but only when the broker or agent has:

(1)   Remitted the fifty dollars ($50.00) annual fee to the Commissioner;

(2)   Submitted a completed license application on a form supplied by the Commissioner, and the application has been approved by the Commissioner;

(3)   Passed a qualifying examination approved by the Commissioner; except that all holders of a license prior to July 11, 1985 shall be deemed to have passed such an examination; and

(4)   Repealed by Session Laws 2004-199, s. 20(c), effective August 17, 2004.

(c)   Corporations shall be eligible to be resident surplus lines licensees, upon the following conditions:

(1)   The corporate licensee shall list individuals within the corporation who have satisfied all requirements of this Article to become surplus lines licensees; and

(2) Only those individuals listed on the corporate license and who are surplus lines licensees shall transact surplus lines business.

(d) Each surplus lines license shall be issued on September 1 of each year and expire August 31 of the following year unless renewed. Application for renewal shall be made 30 days before the expiration date. The license shall be renewed upon payment of the annual license fee and compliance with the other applicable provisions of this section. Any person who places surplus lines insurance without a valid surplus lines license in effect shall pay a penalty of one thousand dollars ($1,000) and be subject to such other penalties as provided by law.

The clear proceeds of civil penalties provided for in this subsection shall be remitted to the Civil Penalty and Forfeiture Fund in accordance with G.S. 115C-457.2.

(e) Any person who does not renew a surplus lines license and applies for another surplus lines license more than two years after the expiration date of the previous license shall be required to satisfy every condition in this section, including the written exam, before the Commissioner issues another surplus lines license to that person. Nonresident surplus lines licensees shall be licensed in accordance with Article 33 of this Chapter.

(f) Repealed by Session Laws 2011-120, s. 8, effective July 21, 2011. (1985, c. 688, s. 1; 1985 (Reg. Sess., 1986), c. 928, s. 6; c. 1013, ss. 4, 16; 1987, c. 629, s. 18; c. 752, s. 6; 1987 (Reg. Sess., 1988), c. 975, s. 14; 1991, c. 212, s. 1; c. 644, s. 41; 1998-215, s. 85; 2004-199, s. 20(c); 2008-124, s. 10.2; 2009-566, s. 11; 2011-120, s. 8.)

§ 58-21-70. Surplus lines licensees may accept business from other agents or brokers; countersignatures required; remittance of premium tax.

(a) A surplus lines licensee may originate surplus lines insurance or accept such insurance from any other duly licensed agent or broker, and the surplus lines licensee may compensate such agent or broker therefor.

(b) Every report filed by a nonresident licensee under G.S. 58-21-35(a) shall, before being filed with the Commissioner, be countersigned by a resident licensee or by a regulatory support organization. The resident licensee or regulatory support organization may charge the nonresident licensee a countersignature fee.

(c) Every resident licensee and regulatory support organization that countersigns a report under subsection (b) of this section is responsible for remitting the premium tax for the coverage, as specified in G.S. 58-21-85, to the Commissioner. (1985, c. 688, s. 1; 2001-451, s. 2.)

§ 58-21-75. Records of surplus lines licensee.

Each surplus lines licensee shall keep in his or her office in this State a full and true record of each surplus lines insurance contract placed by or through the licensee, including a copy of the policy, certificate, cover note, or other evidence of insurance. The record shall include the following items:

(1) Amount of the insurance and perils insured;

(2) Brief description of the property insured and its location;

(3) Gross premium charged;

(4) Any return premium paid;

(5) Rate of premium charged upon the several items of property;

(6) Effective date of the contract, and the terms of the contract;

(7) Name and address of the insured;

(8) Name and address of the insurer;

(9) Amount of tax and other sums to be collected from the insured; and

(10) Identity of the producing broker, any confirming correspondence from the insurer or its representative, and the application.

The record of each contract shall be kept open at all reasonable times to examination by the Commissioner without notice for a period not less than three years following termination of the contract. (1985, c. 688, s. 1; 1991, c. 644, s. 42.)

§ 58-21-80. Quarterly reports; summary of exported business.

On or before the end of January, April, July, and October of each year, each surplus lines licensee shall file with the Commissioner, on a form prescribed by the Commissioner, a verified report of all surplus lines insurance transacted during the preceding three months showing:

(1)   Aggregate gross premiums written;

(2)   Aggregate return premiums; and

(3)   Amount of aggregate tax to be remitted. (1985, c. 688, s. 1; 1987, c. 864, s. 36.)

§ 58-21-85. Surplus lines tax.

(a)   Gross premiums charged, less any return premiums, for surplus lines insurance on insureds for whom North Carolina is the home state are subject to a premium receipts tax of five percent (5%), which shall be collected by the surplus lines licensee as specified by the Commissioner, in addition to the full amount of the gross premium charged by the insurer for the insurance. The tax on any portion of the premium unearned at termination of insurance having been credited by the State to the licensee shall be returned to the policyholder directly by the surplus lines licensee or through the producing broker, if any. The surplus lines licensee is prohibited from absorbing such tax and from rebating for any reason, any part of such tax. To the extent that other states in which portions of the properties, risks, or exposures reside have failed to enter into a compact or reciprocal allocation procedure with this State, the premium tax collected shall be retained by this State.

(b)   At the same time that he files his quarterly report as set forth in G.S. 58-21-80, each surplus lines licensee shall pay the premium receipts tax due for the period covered by the report.

(c) This section does not apply to risks of State government agencies nor to risks of local government risk pools created and operating under Article 23 of this Chapter.

(d) The surplus lines licensee placing the insurance and claiming the exemption in subsection (c) of this section shall affirmatively show in writing to the Commissioner that the risk qualifies for the exemption. (1985, c. 688, s. 1; 1985 (Reg. Sess., 1986), c. 928, s. 11; 1987, c. 727, ss. 2, 3; c. 864, s. 37; 2011-120, s. 9.)

§ 58-21-90. Collection of tax.

All provisions of Chapter 105 of the General Statutes, not inconsistent with this Article, relating to administration, auditing and making returns, the imposition and collection of tax and the lien thereon, assessments, refunds, and penalties, shall be applicable to the tax imposed by this Article; and with respect thereto, the Commissioner has the same power and authority as is given to the Secretary of Revenue under the provisions of Chapter 105 of the General Statutes. (1985, c. 688, s. 1; 1985 (Reg. Sess., 1986), c. 928, s. 7.)

§ 58-21-95. Suspension, revocation or nonrenewal of surplus lines licensee's license.

The Commissioner may suspend, revoke, or refuse to renew the license of a surplus lines licensee after notice and hearing as provided under G.S. 58-2-70 upon any one or more of the following grounds:

(1) Removal of the surplus lines licensee's office from this State;

(2) Removal of the surplus lines licensee's office accounts and records from this State during the period during which such accounts and records are required to be maintained under G.S. 58-21-75;

(3) Closing of the surplus lines licensee's office for a period of more than 30 business days, unless permission is granted by the Commissioner;

(4) Failure to make and file required reports;

(5)　Failure to transmit the required tax on surplus lines premiums;

(6)　Failure to maintain the required bond;

(7)　Violation of any provision of this Article; or

(8)　For any other cause for which an insurance license could be denied, revoked, suspended, or renewal refused under the Insurance Law. (1985, c. 688, s. 1.)

§ 58-21-100.　Actions against surplus lines insurer; service of process.

(a)　A surplus lines insurer may be sued upon any cause of action arising in this State, under any surplus lines insurance contract made by it or evidence of insurance issued or delivered by the surplus lines licensee, pursuant to the procedure provided in G.S. 58-16-30. Any such policy issued by the surplus lines licensee shall contain a provision stating the substance of this section and designating the person to whom the Commissioner shall mail process.

(b)　Each surplus lines insurer engaging in surplus lines insurance shall be deemed thereby to have subjected itself to this Article.

(c)　The remedies and procedures provided in this section are in addition to any other methods provided by law for service of process upon insurers. (1985, c. 688, s. 1; 1991, c. 720, s. 43.)

§ 58-21-105.　Penalties.

(a)　Any surplus lines licensee who in this State represents or aids a nonadmitted insurer in violation of this Article shall be guilty of a Class 1 misdemeanor.

(b)　In addition to any other penalty provided for in this section or otherwise provided by law, including any suspension, revocation, or refusal to renew a license, any person violating any provision of this Article shall be subject to a civil penalty, payment of restitution, or both, in accordance with G.S. 58-2-70. (1985, c. 688, s. 1; 1993, c. 539, s. 450; 1994, Ex. Sess., c. 24, s. 14(c).)

Article 22.

Liability Risk Retention.

§ 58-22-1. Purpose.

The purpose of this Article is to regulate the formation and operation of risk retention and purchasing groups in this State that are formed pursuant to the provisions of the Product Liability Risk Retention Act of 1981, as amended by the Risk Retention Amendments of 1986 (15 U.S.C. §3901 et seq.). (1985 (Reg. Sess., 1986), c. 1013, s. 8; 1987, c. 310, s. 1.)

§ 58-22-5: Reserved for future codification purposes.

§ 58-22-10. Definitions.

As used in this Article:

(1) "Completed operations liability" means liability arising out of the installation, maintenance, or repair of any product at a site that is not owned or controlled by:

a. Any person who performs that work; or

b. Any person who hires an independent contractor to perform that work;

but includes liability for activities that are completed or abandoned before the date of the occurrence giving rise to the liability.

(2) "Domicile", for purposes of determining the state in which a purchasing group is domiciled, means:

a. For a corporation, the state in which the purchasing group is incorporated; and

b. For an unincorporated entity, the state of its principal place of business.

(3) "Hazardous financial condition" means that, based on its present or reasonably anticipated financial condition, a risk retention group is insolvent or, although not yet financially impaired or insolvent, is unlikely to be able:

a. To meet obligations to policyholders with respect to known claims and reasonably anticipated claims; or

b. To pay other obligations in the normal course of business.

(4) "Insurance" means primary insurance, excess insurance, reinsurance, surplus lines insurance, and any other arrangement for shifting and distributing risk that is determined to be insurance under the laws of this State.

(5) "Liability" means legal liability for damages, including costs of defense, legal costs and fees, and other claims expenses, because of injuries to other persons, damage to their property, or other damage or loss to such other persons resulting from or arising out of any profit or nonprofit business, trade, product, professional or other services, premises, or operations; or any activity of any state or local government, or any agency or political subdivision thereof. Liability does not include personal risk liability or an employer's liability with respect to its employees other than legal liability under the Federal Employers' Liability Act (45 U.S.C. § 51 et seq.).

(6) "Personal risk liability" means liability for damage because of injury to any person, damage to property, or other loss or damage resulting from any personal, familial, or household responsibilities or activities. Personal risk liability does not include liability as defined in subdivision (5) of this section.

(7) "Plan of operation" or "feasibility study" means an analysis that presents the expected activities and results of a risk retention group including, at a minimum:

a. For each state in which the group intends to do business, the coverages, deductibles, coverage limits, rates, and rating classification systems for each kind of insurance the group intends to offer;

b. Historical and expected loss experience of the proposed members and national experience of similar exposures;

c. Prospective financial statements and projections;

d. Appropriate opinions by a qualified, independent casualty actuary, including a determination of minimum premium or participation levels required to commence operations and to prevent a hazardous financial condition;

e. Identification of management, underwriting and claim procedures, marketing methods, managerial oversight methods, reinsurance agreements, and investment policies;

f. Identification of each state in which the group has obtained, or sought to obtain, a charter and license, and a description of its status in each such state;

g. Information sufficient to verify that the group's members are engaged in businesses or activities similar or related with respect to the liability to which those members are exposed by virtue of any related, similar, or common business, trade, product, services, premises, or operations; and

h. Such other matters that are prescribed by the Commissioner for liability insurance companies authorized by this Chapter.

(8) "Product liability" means liability for damages because of any personal injury, death, emotional harm, consequential economic damage, or property damage, including damages resulting from the loss of use of property, arising out of the manufacture, design, importation, distribution, packaging, labeling, lease, or sale of a product; but does not include the liability of any person for those damages if the product involved was in the possession of such person when the incident giving rise to the claim occurred.

(9) "Purchasing group" means any group that:

a. Has as one of its purposes the purchase of liability insurance on a group basis;

b.   Purchases such insurance only for its group members and only to cover their similar or related liability exposure, as described in sub-subdivision c. of this subdivision;

c.   Is composed of members whose businesses or activities are similar or related with respect to the liability to which the members are exposed by virtue of any related, similar, or common business, trade, product, services, premises, or operations; and

d.   Is domiciled in any state.

(10)   "Risk retention group" means any corporation or other limited liability association:

a.   Whose primary activity consists of assuming and spreading all or any portion of the liability exposure of its group members;

b.   That is organized for the primary purpose of conducting the activity described under sub-subdivision a. of this subdivision;

c.   That

1.   Is chartered and licensed as a liability insurance company and authorized to engage in the business of insurance under the laws of any state; or

2.   Before January 1, 1985, was chartered or licensed and authorized to engage in the business of insurance under the laws of Bermuda or the Cayman Islands and, before that date, had certified to the insurance regulator of at least one state that it satisfied the capitalization requirements of such state; except that any such group shall be considered to be a risk retention group only if it has been engaged in business continuously since that date and only for the purpose of continuing to provide insurance to cover product liability or completed operations liability, as such terms were defined in the Product Liability Risk Retention Act of 1981 before the effective date of the Risk Retention Act of 1986;

d.   That does not exclude any person from membership in the group solely to provide for members of such a group a competitive advantage over such person;

e. That

1. Has as it [its] owners only persons who comprise the membership of the risk retention group and who are provided insurance by such group; or

2. Has as its sole owner an organization that meets all of the following:

I. Its members are only persons who comprise the membership of the risk retention group; and

II. Its owners are only persons who comprise the membership of the risk retention group and who are provided insurance by such group;

f. Whose members are engaged in businesses or activities similar or related with respect to the liability of which such members are exposed by virtue of any related, similar, or common business trade, product, services, premises, or operations;

g. Whose activities do not include the provision of insurance other than:

1. Liability insurance for assuming and spreading all or any portion of the similar or related liability exposure of its group members; and

2. Reinsurance with respect to the similar or related liability exposure of any other risk retention group, or any member of such other group, that is engaged in businesses or activities so that such group or member meets the requirement described in sub-subdivision f. of this subdivision from membership in the risk retention group that provides such reinsurance; and

h. The name of which includes the phrase "Risk Retention Group". (1985 (Reg. Sess., 1986), c. 1013, s. 8; 1987, c. 310, s. 1; 1993, c. 452, s. 35; 2001-223, s. 18; 2011-120, s. 10.)

§ 58-22-15. Risk retention groups chartered in this State.

(a) A risk retention group shall, pursuant to the provisions of Part 9 of Article 10 of this Chapter, be chartered and licensed to write only liability insurance pursuant to this Article and, except as provided elsewhere in this Article, must comply with all of the laws and rules applicable to such insurers chartered and licensed in this State and with G.S. 58-22-20 to the extent such requirements are not a limitation on laws, administrative rules, or requirements of this State.

(b) Before it may offer insurance in any state, each risk retention group shall also submit for approval to the Commissioner of this State a plan of operation or feasibility study. The risk retention group shall submit an appropriate revision in the event of any subsequent material change in any item of the plan of operation or feasibility study, within 10 days after any such change. The group shall not offer any additional kinds of liability insurance, in this State or in any other state, until a revision of such plan or study is approved by the Commissioner.

(c) At the time of filing its application for a charter, the risk retention group shall provide to the Commissioner in summary form the following information: the identity of the initial members of the group, the identity of those individuals who organized the group or who will provide administrative services or otherwise influence or control the activities of the group, the amount and nature of initial capitalization, the coverages to be afforded, and the states in which the group intends to operate. Upon receipt of this information, the Commissioner shall forward such information to the NAIC. Providing notification to the NAIC is in addition to and shall not be sufficient to satisfy the requirements of G.S. 58-22-20 or any other sections of this Article. (1985 (Reg. Sess., 1986), c. 1013, s. 8; 1987, c. 310, s. 1; c. 727, s. 13; 1993, c. 452, s. 36; 1995 (Reg. Sess., 1996), c. 747, s. 8; 2013-116, s. 2.)

§ 58-22-20. Risk retention groups not chartered in this State.

Risk retention groups that have been chartered in states other than this State and that seek to do business as risk retention groups in this state must observe and abide by the laws of this State as follows:

(1) Notice of Operations and Designation of Commissioner as Agent. - Before offering insurance in this State, a risk retention group shall submit to the Commissioner:

a. A statement identifying the state or states in which the risk retention group is chartered and licensed as a liability insurance company, date of chartering, its principal place of business, and such other information including information on its membership, as the Commissioner may require to verify that the risk retention group is qualified under G.S. 58-22-10(10);

b. A copy of its plan of operations or a feasibility study and revisions of such plan or study submitted to its state of domicile; provided, however, that the provision relating to the submission of a plan of operation or a feasibility study shall not apply with respect to any line or classification of liability insurance that (i) was defined in the Product Liability Risk Retention Act of 1981 before October 27, 1986, and (ii) was offered before that date by any risk retention group that had been chartered and operating for not less than three years before that date;

c. The risk retention group shall submit a copy of any revision to its plan of operation or feasibility study required by G.S. 58-22-15(b) at the same time that such revision is submitted to the Commissioner of its chartering state; and

d. A statement of registration that designates the Commissioner as its agent for the purpose of receiving service of legal process.

(2) Financial Condition. - A risk retention group doing business in this State shall file with the Commissioner:

a. A copy of the group's financial statement submitted to its state of domicile, which shall be certified by an independent public accountant and contain a statement of opinion on loss and loss adjustment expense reserves made by a member of the American Academy of Actuaries or a qualified loss reserve specialist, under criteria established by the NAIC or by the Commissioner;

b. A copy of each examination of the risk retention group as certified by the State insurance regulator or public official conducting the examination;

c. Upon request by the Commissioner, a copy of any audit performed with respect to the risk retention group; and

d. Such information as may be required to verify its continuing qualification as a risk retention group under G.S. 58-22-10(10).

(3) Taxation.

a. All premiums paid for coverages within this State to risk retention groups shall be subject to taxation at the same rate and subject to the same payment procedures and to the same interest, fines, and penalties for nonpayment as those applicable to surplus lines insurance under Article 21 of this Chapter. Premiums paid by purchasing groups are, however, taxed as provided in G.S. 58-22-35(b).

b. To the extent licensed agents or brokers are utilized pursuant to G.S. 58-22-60, they shall report and pay the taxes for the premiums for risks that they have placed with or on behalf of a risk retention group not chartered in this State. Such agent or broker shall keep a complete and separate record of all policies procured from each such risk retention group, which record shall be open to examination by the Commissioner, as provided in G.S. 58-2-185. These records shall, for each policy and each kind of insurance provided thereunder, include the following:

1. The limit of liability;

2. The time period covered;

3. The effective date;

4. The name of the risk retention group that issued the policy;

5. The gross premium charged; and

6. The amount of return premiums, if any.

c. To the extent that insurance agents or brokers are not utilized or fail to pay the tax, each risk retention group shall pay the tax for risks insured within the State. Each risk retention group shall report to the Commissioner all premiums paid to it for risks insured within the State.

(4) Compliance With Unfair Claims Settlement Practices Law. - A risk retention group and its agents and representatives shall comply with G.S. 58-3-100(a)(5) and G.S. 58-63-15(11).

(5) Deceptive, False, or Fraudulent Practices. - A risk retention group shall comply with the provisions of Article 63 of this Chapter and Chapter 75 of the General Statutes regarding deceptive, false, or fraudulent acts or practices.

(6) Examination Regarding Financial Condition. - A risk retention group must submit to an examination by the Commissioner to determine its financial condition if the insurance regulator of the jurisdiction in which the group is chartered has not initiated an examination or does not initiate an examination within 60 days after a request by the Commissioner. This examination shall be coordinated to avoid unjustified repetition and conducted in an expeditious manner and in accordance with the Examiner Handbook of the NAIC.

(7) Notice to Purchasers. - Any policy issued by a risk retention group shall contain in 10 point type and contrasting color on the front page and the declaration page, the following notice:

"NOTICE

This policy is issued by your risk retention group. Your risk retention group is not subject to all of the insurance laws and regulations of your state. In the event of the insolvency of your risk retention group, losses under this policy will not be paid by any insurance insolvency or guaranty fund in this State."

(8) Prohibited Acts Regarding Solicitation or Sale. - The following acts by a risk retention group are prohibited:

a. The solicitation or sale of insurance by a risk retention group to any person who is not eligible for membership in such group; and

b. The solicitation or sale of insurance by, or operation of, a risk retention group that is in a hazardous financial condition or is financially impaired.

(9) Prohibition of Ownership By An Insurance Company. - No risk retention group shall be allowed to do business in this State if an insurance company is directly or indirectly a member or owner of such risk retention group, other than in the case of a risk retention group all of whose members are insurance companies.

(10) Prohibited Coverage. - No risk retention group may offer insurance policy coverage prohibited or not authorized by this Chapter or declared unlawful by the appellate courts of this State.

(11) Delinquency Proceedings. - A risk retention group not chartered in this State and doing business in this State must comply with a lawful order issued in a voluntary dissolution proceeding or in a delinquency proceeding commenced by a state insurance commissioner if there has been a finding of financial impairment after an examination under G.S. 58-22-20(6).

(12) Penalties. - A risk retention group that violates any provision of this Article is subject to G.S. 58-2-70. (1985 (Reg. Sess., 1986), c. 1013, s. 8; 1987, c. 310, s. 1; c. 727, ss. 1, 2; 1993, c. 452, s. 37; 1995 (Reg. Sess., 1996), c. 747, s. 9; 2004-199, s. 20(d).)

§ 58-22-25. Compulsory association.

(a) No risk retention group is required to join or contribute financially to any insurance insolvency or guaranty fund or similar mechanism in this State; nor shall any risk retention group or its insureds receive any benefit from any such fund for claims arising out of the operations of such risk retention group.

(b) A risk retention group may be required to participate in residual market mechanisms under Articles 37 and 42 of this Chapter. (1987, c. 310.)

§ 58-22-30. Countersignature not required.

A policy of insurance issued to a risk retention group or any member of that group is not required to be countersigned as otherwise provided in Articles 1 through 64 of this Chapter. (1985 (Reg. Sess., 1986), c. 1013, s. 8; 1987, c. 310.)

§ 58-22-35. Purchasing groups; exemption from certain laws relating to the group purchase of insurance.

(a) Any purchasing group meeting the criteria established under the provisions of 15 U.S.C. § 3901 et seq. is exempt from any law of this State relating to the creation of groups for the purchase of insurance, prohibition of group purchasing, or any law that discriminates against a purchasing group or its members. In addition, an insurer is exempt from any law of this State that prohibits providing, or offering to provide, to a purchasing group or its members, advantages based on their loss and expense experience not afforded to other persons with respect to rates, policy forms, coverages, or other matters. A purchasing group is subject to all other applicable laws of this State.

(b) Taxes on premiums paid for coverage of risks resident or located in this State by a purchasing group or any members of the purchasing group shall be:

(1) Imposed at the same rate and subject to the same interest, fines, and penalties as those applicable to premium taxes on similar coverage from a similar insurance source by other insureds. For example, coverage provided by a surplus lines licensee is taxed under Article 21 of this Chapter, coverage provided by an insurance company is taxed under Article 8B of Chapter 105 of the General Statutes, and coverage provided by an unlicensed insurer is taxed under G.S. 58-28-5(b).

(2) Paid first by such insurance source, and if not by such source then by the agent or broker for the purchasing group, and if not by such agent or broker then by the purchasing group, and if not by such group then by each of its members. (1987, c. 310, s. 1; c. 727, s. 9; 1995 (Reg. Sess., 1996), c. 747, s. 10.)

§ 58-22-40. Notice and registration requirements of purchasing groups.

(a) A purchasing group that intends to do business in this State shall, before doing business, furnish notice to the Commissioner that shall:

(1) Identify the state in which the group is domiciled;

(2) Specify the lines and classifications of liability insurance that the purchasing group intends to purchase;

(3) Identify the insurer from which the group intends to purchase its insurance and the domicile of such insurer;

(4) Identify the principal place of business of the group;

(5) Provide such other information as may be required by the Commissioner to verify that the purchasing group is qualified under G.S. 58-22-10(9);

(6) Specify the method by which and the person or persons, if any, through whom insurance will be offered to its members whose risks are resident or located in this State; and furnish such information as may be required by the Commissioner to determine the appropriate premium tax treatment; and

(7) Identify all other states in which the group intends to do business.

(b) The purchasing group shall register with and designate the Commissioner as its agent solely for the purpose of receiving service of legal documents or process, except that such requirement does not apply in the case of a purchasing group:

(1) That

a. Was domiciled before April 2, 1986, in any state of the United States; and

b. Is domiciled on and after October 27, 1986, in any state of the United States;

(2) That before October 27, 1986, purchased insurance from an insurer licensed in any state; and since October 27, 1986, purchased its insurance from an insurer licensed in any state;

(3) That was a purchasing group under the requirements of the Product Liability Retention Act of 1981 before October 27, 1986; and

(4) That does not purchase insurance that was not authorized for purposes of an exemption under that act, as in effect before October 27, 1986.

(c) A purchasing group shall notify the Commissioner of any changes in any of the items in subsection (a) of this section within 10 days after those changes.

(d) Each purchasing group that is required to give notice under subsection (a) of this section shall also furnish such information as may be required by the Commissioner to:

(1) Verify that the entity qualifies as a purchasing group;

(2) Determine where the purchasing group is located; and

(3) Determine appropriate tax treatment. (1987, c. 310, c. 727, s. 10; 1993, c. 452, s. 38.)

§ 58-22-45. Restriction on insurance purchased by purchasing groups.

(a) A purchasing group may not purchase insurance from a risk retention group that is not chartered in a state nor from an insurer not admitted in the state in which the purchasing group is located, unless the purchase is effected through a licensed agent or broker acting pursuant to the surplus lines laws and regulations of such state.

(b) A purchasing group that obtains liability insurance from a nonadmitted insurer or from a risk retention group shall provide each member of the purchasing group that has a risk resident or located in this State with the notice specified in G.S. 58-21-45(f) or G.S. 58-22-20(7), whichever is applicable.

(c) No purchasing group may purchase insurance that provides for a deductible or for a self-insured retention applicable to the group as a whole; provided, however, that coverage may provide for a deductible or for self-insured retention applicable to members of the group. (1987, c. 310, c. 727, s. 11.)

§ 58-22-50. Administrative and procedural authority regarding risk retention groups and purchasing groups.

The Commissioner is authorized to make use of any of the powers established under Articles 1 through 64 of this Chapter to enforce the laws of this State as long as those powers are not specifically preempted by the Product Liability Risk Retention Act of 1981, as amended by the Risk Retention Act of 1986.

This includes, but is not limited to, the Commissioner's administrative authority to investigate, issue subpoenas, conduct depositions and hearings, issue orders, and seek or impose penalties. With regard to any investigation, administrative proceeding, or litigation, the Commissioner can rely on the procedural law and regulations of the State. The injunctive authority of the Commissioner in regard to risk retention groups is restricted by the requirement that any injunction be issued by a court of competent jurisdiction. (1987, c. 310.)

§ 58-22-55. Penalties.

A risk retention group that violates any provision of this Article is subject to G.S. 58-2-70. (1985 (Reg. Sess., 1986), c. 1013, s. 8; 1987, c. 310.)

§ 58-22-60. Duty of agents or brokers to obtain license.

Any person acting, or offering to act, as an agent or broker for a risk retention group or purchasing group, that solicits members, sells insurance coverage, purchases coverage for its members located within the State, or otherwise does business in this State shall, before commencing any such activity, obtain a license from the Commissioner. (1987, c. 310.)

§ 58-22-65. Binding effect of orders issued in U.S. District Court.

An order issued by any district court of the United States enjoining a risk retention group from soliciting or selling insurance, or operating, in any state, or in all states or in any territory or possession of the United States, upon a finding that such a group is in a hazardous financial condition, is enforceable in the courts of this State. (1987, c. 310.)

§ 58-22-70. Registration and renewal fees.

Every risk retention group and purchasing group that registers with the Commissioner under this Article shall pay the following fees:

Risk retention group registration.. $ 500.00

Purchasing group registration.. 500.00

Risk retention group renewal.. 1,500.00

Purchasing group renewal... 100.00

Registration fees shall not be prorated and must be submitted with the application for registration. Renewal fees shall not be prorated and shall be paid on or before January 1 of each year. (1989 (Reg. Sess., 1990), c. 1069, s. 12; 1995, c. 507, s. 11A(c); 1999-435, s. 3; 2009-451, s. 21.12(a).)

Article 23.

Local Government Risk Pools.

§ 58-23-1. Short title; definition.

This Article shall be known and may be cited as the Local Government Risk Pool Act. As used in this Article, "local government" means any county, city, or housing authority located in this State. (1985 (Reg. Sess., 1986), c. 1027, s. 26; 1987, c. 864, s. 30.)

§ 58-23-5. Local government pooling of property, liability and workers' compensation coverages.

(a)   In addition to other authority granted to local governments under Chapters 153A and 160A of the General Statutes to jointly purchase insurance or pool retention of their risks, two or more local governments may enter into contracts or agreements under this Article for the joint purchasing of insurance or to pool retention of their risks for property losses and liability claims and to provide for the payment of such losses of or claims made against any member of the pool on a cooperative or contract basis with one another, or may enter into a trust agreement to carry out the provisions of this Article.

(b) In addition to other authority granted to local governments under Chapters 153A and 160A of the General Statutes or under G.S. 97-7 to jointly purchase insurance or pool retention of their risks, two or more local governments may enter into contracts or agreements pursuant to this Article to establish a separate workers' compensation pool to provide for the payment of workers' compensation claims under Chapter 97 of the General Statutes.

(c) In addition to other authority granted to local governments under Chapters 153A and 160A of the General Statutes to pool retention of their risks, two or more local governments may enter into contracts or agreements under this Article to establish pools providing for life or accident and health insurance for their employees on a cooperative or contract basis with one another; or may enter into a trust agreement to carry out the provisions of this Article.

(d) A workers' compensation pool established under this Article may only provide coverage for workers' compensation, employers' liability, and occupational disease claims.

(e) Local governments that intend to operate under this Article shall give the Commissioner 30 days' advance written notification, in a form prescribed by the Commissioner, that they intend to organize and operate risk pools pursuant to this Article. Local governments that jointly purchase insurance or pool retention of their risks under authority granted to them in Chapters 153A and 160A of the General Statutes or under G.S. 97-7 and that do not provide the Commissioner with the notification prescribed by this subsection shall not be subject to regulation by the Commissioner and shall not be under the jurisdiction of the Commissioner. (1985 (Reg. Sess., 1986), c. 1027, s. 26; 1987, c. 441, s. 14; 2001-334, s. 18.3.)

§ 58-23-10. Board of trustees.

(a) Each pool will be operated by a board of trustees consisting of at least five persons who are elected officials or employees of local governments within this State. The board of trustees of each pool will:

(1) Establish terms and conditions of coverage within the pool, including underwriting criteria and exclusions of coverage;

(2) Ensure that all valid claims are paid promptly;

(3) Take all necessary precautions to safeguard the assets of the pool;

(4) Maintain minutes of its meeting and make those minutes available to the Commissioner;

(5) Designate an administrator to carry out the policies established by the board of trustees and to provide day to day management of the group and delineate in written minutes of its meetings the areas of authority it delegates to the administrator; and

(6) Establish guidelines for membership in the pool.

(b) The board of trustees may not:

(1) Extend credit to individual members for payment of a premium, except pursuant to payment plans approved by the Commissioner.

(2) Borrow any moneys from the pool or in the name of the pool, except in the ordinary course of business, without first advising the Commissioner of the nature and purpose of the loan and obtaining prior approval from the Commissioner. (1985 (Reg. Sess., 1986), c. 1027, s. 26.)

§ 58-23-15. Contract.

A contract or agreement made pursuant to this Article must contain provisions:

(1) For a system or program of loss control;

(2) For termination of membership including either:

a. Cancellation of individual members of the pool by the pool; or

b. Election by an individual member of the pool to terminate its participation;

(3) Requiring the pool to pay all claims for which each member incurs liability during each member's period of membership, except where a member has individually retained the risk, where the risk is not covered, and except for amount of claims above the coverage provided by the pool.

(4) For the maintenance of claim reserves equal to known incurred losses and loss adjustment expenses and to an estimate of incurred but not reported losses;

(5) For a final accounting and settlement of the obligations of or refunds to a terminating member to occur when all incurred claims are concluded, settled, or paid;

(6) That the pool may establish offices where necessary in this State and employ necessary staff to carry out the purposes of the pool;

(7) That the pool may retain legal counsel, actuaries, claims adjusters, auditors, engineers, private consultants, and advisors, and other persons as the board of trustees or the administrator deem to be necessary;

(8) That the pool may make and alter bylaws and rules pertaining to the exercise of its purpose and powers;

(9) That the pool may purchase, lease, or rent real and personal property it deems to be necessary; and

(10) That the pool may enter into financial services agreements with financial institutions and that it may issue checks in its own name. (1985 (Reg. Sess., 1986), c. 1027, s. 26.)

§ 58-23-20. Termination.

A pool or a terminating member must provide at least 90 days' written notice of the termination or cancellation. A workers' compensation pool must notify the Commissioner of the termination or cancellation of a member within 10 days after notice of termination or cancellation is received or issued. (1985 (Reg. Sess., 1986), c. 1027, s. 26.)

§ 58-23-25: Repealed by Session Laws 1993, c. 452, s. 65.

§ 58-23-26. Financial monitoring and evaluation of pools.

(a) Each pool shall have an annual audit by an independent certified public accountant, pursuant to Part 7 of Article 10 of this Chapter, at the expense of the pool, and shall make a copy of the audit available to the governing body or chief executive officer of each member of the pool. A copy of the audit shall be filed with the Commissioner within 130 days after the end of the pool's fiscal year, unless that time is extended by the Commissioner. The annual audit shall report the financial position of the pool in conformity with statutory accounting practices prescribed or permitted by the Commissioner.

(b) Each pool shall have an actuarial evaluation of its loss and loss adjustment expense reserves, including reserves for loss and loss adjustment expenses incurred but not reported, performed annually by a qualified actuary. A copy of the evaluation shall be filed with the Commissioner along with the annual audit submitted pursuant to subsection (a) of this section. A "qualified actuary" shall be as defined or prescribed by the Commissioner.

(c) Each pool is subject to G.S. 58-2-131, 58-2-132, 58-2-133, 58-2-134, 58-2-150, 58-2-155, 58-2-165, 58-2-180, 58-2-185, 58-2-190, 58-2-200, 58-3-71, 58-3-75, 58-3-81, 58-3-105, 58-6-5, 58-7-21, 58-7-26, 58-7-30, 58-7-31, 58-7-50, 58-7-55, 58-7-140, 58-7-160, 58-7-162, 58-7-163, 58-7-165, 58-7-167, 58-7-168, 58-7-170, 58-7-172, 58-7-173, 58-7-175, 58-7-179, 58-7-180, 58-7-183, 58-7-185, 58-7-187, 58-7-188, 58-7-192, 58-7-193, 58-7-197, 58-7-200, Part 7 of Article 10, and Articles 13, 19, and 34 of this Chapter. Annual financial statements required by G.S. 58-2-165 shall be filed by each pool within 60 days after the end of the pool's fiscal year, subject to extension by the Commissioner. (1993, c. 452, s. 39; c. 504, s. 45; 1999-132, s. 11.4; 2001-223, s. 8.10; 2003-212, s. 12; 2009-384, s. 2.)

§ 58-23-30. Insolvency or impairment of pool.

(a) If, as a result of the annual audit or an examination by the Commissioner, it appears that the assets of a pool are insufficient to enable the pool to discharge its legal liabilities and other obligations, the Commissioner must notify the administrator and the board of trustees of the pool of the deficiency and his list of recommendations to abate the deficiency, including a recommendation not to add any new members until the deficiency is abated. If the pool fails to comply with the recommendations within 30 days after the date of the notice, the Commissioner may apply to the Superior Court of Wake County for an order requiring the pool to abate the deficiency and authorizing the Commissioner to appoint one or more special deputy commissioners, counsel, clerks, or assistants to oversee the implementation of the Court's order. The compensation and expenses of such persons shall be fixed by the Commissioner, subject to the approval of the Court, and shall be paid out of the funds or assets of the pool.

(b) If a pool is determined to be insolvent, financially impaired, or is otherwise found to be unable to discharge its legal liabilities and other obligations, each pool contract will provide that the members of the pool shall be assessed on a pro rata basis as calculated by the amount of each member's average annual contribution in order to satisfy the amount of deficiency. Members of a pool may, by contract, agree to limit the assessment to the amount of each member's annual contribution to the pool. Such a contractual agreement shall not impair the authority granted the Commissioner by this section. (1985 (Reg. Sess., 1986), c. 1027, s. 26; 1987, c. 441, ss. 16, 17.)

§ 58-23-35. Immunity of administrators and boards of trustees.

There is no liability on the part of and no cause of action arises against any board of trustees established or administrator appointed pursuant to G.S. 58-23-10, their representatives, or any pool, its members, or its employees, agents, contractors, or subcontractors for any good faith action taken by them in the performance of their powers and duties in creating or administering any pool under this Article. (1985 (Reg. Sess., 1986), c. 1027, s. 26.)

§ 58-23-40. Pools not covered by guaranty associations.

The provisions of Articles 48 and 62 of this Chapter and of Article 4 of Chapter 97 of the General Statutes do not apply to any risks retained by local governments pursuant to this Article. (1985 (Reg. Sess., 1986), c. 1027, s. 26; 1987, c. 441, s. 18; 1993, c. 504, s. 16.)

§ 58-23-45. Relationship to other insurance laws.

Unless local government risk pools are specifically referenced in a particular section of this Chapter, no provisions in this Chapter other than this Article apply to local government risk pools. (1999-351, s. 6.)

Article 24.

Fraternal Benefit Societies.

§ 58-24-1. Fraternal benefit societies.

Any incorporated society, order or supreme lodge, without capital stock, including one exempted under the provisions of G.S. 58-24-185(a)(2) whether incorporated or not, conducted solely for the benefit of its members and their beneficiaries and not for profit, operated on a lodge system with ritualistic form of work, having a representative form of government, and which provides benefits in accordance with this Article, is hereby declared to be a fraternal benefit society. (1987, c. 483, s. 2.)

§ 58-24-5. Lodge system.

(a) A society is operating on the lodge system if it has a supreme governing body and subordinate lodges into which members are elected, initiated or admitted in accordance with its laws, rules and ritual. Subordinate lodges shall be required by the laws of the society to hold regular meetings periodically in futherance of the purposes of the society.

(b) A society may, at its option, organize and operate lodges for children under the minimum age for adult membership. Membership and initiation in local lodges shall not be required of such children, nor shall they have a voice or vote in the management of the society. (1987, c. 483, s. 2.)

§ 58-24-10. Representative form of government.

A society has a representative form of government when:

(a) It has a supreme governing body constituted in one of the following ways:

(1) Assembly. - The supreme governing body is an assembly composed of delegates elected directly by the members or at intermediate assemblies or conventions of members or their representatives, together with other delegates as may be prescribed in the society's laws. A society may provide for election of delegates by mail. The elected delegates shall constitute a majority in number and shall not have less than two-thirds of the votes and not less than the number of votes required to amend the society's laws. The assembly shall be elected and shall meet at least once every four years and shall elect a board of directors to conduct the business of the society between meetings of the assembly. Vacancies on the board of directors between elections may be filled in the manner prescribed by the society's laws.

(2) Direct Election. - The supreme governing body is a board composed of persons elected by the members, either directly or by their representatives in intermediate assemblies, and any other persons prescribed in the society's laws. A society may provide for election of the board by mail. Each term of a board member may not exceed four years. Vacancies on the board between elections may be filled in the manner prescribed by the society's laws. Those persons elected to the board shall constitute a majority in number and not less than the number of votes required to amend the society's laws. A person filling the unexpired term of an elected board member shall be considered to be an elected member. The board shall meet at least quarterly to conduct the business of the society.

(b) The officers of the society are elected either by the supreme governing body or by the board of directors;

(c) Only benefit members are eligible for election to the supreme governing body, the board of directors or any intermediate assembly; and

(d) Each voting member shall have one vote; no vote may be cast by proxy. (1987, c. 483, s. 2; 1989, c. 364, s. 1.)

§ 58-24-15. Terms used.

Whenever used in this Article:

(a) "Benefit contract" shall mean the agreement for provision of benefits authorized by G.S. 58-24-75, as that agreement is described in G.S. 58-24-90(a).

(b) "Benefit member" shall mean an adult member who is designated by the laws or rules of the society to be a benefit member under a benefit contract.

(c) "Certificate" shall mean the document issued as written evidence of the benefit contract.

(d) "Premiums" shall mean premiums, rates, dues or other required contributions by whatever name known, which are payable under the certificate.

(e) "Laws" shall mean the society's articles of incorporation, constitution and bylaws, however designated.

(f) "Rules" shall mean all rules, regulations or resolutions adopted by the supreme governing body or board of directors which are intended to have general application to the members of the society.

(g) "Society" shall mean fraternal benefit society, unless otherwise indicated.

(h) "Lodge" shall mean subordinate member units of the society, known as camps, courts, councils, branches or by any other designation. (1987, c. 483, s. 2.)

§ 58-24-20. Purposes and powers.

(a) A society shall operate for the benefit of members and their beneficiaries by:

(1) Providing benefits as specified in G.S. 58-24-75; and

(2) Operating for one or more social, intellectual, educational, charitable, benevolent, moral, fraternal, patriotic or religious purposes for the benefit of its members, which may also be extended to others.

Such purposes may be carried out directly by the society, or indirectly through subsidiary corporations or affiliated organizations.

(b) Every society shall have the power to adopt laws and rules for the government of the society, the admission of its members, and the management of its affairs. It shall have the power to change, alter, add to or amend such laws and rules and shall have such other powers as are necessary and incidental to carrying into effect the objects and purposes of the society. (1987, c. 483, s. 2.)

§ 58-24-25. Qualifications for membership.

(a) A society shall specify in its laws or rules:

(1) Eligibility standards for each and every class of membership, provided that if benefits are provided on the lives of children, the minimum age for adult membership shall be set at not less than age 15 and not greater than age 21;

(2) The process for admission to membership for each membership class; and

(3) The rights and privileges of each membership class, provided that only benefit members shall have the right to vote on the management of the insurance affairs of the society.

(b) A society may also admit social members who shall have no voice or vote in the management of the insurance affairs of the society.

(c) Membership rights in the society are personal to the member and are not assignable. (1987, c. 483, s. 2.)

§ 58-24-30. Location of office, meetings, communications to members, grievance procedures.

(a) The principal office of any domestic society shall be located in this State. The meetings of its supreme governing body may be held in any state, district, province or territory wherein such society has at least one subordinate lodge, or in such other location as determined by the supreme governing body, and all business transacted at such meetings shall be as valid in all respects as if such meetings were held in this State. The minutes of the proceedings of the supreme governing body and of the board of directors shall be in the English language.

(b) A society may provide in its laws for an official publication in which any notice, report, or statement required by law to be given to members, including notice of election, may be published. Such required reports, notices and statements shall be printed conspicuously in the publication. If the records of a society show that two or more members have the same mailing address, an official publication mailed to one member is deemed to be mailed to all members at the same address unless a member requests a separate copy.

(c) Not later than June 1 of each year, a synopsis of the society's annual statement providing an explanation of the facts concerning the condition of the society thereby disclosed shall be printed and mailed to each benefit member of the society or, in lieu thereof, such synopsis may be published in the society's official publication.

(d) A society may provide in its laws or rules for grievance or complaint procedures for members. (1987, c. 483, s. 2.)

§ 58-24-35. No personal liability.

(a) The officers and members of the supreme governing body or any subordinate body of a society shall not be personally liable for any benefits provided by a society.

(b) Any person may be indemnified and reimbursed by any society for expenses reasonably incurred by, and liabilities imposed upon, such person in connection with or arising out of any action, suit or proceeding, whether civil, criminal, administrative or investigative, or threat thereof, in which the person may be involved by reason of the fact that he or she is or was a director, officer, employee or agent of the society or of any firm, corporation or organization which he or she served in any capacity at the request of the society. A person shall not be so indemnified or reimbursed (1) in relation to any matter in such action, suit or proceeding as to which he or she shall finally be adjudged to be or have been guilty of breach of a duty as a director, officer, employee or agent of the society or (2) in relation to any matter in such action, suit or proceeding, or threat thereof, which has been made the subject of a compromise settlement; unless in either such case the person acted in good faith for a purpose the person reasonably believed to be in or not opposed to the best interests of the society and, in a criminal action or proceeding, in addition, had no reasonable cause to believe that his or her conduct was unlawful. The determination whether the conduct of such person met the standard required in order to justify indemnification and reimbursement in relation to any matter described in subpoints (1) or (2) of the preceding sentence may only be made by the supreme governing body or board of directors by a majority vote of a quorum consisting of persons who were not parties to such action, suit or proceeding or by a court of competent jurisdiction. The termination of any action, suit or proceeding by judgment, order, settlement, conviction, or upon a plea of no contest, as to such person shall not in itself create a conclusive presumption that the person did not meet the standard of conduct required in order to justify indemnification and reimbursement. The foregoing right of indemnification and reimbursement shall not be exclusive of other rights to which such person may be entitled as a matter of law and shall inure to the benefit of his or her heirs, executors and administrators.

(c) A society shall have power to purchase and maintain insurance on behalf of any person who is or was a director, officer, employee or agent of the society, or who is or was serving at the request of the society as a director, officer, employee or agent of any other firm, corporation, or organization against any liability asserted against such person and incurred by him or her in any such capacity or arising out of his or her status as such, whether or not the society would have the power to indemnify the person against such liability under this section.

(d) A person serving as an officer or a member of a supreme governing body of a society shall be immune individually from civil liability for monetary damages, except to the extent covered by insurance, for any act or failure to act, except where the person:

(1) Is compensated for his services beyond reimbursement for expenses,

(2) Was not acting within the scope of his official duties,

(3) Was not acting in good faith,

(4) Committed gross negligence or willful or wanton misconduct that resulted in the damage or injury,

(5) Derived an improper personal financial benefit from the transaction,

(6) Incurred the liability from the operation of a motor vehicle, or

(7) Is sued in an action that would qualify as a derivative action if the organization were a for-profit corporation or as a member's or director's derivative action under G.S. 55A-28.1 or G.S. 55A-28.2 if the organization were a nonprofit corporation.

The immunity in this subsection is personal to the individual officers and members of the supreme governing body and does not immunize the organization for the acts or omissions of those officers or members. (1987, c. 483, s. 2, c. 799, s. 2.)

§ 58-24-40. Waiver.

The laws of the society may provide that no subordinate body, nor any of its subordinate officers or members shall have the power or authority to waive any of the provisions of the laws of the society. Such provision shall be binding on the society and every member and beneficiary of a member. (1987, c. 483, s. 2.)

§ 58-24-45. Organization.

A domestic society organized on or after January 1, 1988 shall be formed as follows:

(a) Ten or more citizens of the United States, a majority of whom are citizens of this State, who desire to form a fraternal benefit society, may make, sign and acknowledge before some officer competent to take acknowledgement of deeds, articles of incorporation, in which shall be stated:

(1) The proposed corporate name of the society, which shall not so closely resemble the name of any society or insurance company as to be misleading or confusing;

(2) The purposes for which it is being formed and the mode in which its corporate powers are to be exercised. Such purposes shall not include more liberal powers than are granted by this Article;

(3) The names and residences of the incorporators and the names, residences and official titles of all the officers, trustees, directors, or other persons who are to have and exercise the general control of the management of the affairs and funds of the society for the first year or until the ensuing election at which all such officers shall be elected by the supreme governing body, which election shall be held not later than one year from the date of issuance of the permanent license.

(b) Such articles of incorporation, duly certified copies of the society's bylaws and rules, copies of all proposed forms of certificates, applications therefor, and circulars to be issued by the society and a bond conditioned upon the return to applicants of the advanced payments if the organization is not completed within one year shall be filed with the Commissioner, who may require such further information as the Commissioner deems necessary. The bond with sureties approved by the Commissioner shall be in such amount, not less than three hundred thousand dollars ($300,000) nor more than one million five hundred thousand dollars ($1,500,000), as required by the Commissioner. All documents filed are to be in the English language. If the purposes of the society conform to the requirements of this chapter and all provisions of the law have been complied with, the Commissioner shall so certify, retain and file the articles of incorporation and furnish the incorporators a preliminary license authorizing the society to solicit members as hereinafter provided.

(c) No preliminary license granted under the provisions of this section shall be valid after one year from its date or after such further period, not exceeding one year, as may be authorized by the Commissioner upon cause shown, unless the 500 applicants hereinafter required have been secured and the organization has been completed as herein provided. The articles of incorporation and all other proceedings thereunder shall become null and void in one year from the date of the preliminary license, or at the expiration of the extended period, unless the society shall have completed its organization and received a license to do business as hereinafter provided.

(d)   Upon receipt of a preliminary license from the Commissioner, the society may solicit members for the purpose of completing its organization, shall collect from each applicant the amount of not less than one regular monthly premium in accordance with its table of rates, and shall issue to each such applicant a receipt for the amount so collected. No society shall incur any liability other than for the return of such advance premium, nor issue any certificate, nor pay, allow, or offer or promise to pay or allow, any benefit to any person until:

(1)   Actual bona fide applications for benefits have been secured on not less than 500 applicants, and any necessary evidence of insurability has been furnished to and approved by the society;

(2)   At least 10 subordinate lodges have been established into which the 500 applicants have been admitted;

(3)   There has been submitted to the Commissioner, under oath of the president or secretary, or corresponding officer of the society, a list of such applicants, giving their names, addresses, date each was admitted, name and number of the subordinate lodge of which each applicant is a member, amount of benefits to be granted and premiums therefor; and

(4)   It shall have been shown to the Commissioner, by sworn statement of the treasurer, or corresponding officer of such society, that at least 500 applicants have each paid in cash at least one regular monthly premium as herein provided, which premiums in the aggregate shall amount to at least one hundred and fifty thousand dollars ($150,000). Said advance premiums shall be held in trust during the period of organization and if the society has not qualified for a license within one year, as herein provided, such premiums shall be returned to said applicants.

(e)   The Commissioner may make such examination and require such further information as the Commissioner deems advisable. Upon presentation of satisfactory evidence that the society has complied with all the provisions of law, the Commissioner shall issue to the society a license to that effect and that the society is authorized to transact business pursuant to the provisions of this Article. The license shall be prima facie evidence of the existence of the society at the date of such certificate. The Commissioner shall cause a record of such license to be made. A certified copy of such record may be given in evidence with like effect as the original license.

(f) Any incorporated society authorized to transact business in this State at the time this Article becomes effective shall not be required to reincorporate. (1987, c. 483, s. 2; 1991, c. 720, s. 4; 1999-132, s. 9.1.)

§ 58-24-50. Amendments to laws.

(a) A domestic society may amend its laws in accordance with the provisions thereof by action of its supreme governing body at any regular or special meeting thereof or, if its laws so provide, by referendum. Such referendum may be held in accordance with the provisions of its laws by the vote of the voting members of the society, by the vote of delegates or representatives of voting members or by the vote of local lodges. A society may provide for voting by mail. No amendment submitted for adoption by referendum shall be adopted unless, within six months from the date of submission thereof, a majority of the members voting shall have signified their consent to such amendment by one of the methods herein specified.

(b) No amendment to the laws of any domestic society shall take effect unless approved by the Commissioner who shall approve such amendment if the Commissioner finds that it has been duly adopted and is not inconsistent with any requirement of the laws of this State or with the character, objects and purposes of the society. Unless the Commissioner shall disapprove any such amendment within 60 days after the filing of same, such amendment shall be considered approved. The approval or disapproval of the Commissioner shall be in writing and mailed to the secretary or corresponding officer of the society at its principal office. In case the Commissioner disapproves such amendment, the reasons therefor shall be stated in such written notice.

(c) Within 90 days from the approval thereof by the Commissioner, all such amendments, or a synopsis thereof, shall be furnished to all members of the society either by mail or by publication in full in the official publication of the society. The affidavit of any officer of the society or of anyone authorized by it to mail any amendments or synopsis thereof, stating facts which show that same have been duly addressed and mailed, shall be prima facie evidence that such amendments or synopsis therof, have been furnished the addressee.

(d)   Every foreign or alien society authorized to do business in this State shall file with the Commissioner a duly certified copy of all amendments of, or additions to, its laws within 90 days after the enactment of same.

(e)   Printed copies of the laws as amended, certified by the secretary or corresponding officer of the society shall be prima facie evidence of the legal adoption thereof. (1987, c. 483, s. 2; 1991, c. 720, s. 4.)

§ 58-24-55. Institutions.

A society may create, maintain and operate, or may establish organizations to operate, not for profit institutions to further the purposes permitted by G.S. 58-24-20(a)(2). Such institutions may furnish services free or at a reasonable charge. Any real or personal property owned, held or leased by the society for this purpose shall be reported in every annual statement. (1987, c. 483, s. 2.)

§ 58-24-60. Reinsurance.

(a)   A domestic society may, by a reinsurance agreement, cede any individual risk or risks in whole or in part to an insurer (other than another fraternal benefit society) having the power to make such reinsurance and authorized to do business in this State, or if not so authorized, one which is approved by the Commissioner, but no such society may reinsure substantially all of its insurance in force without the written permission of the Commissioner. It may take credit for the reserves on such ceded risks to the extent reinsured, but no credit shall be allowed as an admitted asset or as a deduction from liability, to a ceding society for reinsurance made, ceded, renewed, or otherwise becoming effective after January 1, 1988, unless the reinsurance is payable by the assuming insurer on the basis of the liability of the ceding society under the contract or contracts reinsured without diminution because of the insolvency of the ceding society.

(b) Notwithstanding the limitation in subsection (a), a society may reinsure the risks of another society in a consolidation or merger approved by the Commissioner under G.S. 58-24-65. (1987, c. 483, s. 2; 1991, c. 720, s. 4.)

§ 58-24-65. Consolidations and mergers.

(a) A domestic society may consolidate or merge with any other society by complying with the provisions of this section. It shall file with the Commissioner:

(1) A certified copy of the written contract containing in full the terms and conditions of the consolidation or merger;

(2) A sworn statement by the president and secretary or corresponding officers of each society showing the financial condition thereof on a date fixed by the Commissioner but not earlier than December 31, next preceding the date of the contract;

(3) A certificate of such officers, duly verified by their respective oaths, that the consolidation or merger has been approved by a two-thirds vote of the supreme governing body of each society, such vote being conducted at a regular or special meeting of each such body, or, if the society's laws so permit, by mail; and

(4) Evidence that at least 60 days prior to the action of the supreme governing body of each society, the text of the contract has been furnished to all members of each society either by mail or by publication in full in the official publication of each society.

(b) If the Commissioner finds that the contract is in conformity with the provisions of this section, that the financial statements are correct and that the consolidation or merger is just and equitable to the members of each society, the Commissioner shall approve the contract and issue a certificate to such effect. Upon such approval, the contract shall be in full force and effect unless any society which is a party to the contract is incorporated under the laws of any other state or territory. In such event the consolidation or merger shall not become effective unless and until it has been approved as provided by the laws of such state or territory and a certificate of such approval filed with the Commissioner of this State or, if the laws of such state or territory contain no such provision, then the consolidation or merger shall not become effective unless and until it has been approved by the Commissioner of such state or territory and a certificate of such approval filed with the Commissioner of this State. In case such contract is not approved it shall be inoperative, and the fact of the submission and its contents shall not be disclosed by the Commissioner.

(c)   Upon the consolidation or merger becoming effective as herein provided, all the rights, franchises and interests of the consolidated or merged societies in and to every species of property, real, personal or mixed, and things in action thereunto belonging shall be vested in the society resulting from or remaining after the consolidation or merger without any other instrument, except that conveyances of real property may be evidenced by proper deeds, and the title to any real estate or interest therein, vested under the laws of this State in any of the societies consolidated or merged, shall not revert or be in any way impaired by reason of the consolidation or merger, but shall vest absolutely in the society resulting from or remaining after such consolidation or merger.

(d)   The affidavit of any officer of the society or of anyone authorized by it to mail any notice or document, stating that such notice or document has been duly addressed and mailed, shall be prima facie evidence that such notice or document has been furnished the addressees.

(e)   All necessary and actual expenses and compensation incident to the proceedings provided in this section shall be paid as provided by such contract of consolidation or merger: Provided, however, that no brokerage or commission shall be included in such expenses and compensation or shall be paid to any person by either of the parties to any such contract in connection with the negotiation therefor or execution thereof, nor shall any compensation be paid to any officer or employee of either of the parties to such contract for directly or indirectly aiding in effecting such contract of consolidation or merger. An itemized statement of all such expenses shall be filed with the Commissioner, subject to approval, and when approved the same shall be binding on the parties thereto. Except as fully expressed in the contract of consolidation or merger, or itemized statement of expenses, as approved by the Commissioner, or commissioners, as the case may be, no compensation shall be paid to any person or persons, and no officer or employee of the State shall receive any compensation, directly or indirectly, for in any manner aiding, promoting, or assisting any such consolidation or merger. (1987, c. 483, s. 2; 1991, c. 720, s. 4.)

§ 58-24-70. Conversion of fraternal benefit society into mutual life insurance company.

Any domestic fraternal benefit society may be converted and licensed as a mutual life insurance company by compliance with all the requirements of the general insurance laws for mutual life insurance companies. A plan of conversion shall be prepared in writing by the board of directors setting forth in full the terms and conditions of conversion. The affirmative vote of two-thirds of all members of the supreme governing body at a regular or special meeting shall be necessary for the approval of such plan. No such conversion shall take effect unless and until approved by the Commissioner who may give such approval if the Commissioner finds that the proposed change is in conformity with the requirements of law and not prejudicial to the certificateholders of the society. (1987, c. 483, s. 2; 1991, c. 720, s. 4.)

§ 58-24-75. Benefits.

(a)   A society may provide the following contractual benefits in any form:

(1)   Death benefits;

(2)   Endowment benefits;

(3)   Annuity benefits;

(4)   Temporary or permanent disability benefits;

(5)   Hospital, medical or nursing benefits;

(6)   Monument or tombstone benefits to the memory of deceased members; and

(7)   Such other benefits as authorized for life insurers and which are not inconsistent with this Article.

(b)   A society shall specify in its rules those persons who may be issued, or covered by, the contractual benefits in subsection (a), consistent with providing benefits to members and their dependents. A society may provide benefits on the lives of children under the minimum age for adult membership upon application of an adult person. (1987, c. 483, s. 2.)

§ 58-24-80. Beneficiaries.

(a)   The owner of a benefit contract shall have the right at all times to change the beneficiary or beneficiaries in accordance with the laws or rules of the society unless the owner waives this right by specifically requesting in writing that the beneficiary designation be irrevocable. A society may, through its laws or rules, limit the scope of beneficiary designations and shall provide that no revocable beneficiary shall have or obtain any vested interest in the proceeds of any certificate until the certificate has become due and payable in conformity with the provisions of the benefit contract.

(b)   A society may make provision for the payment of funeral benefits to the extent of such portion of any payment under a certificate as might reasonably appear to be due to any person equitably entitled thereto by reason of having incurred expense occasioned by the burial of the member.

(c)   If, at the death of any person insured under a benefit contract, there is no lawful beneficiary to whom the proceeds shall be payable, the amount of such benefit, except to the extent that funeral benefits may be paid as hereinbefore provided, shall be payable to the personal representative of the deceased insured, provided that if the owner of the certificate is other than the insured, such proceeds shall be payable to such owner. (1987, c. 483, s. 2.)

§ 58-24-85. Benefits not attachable.

No money or other benefit, charity, relief or aid to be paid, provided or rendered by any society, shall be liable to attachment, garnishment or other process, or to be seized, taken, appropriated or applied by any legal or equitable process or operation of law to pay any debt or liability of a member or beneficiary, or any other person who may have a right thereunder, either before or after payment by the society. (1987, c. 483, s. 2.)

§ 58-24-90. The benefit contract.

(a)   Every society authorized to do business in this State shall issue to each owner of a benefit contract a certificate specifying the amount of benefits provided thereby. The certificate, together with any riders or endorsements attached thereto, the laws of the society, the application for membership, the application for insurance and declaration of insurability, if any, signed by the applicant, and all amendments to each thereof, shall constitute the benefit contract, as of the date of issuance, between the society and the owner, and the certificate shall so state. A copy of the application for insurance and declaration of insurability, if any, shall be endorsed upon or attached to the certificate. All statements on the application shall be representations and not warranties. Any waiver of this provision shall be void.

(b)   Any changes, additions or amendments to the laws of the society duly made or enacted subsequent to the issuance of the certificate, shall bind the owner and the beneficiaries, and shall govern and control the benefit contract in all respects the same as though such changes, additions or amendments had been made prior to and were in force at the time of the application for insurance, except that no change, addition or amendment shall destroy or diminish benefits which the society contracted to give the owner as of the date of issuance.

(c)   Any person upon whose life a benefit contract is issued prior to attaining the age of majority shall be bound by the terms of the application and certificate and by all the laws and rules of the society to the same extent as though the age of majority had been attained at the time of application.

(d)   A society shall provide in its laws that if its reserves as to all or any class of certificates become impaired its board of directors or corresponding body may require that there shall be paid by the owner to the society the amount of the owner's equitable proportion of such deficiency as ascertained by its board, and that if the payment is not made either (1) it shall stand as an indebtedness against the certificate and draw interest not to exceed the rate specified for certificate loans under the certificates; or (2) in lieu of or in combination with (1), the owner may accept a proportionate reduction in benefits under the certificate. The society may specify the manner of the election and which alternative is to be presumed if no election is made.

(e)   Copies of any of the documents mentioned in this section, certified by the secretary or corresponding officer of the society, shall be received in evidence of the terms and conditions thereof.

(f) No certificate shall be delivered or issued for delivery in this State unless a copy of the form has been filed with and approved by the Commissioner in the manner provided for like policies issued by life insurers in this State. Every life, accident, health, or disability insurance certificate and every annuity certificate issued on or after one year from the effective date of this Article shall meet the standard contract provision requirements not inconsistent with this Article for like policies issued by life insurers in this State, except that a society may provide for a grace period for payment of premiums of one full month in its certificates. The certificate shall also contain a provision stating the amount of premiums which are payable under the certificate and a provision reciting or setting forth the substance of any sections of the society's laws or rules in force at the time of issuance of the certificate which, if violated, will result in the termination or reduction of benefits payable under the certificate. If the laws of the society provide for expulsion or suspension of a member, the certificate shall also contain a provision that any member so expelled or suspended, except for nonpayment of a premium or within the contestable period for material misrepresentation in the application for membership or insurance, shall have the privilege of maintaining the certificate in force by continuing payment of the required premium.

(g) Benefit contracts issued on the lives of persons below the society's minimum age for adult membership may provide for transfer of control of ownership to the insured at an age specified in the certificate. A society may require approval of an application for membership in order to effect this transfer, and may provide in all other respects for the regulation, government and control of such certificates and all rights, obligations and liabilities incident thereto and connected therewith. Ownership rights prior to such transfer shall be specified in the certificate.

(h) A society may specify the terms and conditions on which benefit contracts may be assigned. (1987, c. 483, s. 2; 1991, c. 720, s. 4.)

§ 58-24-95. Nonforfeiture benefits, cash surrender values, certificate loans and other options.

(a) For certificates issued prior to one year after January 1, 1988, the value of every paid-up nonforfeiture benefit and the amount of any cash surrender value, loan or other option granted shall comply with the provisions of law applicable immediately prior to January 1, 1988.

(b)   For certificates issued on or after one year from January 1, 1988 for which reserves are computed on the Commissioner's 1941 Standard Ordinary Mortality Table, the Commissioner's 1941 Standard Industrial Table or the Commissioner's 1958 Standard Ordinary Mortality Table, or the Commissioner's 1980 Standard Mortality Table, or any more recent table made applicable to life insurers, every paid-up nonforfeiture benefit and the amount of any cash surrender value, loan or other option granted shall not be less than the corresponding amount ascertained in accordance with the laws of this State applicable to life insurers issuing policies containing like benefits based upon such tables. (1987, c. 483, s. 2.)

§ 58-24-100. Investments.

A society shall invest its funds only in investments that are authorized by the laws of this State for the investment of assets of life insurers and subject to the limitations thereon. Any foreign or alien society permitted or seeking to do business in this State must comply in substance with the investment requirements and limitations imposed by Article 7 of this Chapter and applicable to life insurers; provided, that any society that invests its funds in accordance with the laws of the state, district, territory, country, or province in which it is incorporated, shall thereby be deemed to be in compliance with the investment requirements and limitations for a period of two years from January 1, 1988. (1987, c. 483, s. 2; 1995, c. 193, s. 29.)

§ 58-24-105. Funds.

(a)   All assets shall be held, invested and disbursed for the use and benefit of the society and no member or beneficiary shall have or acquire individual rights therein or become entitled to any apportionment on the surrender of any part thereof, except as provided in the benefit contract.

(b)   A society may create, maintain, invest, disburse and apply any special fund or funds necessary to carry out any purpose permitted by the laws of such society.

(c) A society may, pursuant to resolution of its supreme governing body, establish and operate one or more separate accounts and issue contracts on a variable basis, subject to the provisions of law regulating life insurers establishing such accounts and issuing such contracts. To the extent the society deems it necessary in order to comply with any applicable federal or State laws, or any rules issued thereunder, the society may adopt special procedures for the conduct of the business and affairs of a separate account, may, for persons having beneficial interests therein, provide special voting and other rights, including without limitation special rights and procedures relating to investment policy, investment advisory services, selection of certified public accountants, and selection of a committee to manage the business and affairs of the account, and may issue contracts on a variable basis to which G.S. 58-24-90(b) and G.S. 58-24-90(d) shall not apply. (1987, c. 483, s. 2.)

§ 58-24-110. Exemptions.

Except as herein provided, societies shall be governed by this Article and shall be exempt from all other provisions of the general insurance laws of this State unless they be expressly designated therein, or unless it is specifically made applicable by this Article. (1987, c. 483, s. 2.)

§ 58-24-115. Taxation.

Every society organized or licensed under this Article is hereby declared to be a charitable and benevolent institution, and all of its funds shall be exempt from all and every State, county, district, municipal and school tax other than taxes on real estate not occupied by such society in carrying on its business. (1987, c. 483, s. 2.)

§ 58-24-120. Valuation.

(a) Standards of valuation for certificates issued prior to one year after the effective date of this Article shall be those provided by the laws applicable immediately prior to January 1, 1988.

(b) The minimum standards of valuation for certificates issued on or after one year from January 1, 1988, shall be based on the following tables:

(1) For certificates of life insurance - the Commissioner's 1941 Standard Ordinary Mortality Table, the Commissioner's 1941 Standard Industrial Mortality Table, the Commissioner's 1958 Standard Ordinary Mortality Table, the Commissioner's 1980 Standard Ordinary Mortality Table or any more recent table made applicable to life insurers;

(2) For annuity and pure endowment certificates, for total and permanent disability benefits, for accidental death benefits and for non-cancellable accident and health benefits - such tables as are authorized for use by life insurers in this State.

All of the above shall be under valuation methods and standards (including interest assumptions) in accordance with the laws of this State applicable to life insurers issuing policies containing like benefits.

(c) The Commissioner may, in his or her discretion, accept other standards for valuation if the Commissioner finds that the reserves produced thereby will not be less in the aggregate than reserves computed in accordance with the minimum valuation standard herein prescribed. The Commissioner may, in his or her discretion, vary the standards of mortality applicable to all benefit contracts on substandard lives or other extra hazardous lives by any society authorized to do business in this State.

(d) Any society, with the consent of the Commissioner of the state of domicile of the society and under such conditions, if any, which the Commissioner may impose, may establish and maintain reserves on its certificates in excess of the reserves required thereunder, but the contractual rights of any benefit member shall not be affected thereby. (1987, c. 483, s. 2; 1991, c. 720, s. 4.)

§ 58-24-125. Reports.

Reports shall be filed in accordance with the provisions of this section.

(a) Every society transacting business in this State shall annually, on or before the first day of March, unless for cause shown such time has been extended by the Commissioner, file with the Commissioner a true statement of its financial condition, transactions and affairs for the preceding calendar year and pay the fee specified in G.S. 58-6-5 for filing same. The statement shall be in general form and context as approved by the NAIC for fraternal benefit societies and as supplemented by additional information required by the Commissioner.

(b) As part of the annual statement herein required, each society shall, on or before the first day of March, file with the Commissioner a valuation of its certificates in force on December 31st last preceding, provided the Commissioner may, in his or her discretion for cause shown, extend the time for filing such valuation for not more than two calendar months. Such valuation shall be done in accordance with the standards specified in G.S. 58-24-120. Such valuation and underlying data shall be certified by a qualified actuary or, at the expense of the society, verified by the actuary of the Department of the state of domicile of the society.

(c) A society neglecting to file the annual statement in the form and within the time provided by this section shall forfeit one hundred dollars ($100.00) for each day during which such neglect continues, and, upon notice by the Commissioner to that effect, its authority to do business in this State shall cease while such default continues. (1987, c. 483, s. 2; 1991, c. 720, ss. 4, 19.)

§ 58-24-130. Perpetual license.

Subject to timely payment of the annual license continuation fee and subject to any other applicable provisions of the insurance laws of this State, a license, other than a preliminary license, to a fraternal benefit society under this Article shall continue in full force and effect. For each license the society shall pay the Commissioner the fee specified in G.S. 58-6-5. The society shall pay the Commissioner, as an annual license continuation fee and a condition of the continuation of the license, the fee specified in G.S. 58-6-7 on or before the first day of March on a form to be supplied by the Commissioner. A duly certified copy or duplicate of the license shall be prima facie evidence that the licensee is a fraternal benefit society within the meaning of Articles 1 through 64 of this Chapter. (1987, c. 483, s. 2; 1991, c. 720, s. 4; 2003-212, s. 26(g).)

§ 58-24-135. Examination of societies; no adverse publications.

(a) The Commissioner, or any person he or she may appoint, may examine any domestic, foreign or alien society transacting or applying for admission to transact business in this State in the same manner as authorized for examination of domestic, foreign or alien insurers. Requirements of notice and an opportunity to respond before findings are made public as provided in the laws regulating insurers shall also be applicable to the examination of societies.

(b) Repealed by Session Laws 1995, c. 360, s. 2(i). (1987, c. 483, s. 2; 1991, c. 720, s. 4; 1995, c. 360, s. 2(i).)

§ 58-24-140. Foreign or alien society - Admission.

No foreign or alien society shall transact business in this State without a license issued by the Commissioner. Any such society desiring admission to this State shall comply substantially with the requirements and limitations of this Article applicable to domestic societies. Any such society may be licensed to transact business in this State upon filing with the Commissioner:

(a) A duly certified copy of its Articles of Incorporation;

(b) A copy of its bylaws, certified by its secretary or corresponding officer;

(c) A power of attorney to the Commissioner as prescribed in G.S. 58-24-170;

(d) A statement of its business under oath of its president and secretary or corresponding officers in a form prescribed by the Commissioner, duly verified by an examination made by the supervising insurance official of its home state or other state, territory, province or country, satisfactory to the Commissioner of this State;

(e) Certification from the proper official of its home state, territory, province or country that the society is legally incorporated and licensed to transact business therein;

(f)   Copies of its certificate forms; and

(g)   Such other information as the Commissioner may deem necessary;

and upon a showing that its assets are invested in accordance with the provisions of Articles 1 through 64 of this Chapter. (1987, c. 483, s. 2; 1991, c. 720, ss. 4, 20.)

§ 58-24-145. Injunction - Liquidation - Receivership of domestic society.

(a)   When the Commissioner upon investigation finds that a domestic society:

(1)   Has exceeded its powers;

(2)   Has failed to comply with any provision of this Article;

(3)   Is not fulfilling its contracts in good faith;

(4)   Has a membership of less than 400 after an existence of one year or more; or

(5)   Is conducting business fraudulently or in a manner hazardous to its members, creditors, the public or the business;

the Commissioner shall notify the society of such deficiency or deficiencies and state in writing the reasons for his or her dissatisfaction. The Commissioner shall at once issue a written notice to the society requiring that the deficiency or deficiencies which exist are corrected. After such notice the society shall have a 30 day period in which to comply with the Commissioner's request for correction, and if the society fails to comply the Commissioner shall notify the society of such findings of noncompliance and require the society to show cause on a date named why it should not be enjoined from carrying on any business until the violation complained of shall have been corrected, or why an action under Article 41 of Chapter 1 of the General Statutes (quo warranto) should not be commenced against the society.

(b)   If on such date the society does not present good and sufficient reasons why it should not be so enjoined or why such action should not be commenced, the Commissioner may present the facts relating thereto to the Attorney General who shall, if he or she deems the circumstances warrant, commence an action to enjoin the society from transacting business or under Article 41 of Chapter 1 of the General Statutes (quo warranto).

(c)   The court shall thereupon notify the officers of the society of a hearing. If after a full hearing it appears that the society should be so enjoined or liquidated or a receiver appointed, the court shall enter the necessary order. No society so enjoined shall have the authority to do business until:

(1)   The Commissioner finds that the violation complained of has been corrected;

(2)   The costs of such action shall have been paid by the society if the court finds that the society was in default as charged;

(3)   The court has dissolved its injunction; and

(4)   The Commissioner has reinstated the license.

(d)   If the court orders the society liquidated, it shall be enjoined from carrying on any further business, whereupon the receiver of the society shall proceed at once to take possession of the books, papers, money and other assets of the society and, under the direction of the court, proceed forthwith to close the affairs of the society and to distribute its funds to those entitled thereto.

(e)   No action under this section shall be recognized in any court of this State unless brought by the Attorney General upon request of the Commissioner. Whenever a receiver is to be appointed for a domestic society, the court shall appoint the Commissioner as such receiver.

(f)   The provisions of this section relating to hearing by the Commissioner, action by the Attorney General at the request of the Commissioner, hearing by the court, injunction and receivership shall be applicable to a society which shall voluntarily determine to discontinue business. (1987, c. 483, s. 2; 1991, c. 720, s. 4; 1999-132, s. 9.1.)

§ 58-24-150. Suspension, revocation or refusal of license of foreign or alien society.

(a) When the Commissioner upon investigation finds that a foreign or alien society transacting or applying to transact business in this State:

(1) Has exceeded its powers;

(2) Has failed to comply with any of the provisions of this Article;

(3) Is not fulfilling its contracts in good faith; or

(4) Is conducting its business fraudulently or in a manner hazardous to its members or creditors or the public;

the Commissioner shall notify the society of such deficiency or deficiencies and state in writing the reasons for his or her dissatisfaction. The Commissioner shall at once issue a written notice to the society requiring that the deficiency or deficiencies which exist are corrected. After such notice the society shall have a 30 day period in which to comply with the Commissioner's request for correction, and if the society fails to comply the Commissioner shall notify the society of such findings of noncompliance and require the society to show cause on a date named why its license should not be suspended, revoked or refused. If on such date the society does not present good and sufficient reason why its authority to do business in this State should not be suspended, revoked or refused, the Commissioner may suspend or refuse the license of the society to do business in this State until satisfactory evidence is furnished to the Commissioner that such suspension or refusal should be withdrawn or the Commissioner may revoke the authority of the society to do business in this State.

(b) Nothing contained in this section shall be taken or construed as preventing any such society from continuing in good faith all contracts made in this State during the time such society was legally authorized to transact business herein. (1987, c. 483, s. 2; 1991, c. 720, s. 4.)

§ 58-24-155. Injunction.

No application or petition for injunction against any domestic, foreign or alien society, or lodge thereof, shall be recognized in any court of this State unless made by the Attorney General upon request of the Commissioner. (1987, c. 483, s. 2; 1991, c. 720, s. 4.)

§ 58-24-160. Licensing of agents.

(a) Agents of societies shall be licensed in accordance with the provisions of the general insurance laws regulating the licensing, revocation, suspension or termination of license of resident and nonresident agents; provided that agents licensed pursuant to former G.S. 58-268 as of July 1, 1977, shall be exempt from examination.

(b) No examination or license shall be required of any regular salaried officer, employee or member of a licensed society who devotes substantially all of his or her services to activities other than the solicitation of fraternal insurance contracts from the public, and who receives for the solicitation of such contracts no commission or other compensation directly dependent upon the amount of business obtained. (1987, c. 483, s. 2.)

§ 58-24-165. Unfair methods of competition and unfair and deceptive acts and practices.

Every society authorized to do business in this State shall be subject to the provisions of Article 63 of this Chapter relating to unfair methods of competition and unfair or deceptive acts or practices; provided, however, that nothing in such provisions shall be construed as applying to or affecting the right of any society to determine its eligibility requirements for membership, or be construed as applying to or affecting the offering of benefits exclusively to members or persons eligible for membership in the society by a subsidiary corporation or affiliated organization of the society. (1987, c. 483, s. 2.)

§ 58-24-170. Service of process.

(a) Every society authorized to do business in this State shall appoint in writing the Commissioner and each successor in office to be its true and lawful attorney upon whom all lawful process in any action or proceeding against it shall be served, and shall agree in such writing that any lawful process against it which is served on said attorney shall be of the same legal force and validity as if served upon the society, and that the authority shall continue in force so long as any liability remains outstanding in this State. Copies of such appointment, certified by said Commissioner, shall be deemed sufficient evidence thereof and shall be admitted in evidence with the same force and effect as the original thereof might be admitted.

(b) Service shall only be made upon the Commissioner, or if absent, upon the person in charge of the Commissioner's office. It shall be made in duplicate and shall constitute sufficient service upon the society. When legal process against a society is served upon the Commissioner, the Commissioner shall forthwith forward one of the duplicate copies by certified or registered mail, prepaid, directed to the secretary or corresponding officer. No such service shall require a society to file its answer, pleading or defense in less than 30 days from the date of mailing the copy of the service to a society. Legal process shall not be served upon a society except in the manner herein provided. At the time of serving any process upon the Commissioner, the plaintiff or complainant in the action shall pay to the Commissioner a fee in the amount set in G.S. 58-16-30. (1987, c. 483, s. 2; 1989, c. 645, s. 4; 1991, c. 720, s. 4.)

§ 58-24-175. Review.

All decisions and findings of the Commissioner made under the provisions of this Article shall be subject to review under G.S. 58-2-75. (1987, c. 483, s. 2; 1991, c. 720, ss. 4, 21.)

§ 58-24-180. Penalties.

(a) Any person, officer, member, or examining physician of any society authorized to do business under this Article who shall knowingly or willfully make any false or fraudulent statement or representation in or with reference to any application for membership, or for the purpose of obtaining money from or benefit in any society transacting business under this Article, shall be guilty of a Class 1 misdemeanor.

(b) Any person who shall solicit membership for, or in any manner assist in procuring membership in any fraternal benefit society not licensed to do business in this State, or who shall solicit membership for, or in any manner assist in procuring membership in any such society not authorized as herein provided to do business as herein defined in this State, shall be guilty of a Class 3 misdemeanor and upon conviction thereof shall be punished only by a fine of not less than one thousand dollars ($1,000) nor more than five thousand dollars ($5,000).

(c) Any society, or any officer, agent, or employee thereof, neglecting or refusing to comply with, or violating, any of the provisions of this Article, the penalty for which neglect, refusal, or violation is not specified in this section, shall be guilty of a Class 3 misdemeanor, and upon conviction shall be punished only by a fine not to exceed five thousand dollars ($5,000).

(d) Any person violating the provisions of G.S. 58-24-65 shall be guilty of a Class I felony.

(e) Any person who willfully makes any false statement under oath in any verified report or declaration that is required by law from fraternal benefit societies, is guilty of a Class I felony. (1987, c. 483, s. 2; 1989 (Reg. Sess., 1990), c. 1054, s. 3; 1993, c. 539, ss. 451, 1273; 1994, Ex. Sess., c. 24, s. 14(c); 1993 (Reg. Sess., 1994), c. 767, s. 25.)

§ 58-24-185. Exemption of certain societies, orders, and associations.

(a) Nothing contained in this Article shall be so construed as to affect or apply to:

(1) Grand or subordinate lodges of societies, orders or associations now doing business in this State which provide benefits exclusively through local or subordinate lodges;

(2) Orders, societies or associations which admit to membership only persons engaged in one or more crafts or hazardous occupations, in the same or similar lines of business, insuring only their own members and their families, and the ladies' societies or ladies' auxiliaries to such orders, societies or associations;

(3) Domestic societies which limit their membership to employees of a particular city or town, designated firm, business house or corporation which provide for a death benefit of not more than five hundred dollars ($500.00) or

disability benefits of not more than three hundred fifty dollars ($350.00) to any person in any one year, or both;

(4)   Domestic societies or associations of a purely religious, charitable or benevolent description, which provide for a death benefit of not more than five hundred dollars ($500.00) or for disability benefits of not more than three hundred fifty dollars ($350.00) to any one person in any one year, or both;

(5)   An association of local lodges of a society now doing business in this State which provides death benefits not exceeding five hundred dollars ($500.00) to any one person, provided, that the Commissioner may authorize the payment of death benefits not exceeding three thousand dollars ($3,000) to any one person, or may authorize disability benefits not exceeding three hundred dollars ($300.00), or may authorize both payments, in any one year to any one person; or

(6)   Any association, whether a fraternal benefit society or not, which was organized before 1880 and whose members are officers or enlisted, regular or reserve, active, retired, or honorably discharged members of the Armed Forces or Sea Services of the United States, and a principal purpose of which is to provide insurance and other benefits to its members and their dependents or beneficiaries.

(b)   Any such society or association described in subsections (a)(3) or (a)(4) supra which provides for death or disability benefits for which benefit certificates are issued, and any such society or association included in subsection (a)(4) which has more than 1000 members, shall not be exempted from the provisions of this Article but shall comply with all requirements thereof.

(c)   No society which, by the provisions of this section, is exempt from the requirements of this Article, except any society described in subsection (a)(2) supra, shall give or allow, or promise to give or allow to any person any compensation for procuring new members.

(d)   Every society which provides for benefits in case of death or disability resulting solely from accident, and which does not obligate itself to pay natural death or sick benefits shall have all of the privileges and be subject to all the applicable provisions and regulations of this Article except that the provisions thereof relating to medical examination, valuations of benefit certificates, and incontestability, shall not apply to the society.

(e) The Commissioner may require from any society or association, by examination or otherwise, such information as will enable the Commissioner to determine whether the society or association is exempt from the provisions of this Article.

(f) Societies, orders, or associations exempted under the provisions of this section shall also be exempt from all other provisions of the general insurance laws of this State. (1987, c. 483, s. 2; 1989, c. 364, s. 2; c. 485, s. 2; 1991, c. 476, s. 1; c. 720, ss. 4, 45, 55; 2007-27, s. 1; 2008-187, s. 12.)

§ 58-24-190. Severability.

If any provision of this Article or the application of such provision to any circumstance is held invalid, the remainder of the Article or the application of the provision to other circumstances, shall not be affected thereby. (1987, c. 483, s. 2.)

Article 25.

Fraternal Orders.

§ 58-25-1. General insurance law not applicable.

Nothing in the general insurance laws, except such as apply to fraternal orders shall be construed to extend to benevolent associations incorporated under the laws of this State that only levy an assessment on the members to create a fund to pay the family of a deceased member and make no profit therefrom, and do not solicit business through agents. (1987, c. 483, s. 2.)

§ 58-25-5. Fraternal orders defined.

Every incorporated association, order, or society doing business in this State on the lodge system, with ritualistic form of work and representative form of government, for the purpose of making provision for the payment of benefits of three hundred dollars ($300.00) or less in case of death, sickness, temporary or permanent physical disability, either as the result of disease, accident, or old age, formed and organized for the sole benefit of its members and their beneficiaries, and not for profit, is hereby declared to be a "fraternal order". Societies and orders which do not make insurance contracts or collect dues or assessments therefor, but simply pay burial or other benefits out of the treasury of their orders, and use their funds for the purpose of building homes or asylums for the purpose of caring for and educating orphan children and aged and infirm people in this State, shall not be considered as "fraternal orders"; and such order or association paying death or disability benefits may also create, maintain, apply, or disburse among its membership a reserve or emergency fund as may be provided in its constitution or bylaws; but no profit or gain may be added to the payments made by a member. (1987, c. 483, s. 2.)

§ 58-25-10. Funds derived from assessments and dues.

The fund from which the payment of benefits, as provided for in G.S. 58-25-5, shall be made, and the fund from which the expenses of such association, order or society shall be defrayed, shall be derived from assessments or dues collected from its members. Such societies or associations shall be governed by the laws of the State governing fraternal orders or societies, and are exempt from the provisions of all general insurance laws of this State, and no law hereafter passed shall apply to such orders or societies unless fraternal orders or societies are designated therein. (1987, c. 483, s. 2.)

§ 58-25-15. Appointment of member as receiver or collector; appointee as agent for order or society; rights of members.

Assessments and dues referred to in G.S. 58-25-5 and G.S. 58-25-10 may be collected, receipted, and remitted by a member or officer of any local or subordinate lodge of any fraternal order or society when so appointed or designated by any grand, district, or subordinate lodge or officer, deputy, or representative of the same, there being no regular licensed agent or deputy of said grand lodge charged with said duties; but any person so collecting said dues or assessments shall be the agent or representative of such fraternal order or society, or any department thereof, and shall bind them by their acts in collecting and remitting said amounts so collected. Under no circumstances, regardless of any agreement, bylaws, contract, or notice, shall said officer or collector be the agent or representative of the individual member from whom any such collection is made; nor shall said member be responsible for the failure of such officer or collector to safely keep, handle, or remit said dues or assessments so collected, in accordance with the rules, regulations, or bylaws of said order or society; nor shall said member, regardless of any rules, regulations, or bylaws to the contrary, forfeit any rights under his certificate of membership in said fraternal order or society by reason of any default or misconduct of any said officer or member so acting. (1987, c. 483, s. 2.)

§ 58-25-20. Meetings of governing body; principal office.

Any such order or society incorporated and organized under the laws of this State may provide for the meeting of its supreme legislative or governing body in any other state, province, or territory wherein such order or society has subordinate lodges, and all business transacted at such meetings is as valid in all respects as if the meetings were held in this State; but the principal business office of such order or society shall always be kept in this State. (1987, c. 483, s. 2.)

§ 58-25-25. Conditions precedent to doing business.

Any such fraternal order, society, or association as defined by this Article, chartered and organized in this State or organized and doing business under the laws of any other state, district, province, or territory, having the qualifications required of domestic societies of like character, upon satisfying the Commissioner that its business is proper and legitimate and so conducted, may be admitted to transact business in this State upon the same conditions as are prescribed by Articles 1 through 64 of this Chapter for admitting and authorizing foreign insurance companies to do business in this State, except that such fraternal orders shall not be required to have the capital required of such insurance companies. Organizers or agents shall be licensed without requiring an examination; provided, organizers or agents who are engaged in or intend to engage in the sale of individual policies of life insurance shall take the examination required of life insurance agents. Those organizers or agents licensed for the sale of insurance pursuant to former G.S. 58-268 as of July 1, 1977, shall be exempt from examination. (1987, c. 483, s. 2; 1991, c. 720, s. 4.)

§ 58-25-30. Certain lodge systems exempt.

The following beneficial orders or societies shall be exempt from the requirements of this Article, and shall not be required to pay any license tax or fees nor make any report to the Commissioner, unless the assessments collected for death benefits by the supreme lodge amount to at least three hundred dollars ($300.00) in one year: Beneficial fraternal orders, or societies incorporated under the laws of this State, which are conducted under the lodge system which have the supreme lodge or governing body located in this State, and which are so organized that the membership consists of members of subordinate lodges; that the subordinate lodges accept for membership only residents of the county in which such subordinate lodge is located; that each subordinate lodge issues certificates, makes assessments, and collects a fund to pay benefits to the widows and orphans of its own deceased members and their families, each lodge independently of the others, for itself and independently of the supreme lodge; that each lodge controls the fund for this purpose; that in addition to the benefits paid by each subordinate lodge to its own members, the supreme lodge provides for an additional benefit for such of the members of the subordinate lodges as are qualified, at the option of the subordinate lodge members; that such organization is not conducted for profit, has no capital stock, and has been in operation for 10 years in this State.

The Commissioner may require the chief or presiding officer, or the secretary, to file annually an affidavit that such organization is entitled to this exemption. (1987, c. 483, s. 2; 1991, c. 720. s. 4.)

§ 58-25-35. Insurance on children.

Any fraternal order or society authorized pursuant to this Article to do business in this State and operating on the lodge plan may provide in its constitution and bylaws, in addition to other benefits provided for therein, for the payment of death or annuity benefits upon the lives of children between the ages of one and 16 years at next birthday, for whose support and maintenance a member of such order or society is responsible. The order or society may at its option organize and operate branches for such children and membership in local lodges, and initiation therein shall not be required of such children, nor shall they have any voice in the management of the order or society. The total benefits payable as above provided shall in no case exceed the following amounts at ages at next birthday at time of death, respectively, as follows: one year, twenty dollars ($20.00); two years, fifty dollars ($50.00); three years, seventy-five dollars ($75.00); four years, one hundred dollars ($100.00); five years, one hundred twenty-five dollars ($125.00); six years, one hundred fifty dollars ($150.00); seven years, two hundred dollars ($200.00); eight years, two hundred fifty dollars ($250.00); nine years, three hundred dollars ($300.00); 10 years, four hundred dollars ($400.00); 11 years, five hundred dollars ($500.00); 12 years, six hundred dollars ($600.00); 13 years, seven hundred dollars ($700.00); 14 years, eight hundred dollars ($800.00); 15 years, nine hundred dollars ($900.00); 16 years, one thousand dollars ($1,000). (1987, c. 483, s. 2.)

§ 58-25-40. Medical examination; certificates and contributions.

No benefit certificate as to any child shall take effect until after medical examination or inspection by a licensed medical practitioner, in accordance with the laws of the order or society, nor shall any such benefit certificate be issued unless the order or society shall simultaneously put in force at least 500 such certificates, on each of which at least one assessment has been paid, nor where the number of lives represented by such certificate falls below 500. The death benefit contributions to be made upon such certificate shall be based upon the "Standard Mortality Table" or the "English Life Table Number Six," and a rate of interest not greater than four percent (4%) per annum, upon a higher standard or upon such mortality, morbidity, and interest standards permitted by the laws of this State for use by life insurance companies; but contributions may be waived or returns may be made from any surplus held in excess of reserve and other liabilities, as provided in the bylaws; and extra contributions shall be made if the reserves hereafter provided for become impaired. (1987, c. 483, s. 2.)

Vision Books Order Form

Fax Orders:	1-980-299-5965
Phone Orders:	1-704-898-0770
E-mail Orders:	www.visionbooks.org
Mail Orders:	Vision Books, LLC P.O. Box 42406 Charlotte, NC 28215

Shipp To:
Name_____
Address_____
City_____State_____Zip_____
Phone_____Fax_____
Email_____@_____

Bill To: We can bill a third party on your behalf.
Name_____
Address_____
City_____State_____Zip_____
Phone____(_____)_____Fax_____
Email_____@_____

Pamphlet Number ($15.00 Each)	Qty	Total Cost
_____	_____	_____
_____	_____	_____
_____	_____	_____
_____	_____	_____
_____	_____	_____
_____	_____	_____
_____	_____	_____
<u>Full Volume Set 1-92</u>	<u>92 Pamphlets</u>	<u>1,380.00</u>

Free Shipping Shipping & Handling on Full Volume Orders
Add $1.00 Shipping & Handling per pamphlet $_____

Total Cost $_____

DID YOU ENJOY THIS BOOK?

Vision Books, LLC would like to hear from you! If you or someone you know has been fasely imprisoned, we would like to hear your story. If the 'North Carolina Criminal Law and Procedure' has had an effect in your life or if you have suggestions, we would like to hear from you. Send your letters to:

Vision Books, LLC
Attn: Staff Writers
P.O. Box 42406
Charlotte, NC 28215
Email: staff@visionbooks.org

Order Additional Copies:

Fax Orders:	1-980-299-5965
Phone Orders:	1-704-898-0770
E-mail Orders:	www.visionbooks.org
Mail Orders:	Vision Books, LLC P.O. Box 42406 Charlotte, NC 28215

www.ingramcontent.com/pod-product-compliance
Lightning Source LLC
Chambersburg PA
CBHW051629170526
45167CB00001B/116